Advanced Bridge Bidding
for the 21st Century

Advanced Bridge Bidding
for the 21st Century

MAX HARDY

SQueeZe Books
New York

Cover Design by Jay Cookingham

ISBN 1-58776-125-4
Library of Congress catalog number: 2002104136
Printed in the United States of America

 VIVISPHERE PUBLISHING
A division of NetPub Corporation
675 Dutchess Turnpike, Poughkeepsie, NY 12603
www.vivisphere.com   (800) 724-1100

PUBLISHER'S NOTE

Max Hardy has been the acknowledged chronicler of two-over-one bidding methodology for quite a while (almost 30 years).

His last book (SQueeZe's first), *Standard Bridge Bidding for the 21st Century*, was the culmination of all Max's bidding ideas for the average and aspiring player. It was an immediate success, both critically and sales-wise.

But more remains to be done. There are many adjustments and improvements being made continually by experts in the field. In this book, Max brings you his best ideas on those "bells and whistles," as well as contributions by six of America's top two-over-one bidders.

The use of "on-demand" publishing is particularly appropriate here. As changes occur in the "standard" bidding structure or in the "state-of-the-art" improvements, Max (and SQueeZe) can just alter a topic or a chapter in the computer file that represents the book, and from then on we will have up-to-date material. The books will never be out of date and will never go out of print.

It's time to bid like the experts. Go for it!

Ron Garber
for SQueeZe Books

OTHER BOOKS BY MAX HARDY

Five Card Majors—Western Style, 1974 (out of print; replaced by *Two Over One Game Force*)

Play My Card (with Bill Roney), 1980 (out of print)

Two Over One Game Force, 1982 (original out of print; replaced by *Two Over One Game Force Revised and Expanded*)

New Minor Forcing—Fourth Suit Forcing—Forcing Notrump Responses, 1984

Splinters and Other Shortness Bids, 1987

Two Over One Game Force Revised and Expanded, 1989; Winner, "Bridge Book of the Year for Advanced Players," presented by the American Bridge Teachers' Association

Two Over One Game Force: An Introduction (with Steve Bruno), 1993

Two Over One Game Force Quiz Book, 1993

Competitive Bidding With Two Suited Hands, 1997

The Problems With Major Suit Raises and How to Fix Them, 1998

Standard Bridge Bidding for the 21st Century, 2000

ABOUT THE CONTRIBUTORS

GRANT BAZE: Winner of a World Senior Teams, two Pan-American Championships, and seven North American Championships. Has three times won the ACBL trophy for most master points won in a calendar year and stands number six all-time in master points won. Regular Columnist for *OK Bridge*.

MARTY BERGEN: Winner of ten North American Championships. Author (and publisher) of eight successful bridge books, including *Points Schmoints* (1996 ABTA Book of the Year) and his latest, *Marty Sez*. Regular columnist for the *ACBL Bulletin*. Winner of 13,000 master points.

FRED HAMILTON: A two-time World Champion with many other top five finishes in international play. Winner of thirteen North American Championships. Has over 29,000 master points (number eight all-time). Plays professionally and has achieved many of his successes with students. Inventor of a popular convention for bidding over an opponent's one notrump opening.

JEFF MECKSTROTH: Winner of many World Championships and two dozen North American Championships. One of the leading master point holders (number four all-time) and winner of the 2000 and 2001 Barry Crane trophy for most master points won. Author of *Win the Bermuda Bowl with Me*.

MIKE PASSELL: Number two in all-time master points won. Winner of two dozen North American Championships and a recent World Championship. Winner of the Bermuda Bowl.

EDDIE WOLD: Number five in all-time master points. Winner of more than one dozen North American Championships and a recent World Championship.

INTRODUCTION

If one delves into bridge archives and sees the bidding ineptitude of players in the early days, it is easy to appreciate the advances over the years. Ely Culbertson, with a flamboyant style, popularized the new concept that the response of one of a suit to an opening bid was forcing. Approach forcing, he called it. Charles Goren showed the world how to evaluate hands using Milton Work's point count method. But it wasn't until the early 1950's when Alvin Roth and his partner Tobias Stone developed a system based on the requirement that an opening bid in a major suit required five cards that consistent, reliable bidding took hold. A key to the system is that a response in a lower suit at the two level to a major suit opening is forcing to game and the necessary adjunct that a one notrump reponse is forcing one round. Edgar Kaplan and Freddie Shienwold integrated their ideas, including a 12 to 14 high card point one notrump opening, into the system and showed its worth with consistent success in National tournaments. Richard Walsh, Paul Soloway and others incorporated new ideas, adopted the K-S concepts back into the Roth-Stone system and plugged holes in the earlier bidding structures, thereby creating the Walsh System. The success of the Walsh style players made such an impression on the tournament world that it became, by far, the most popular system.

Today this system and its offspring are usually referred to as Two-Over-One or Five Card Majors. There have been many improvements over the years with any number of players contributing. Max Hardy, with the publication of *Five Card Majors—Western Style* in 1974, became the recorder of the system. He has maintained this position by subsequent publication of books which present the new concepts incorporated into the system and also expand on the old ones. Max has also contributed to the system with codification of principles such as equal level correction and has developed conventions such as Hardy major suit raises.

Two years ago Max produced *Standard Bridge Bidding for the 21st Century*. This book itself has become a standard, providing everyone from the novice to the experienced tournament player with a combination teaching manual and reference book for Two-Over-One bidding. Accurate use of the system will allow any partnership to be a force with which to contend in tournament play. Now, with *Advanced Bridge Bidding for the 21st Century*, Max takes players to the next level, bringing them up-to-date with the system of choice of the top players in the world. He presents the concepts with clarity and style worthy of the author and teacher that he is.

In addition to his own writing, Max treats the reader to descriptions of advanced conventions by the developers themselves. Fred Hamilton, Mike Passell, Jeff Meckstroth, Grant Baze, Marty Bergen, and Eddie Wold each contribute. Experienced tournament players will recognize these players as among the very best in the world. Partnerships need not adopt all the ideas presented in order to improve their bidding methods. In fact, Max gives the reader choices by discussing different popular conventions that can be used for the same situation.

The style in the 21st century is to use any reasonable excuse to enter the auction in order to disrupt the opponents' bidding. The reason is that expert partnerships will invariably bid to the best contract when they have the auction to themselves. Study and use the ideas and conventions in this book. Your opponents won't dare leave you alone.

—John Swanson, World Champion, multiple
North American Champion, author,
and co-creator of the Walsh System

CONTENTS

CHAPTER VIII

CHAPTER IX

FOREWORD

This book is part two of *Standard Bridge Bidding for the Twenty First Century*. When half finished, it became apparent that two separate volumes would be needed. Volume I attempted to remain simple enough that a beginner could learn modern bidding without being burdened or confused by excess information. In that volume we promised the reader faithfully that we would complete a second volume which would include upgrades and refinements (the bells and whistles).

When Volume I had been in circulation only a few months we were deluged with requests for information on Volume II. Well, here it is. You will find here not only the refinements that we prefer, but also other ideas from some of the finest bridge minds in the world. You will learn about The Law of Total Tricks from **Marty Bergen**, two way checkbacks after opener's rebid of one notrump from **Grant Baze,** adjuncts to the Forcing Notrump from **Jeff Meckstroth** and **Mike Passell**, a subtle approach to slam bidding from **Eddie Wold**, and new twists on creating forcing auctions from **Fred Hamilton**.

Most of these ideas are widely used at the expert level. There are some areas in which many similar yet different approaches to solving a particular problem exist. In those instances, the solution presented here is the author's choice.

If you do not already have *Standard Bridge Bidding for the Twenty First Century*, it would be wise for you to get a copy. If you ignore the earlier writing you will miss out on the basics. Read the original chapter, then continue with what is added in this volume. Although part one is complete within itself, part two is an extension of part one. Here we begin each chapter with a synopsis of what was presented in Volume I, then continue with further information regarding the same topic.

When you master advanced bidding we are confident that there will be very few bidding problems that you are not equipped to solve. And your solutions will be as complete as possible based upon the techniques that are available in 2002.

So read, study, and enjoy. Continue with each chapter that you began in *Standard Bridge Bidding for the Twenty First Century*, and let your expertise continue to grow.

Advanced Bridge Bidding
for the 21st Century

CHAPTER ONE
Hand Evaluation

Synopsis: You have learned how to integrate the table of "quick tricks" and the 4-3-2-1 point count to get an evaluation of any hand you might be dealt. You have learned NOT to add points for short suits and to amplify your use of the point count based upon these principles:

1. Honor cards are worth more when combined than when isolated.
2. Honor cards are worth more in long suits than in short suits.
3. Give credence to good spot cards to which you have not assigned HCP status.
4. Balanced distribution downgrades the worth of a hand. Good shape upgrades the worth of a hand.
5. Listen to the auction. Your high cards can grow or diminish when their suit is bid in front of you or behind you.

Importantly, you have learned the role of the **splinter** in hand evaluation. When one partner **splinters**, the information conveyed allows complete evaluation of the hand across the table. Partner knows that honor cards facing the announced shortness lose value, but that honor cards in all other suits will combine with honor cards in partner's hand to produce tricks. **Splinter** bids have revolutionized the entire process of hand evaluation.

Our remaining discussion in Chapter One involves the nature in which evaluation can shift during an auction.

There remains yet another method of hand evaluation which has received recognition in some quarters. It is called THE LOSING TRICK COUNT. Although this method has some expert following, it is not recommended here.

Shifting Evaluation

True evaluation requires that the bidder learn to take into account all of the available information. Sometimes one picks up a hand with lots of high cards. The bidder immediately considers this to be a good hand. Often such a hand realizes its promise. But the bidder needs to understand when this apparently good hand shrinks in value. Just because it contains a great deal of high card strength does not make it a good hand when the auction indicates otherwise. Many bidders continue to bid the good hand and fail to make adjustments indicated by the auction. Consider these examples:

Example 1)

♠ AK
♥ QJ
♦ KJ53
♣ KJ1074

With eighteen high card points opener bids one club, planning to rebid by jumping to two notrump. Left hand opponent overcalls one diamond, partner passes, and right hand opponent bids one heart. Suddenly your eighteen point hand has disintegrated. It is likely that your diamond honors are worthless since the diamond bidder is behind you and probably holds the ace-queen and good spot cards in that suit. Right hand opponent holds length and probably honor cards in hearts, which takes away the value of your heart holding. What began as eighteen high card points should now be considered as eleven. Do not let this apparently good hand blind you. Further bidding would be very dangerous.

Example 2)

♠ QJ
♥ AQ6
♦ Q98653
♣ AK

Another very good hand with eighteen high card points and a six card suit. You are admiring it when the auction begins on your left with a bid of one club. Partner passes and RHO bids one spade. It is now your turn. Do you still like your hand? LHO likely holds the heart king and diamond honors.

RHO can probably kill your spades. After this beginning a simple overcall of two diamonds is not without danger. That is probably the call that you must make, but pass is certainly reasonable.

Example 3)

♠ 63
♥ K10754
♦ AK52
♣ KQ

A good hand with shape and fifteen high card points. As dealer you bid one heart. After a pass by LHO partner bids one spade. So far so good. Then the warning signs start to appear. RHO bids two clubs, and you try two diamonds. LHO, who was silent on the previous round, now bids two notrump. After two passes it is again your turn. You know that your side has at least half of the high card strength in the deck. What action do you take?

Pass quickly!!! Do not do anything rash. Be happy that your opponents have not found their cold game. All of the warning signs are present. There are heart honors behind your heart suit. The opposition has stoppers in spades. Your club honors are going to fall quickly. It is likely that your opponents are cold for three notrump. What? You don't believe that? Well, here are all four hands:

Example 4)

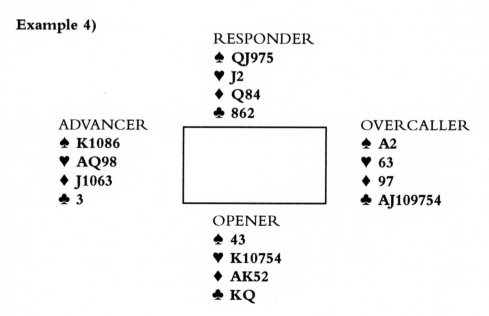

RESPONDER
♠ QJ975
♥ J2
♦ Q84
♣ 862

ADVANCER
♠ K1086
♥ AQ98
♦ J1063
♣ 3

OVERCALLER
♠ A2
♥ 63
♦ 97
♣ AJ109754

OPENER
♠ 43
♥ K10754
♦ AK52
♣ KQ

As you can see your opponents are cold for three notrump, even though their combined total is only nineteen high card points. The repeated message is clear. Do not be blinded by what appear to be good hands. When the auction tells you that your hand has lost its luster, do not chase after a bad result. It is very clear that most bridge players overbid good hands because they do not listen to the auction.

The opposite of this fault is even more apparent. Most bridge players when holding bad hands fail to understand when the auction makes those hands grow. They continue to look at the hand that has already been evaluated as bad and fail to understand that in the current auction the hand has become immense.

I was told about this hand which was bid by World and National Champion Jon Wittes:

Example 5)

♠ 8753
♥ 6
♦ 92
♣ Q97642

Jon's partner opened by bidding one spade. Jon believed that this hand would be a good dummy at a spade contract, so despite holding only two high card points he raised to two spades. Partner's next call was a help suit game try of three clubs. Jon had help in clubs, so he jumped to four spades. I was never given the exact hand, but it might have been this:

Example 6)

♠ AK9642
♥ 84
♦ A6
♣ AJ5

Notice that the double fits in spades and clubs produce ten tricks despite the fact that only eighteen high card points are present between the two hands. Jon correctly upgraded a poor hand at each turn to bid and understood that despite meager high card values his hand was good for the auction.

My Editor, Ron Garber, a very fine player, submits this hand that he bid:

Example 7)

♠ 953
♥ AJ
♦ Q976
♣ A953

Partner opened with one heart and Ron bid a **forcing notrump**. When his partner rebid two diamonds Ron considered the classic rebid of two spades (showing game invitational values and a diamond fit, but denying a spade stopper) but decided instead to show heart support by jumping invitationally to three hearts. Partner next jumped to four spades to show a good hand with spade shortness. Notice how this hand increased in value every time partner bid. Ron considered a cue bid of five clubs but feared that partner would jump to six hearts when Ron knew the hand should play in diamonds. So, Ron jumped to six diamonds. Question: should partner bid seven holding:

Example 8)

♠ —
♥ KQ10984
♦ AKJ3
♣ K74 ?

Playing in a Regional Knockout you hold:

Example 9)

♠ J874
♥ 9764
♦ J1062
♣ 5

The auction begins with one heart on your left, and partner makes a take-out double. After a pass at your right you bid one spade. LHO rebids two clubs and partner cue bids two hearts. RHO bids three clubs followed by two passes. Partner's next call is five spades. What action do you take?

Do you believe partner? The auction says that if you have second round control of clubs, a slam should be bid. Partner has shown first round heart control, and this jump to the five level announces that the club suit is his only problem—not to worry about spades or diamonds. Do you have the guts to bid six spades? Here is the complete hand which was bid extremely well by Canadian expert Barry Harper:

Example 10)

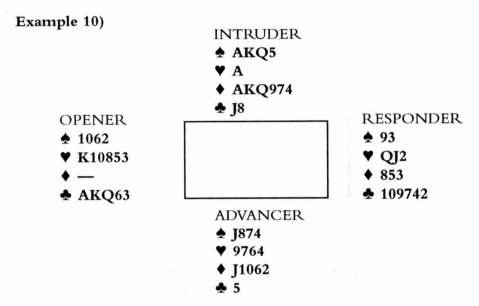

INTRUDER
- ♠ AKQ5
- ♥ A
- ♦ AKQ974
- ♣ J8

OPENER
- ♠ 1062
- ♥ K10853
- ♦ —
- ♣ AKQ63

RESPONDER
- ♠ 93
- ♥ QJ2
- ♦ 853
- ♣ 109742

ADVANCER
- ♠ J874
- ♥ 9764
- ♦ J1062
- ♣ 5

Dummy was quick to point out the presence of the valuable jack of clubs. If West had underled in clubs to try for a diamond ruff, declarer would have had to play that jack to make the hand. At the table the lead was a high club and another club which was ruffed—the rest was easy.

This hand was dealt in a lesson situation. My wife Mary reevaluated at each turn and bid to the best contract:

Example 11)

- ♠ 6
- ♥ 87432
- ♦ K75
- ♣ A843

The bidding went one spade by LHO and partner overcalled two hearts. RHO raised to two spades and Mary jumped to four hearts. Opener rebid four spades and partner next bid five diamonds. With a fitting honor in diamonds and controls in both spades and clubs, Mary jumped to six hearts. Partner's hand was:

Example 12)

♠ 1083
♥ AKJ106
♦ AQ832
♣ —

The slam was cold despite only 21 high card points including a wasted ace.

Here you have seen a series of little hands that became big because of the auction. Do not let your initial evaluation remain constant. When your hand grows because of the auction, you must upgrade that poor hand and bid the value that it assumes. In this last example Mary took a poor hand with seven high card points and first jumped to game, then jumped to slam. You must be able to change your evaluation and downgrade good hands that become bad, but more importantly you must learn to upgrade poor hands that grow when the auction tells you so.

Simon Says _____

One of the greatest bridge books ever written is *Why You Lose at Bridge*, by British expert S. J. Simon, which was first published in 1946. Simon points out that the player who overbids a good hand is usually opposite a player who similarly underbids a bad hand. These are his words:

"The average player overbids big hands and underbids his small ones. When the two hands are opposite each other this cancels out and a normal result is attained, so the loss on balance is not so large as it might be. Which is the reason for its continuance. On the cancelled hands, both overbidder and underbidder remain oblivious of their errors, while the others are dismissed as lucky or pass unnoticed.

"The trouble occurs when a collection of Aces and Kings goes to the hand of any but a very experienced holder. The ordinary holder, after he has finished gloating over them, will announce his strength with his opening bid of, say, two Clubs. And, if he gets a positive response from his partner, he promptly forgets what he has announced and keeps on rebidding the same values. Fortunately the opposite hand will usually underbid and so adjust matters. But when that hand is so weak that it cannot underbid; or more rarely, its owner believes his partner and bids the full value, then the loss is very large indeed."

After several examples, Simon concludes:

"Finally, as the supreme example of bidding bad hands, let me ressurect a hand from my once notorious article 'Master Bids' published in the British Bridge World in 1936. This article, which was entirely devoted to examples of bidding up bad hands, excited a great many jeers at the time and some of the 'master bids' I suggested were brushed aside as 'too fantastic for discussion.' But this particular bid, at first sight the most fantastic of all, was reluctantly admitted to be correct.

"Briefly, it was suggested that you should bid a grand slam holding one King and a complete Yarborough. This was the hand:

♠ xxx
♥ Kx
♦ xxxx
♣ xxxx

"You were East and the bidding went as follows:

NORTH	EAST	SOUTH	WEST
1♦	Pass	2♣	2♦
3♣	Pass	3♦	4♣!
4♦	Pass	5♣	5♦!!
Pass	5♠	Pass	6♠!!!
Pass	?		

"I suggested that a bid of seven Spades from you now stands out a mile.

"What it boiled down to was this. Partner, by sheer bullying, has pulled out of you a tepid preference for Spades rather than Hearts. On the strength of this tepid preference, he has bid six Spades. And you have the King of Hearts—the King of the other suit he is interested in. There is no reason why you should hold that King. Nothing in your bidding has suggested that you can conceivably be holding it. Therefore, he is quite prepared for you to make six Spades without it. Therefore, equally clearly, you can make seven Spades with it."

(Author's note: In modern bidding the first cuebid of two diamonds would be treated as natural by most experts. In a modern auction a takeout double would probably replace that call.)

Simon's logic is irrefutable. Your thinking must be as logical as his if you are to bid your little hands appropriately. It is clear that true hand evaluation requires that you listen to the auction and understand when your small hand grows, or, conversely, when a big hand becomes a death trap.

CHAPTER TWO
Opener Bids to Describe

Synopsis: You have learned:

1. To describe balanced and unbalanced hands as opener. The first priority is seeking a major suit fit, then trying for notrump, and playing in a minor suit only when both searches have failed.
2. To prepare a rebid when you open in a suit and partner has not yet passed, and how to describe size and shape with a rebid as opener.
3. To know when it is right to open one notrump holding the right values and a 5-3-3-2 which includes a five card major.
4. How to use the **reverse**.
5. How to use the **jump reverse**.

As Chapter Two continues we discuss how opener bids hands with both minors, and hands with a six card major and a four card suit. Problem rebids are discussed, then opener's jump rebid of four in the original minor, and the jump rebid of three notrump.

Hands with Both Minor Suits

A balanced minimum opening bid which contains two four card minors should present no problem. The opening bidder intends to rebid one notrump. However, there is disagreement as to the choice of opening bid.

One school of thought insists that these hands be opened with one diamond. The premise is that if there is a major suit overcall and a **negative**

double, opener's planned rebid may no longer be possible. Opener will then need to rebid in the unbid minor suit. When the opening bid has been in clubs and opener must now bid diamonds, the auction is quite awkward.

The other school of thought insists that these hands be opened with one club. The premise is that responder may have a hand which needs to raise clubs, and that becomes impossible when the opening bid has been one diamond (see Example 6 in Volume I).

We believe that both of these ideas have merit, and that on a given hand either choice of opening bid might work out for the best. We suggest that the opener select the minor suit that would be the best lead director if the bidder's side eventually defends.

Example 13)

<table>
<tr><td>a)</td><td>♠ K5</td><td>b)</td><td>♠ K5</td></tr>
<tr><td></td><td>♥ QJ6</td><td></td><td>♥ QJ6</td></tr>
<tr><td></td><td>♦ J743</td><td></td><td>♦ AQ105</td></tr>
<tr><td></td><td>♣ AQ105</td><td></td><td>♣ J743</td></tr>
</table>

Both hands of Example 13) are the same except that the minor suits have been interchanged. We suggest an opening bid of one club with 13a) and one diamond with 13b). Rigid adherents to either school of thought will get the auction wrong on one of the two hands shown.

When the opening hand with both four card minors is unbalanced, there will be a major suit singleton. In all such hands opener must bid one diamond. If responder bids one notrump or in opener's singleton spade suit, opener will then have an easy rebid of two clubs. If opener makes the error of opening one club, no accurate rebid will be available.

When opener has five diamonds and four clubs, opener easily starts with one diamond and has a two club rebid available. Hands with five clubs and four diamonds may not be so easy to bid.

With minimum values, opener must look to the respective quality of the two suits. With four good diamonds and five mediocre clubs, it is best to start by bidding one diamond and then rebidding two clubs. With four mediocre diamonds and five good clubs it is best to open one club and plan to rebid two clubs, if necessary. It would be wrong to start with diamonds and rebid clubs, since a minimum responder would take a preference to diamonds holding equal length, or even with a doubleton diamond and three clubs (see page 27 in Volume I).

Example 14)

a)
♠ A53
♥ 7
♦ KQ105
♣ K8643

b)
♠ AJ5
♥ 7
♦ K754
♣ KQ1053

c)
♠ AJ65
♥ 3
♦ KQ105
♣ K864

d)
♠ 3
♥ AQ65
♦ Q864
♣ KQ105

Example 14a) opens one diamond, preparing a rebid of two clubs. With good diamonds this opener does not fear a preference to the first suit.

Example 14b) opens one club. If the response is one heart, rebid two clubs on the good five card suit. If the response is one spade, the better bridge bid is to raise despite holding only three spades since they are of good quality. If the spades were poor, the rebid of the good club suit would be superior.

Example 14c) and 14d) must both open one diamond despite the difference in quality. A rebid of two clubs must be available if the response is one notrump, or one spade (in 14d).

Hands with a Six Card Major and a Four Card Suit _____

Minimum hands with six hearts and four spades present no problem. Opener is not strong enough to reverse. Opener bids and rebids hearts unless responder bids spades. Hands with six spades and four hearts are not so easy.

Mike Lawrence has suggested that opener's rebid should be based on the quality of the two suits. When spades have more high card points than hearts, rebid spades. When the suits are equal in strength or the hearts are stronger, rebid hearts. With six good spades and four mediocre hearts opener should bid and rebid spades. With another call needed, opener then bids the four card heart suit. If opener bids spades, then hearts, and at a third turn bids spades again, the heart suit is known to be of good quality.

When opener holds a six card major and a four card minor, the rebid choice should be based on the quality of the major. When the major is a good enough suit to play facing a singleton in dummy, rebid the major. When the major is of lesser quality, rebid the minor.

Example 15)

a) ♠ AQJ953
♥ KJ106
♦ 7
♣ Q6

b) ♠ KJ10653
♥ AQJ4
♦ 7
♣ Q6

c) ♠ J98754
♥ A4
♦ AKJ6
♣ 3

d) ♠ 6
♥ KQJ1064
♦ A874
♣ Q9

With Example 15a) opener bids one spade and rebids two spades because of 7HCP in spades and 4HCP in hearts.

With Example 15b) opener bids one spade and rebids two hearts because of 4HCP in spades and 7HCP in hearts.

With Example 15c) opener bids one spade and rebids two diamonds because of the poor spade quality.

With Example 15d) opener bids one heart and rebids two hearts since the suit is self-sufficient.

Other Problem Rebids

Hands will often occur which present true rebid problems. When this happens, our motto is to find and make "the least worst bad bid." There will often be more than one solution, but usually one stands out. Here are a few such situations.

Example 16)

a) ♠ K
   ♥ AQ84
   ♦ Q76
   ♣ Q9852

b) ♠ K
   ♥ AJ84
   ♦ KQ6
   ♣ Q9852

c) ♠ K104
   ♥ AJ93
   ♦ A
   ♣ J8432

d) ♠ 8
   ♥ K873
   ♦ KJ1064
   ♣ AQ9

e) ♠ 95
   ♥ KQ8
   ♦ A1074
   ♣ K982

f) ♠ KQ107
   ♥ 9654
   ♦ J6
   ♣ Q105

Example 16a) opens one club. If the response is in diamonds or hearts, there is no rebid problem. If the response is one spade, opener must choose between two clubs and one notrump. We regard one notrump with the singleton spade king as better than two clubs on a bad five card suit.

Example 16b) anticipates a similar rebid problem. However opener's values are too great for the rebid of one notrump and not appropriate for a reverse of two hearts. Opener forestalls the rebid problem by opening one notrump despite having an unbalanced hand. This solution becomes viable only when opener's singleton is a high honor, and other descriptive rebids are not possible.

Example 16c) opens one club and responder bids one spade. Opener's rebid choices are the rebid of the bad five card club

suit or a raise to two spades. The spade raise with a good three card holding is the superior bridge action.

Example 16d) opens one diamond and responder bids one spade. Rather than rebid diamonds, opener rebids two clubs on the three card holding. Opener knows that responder will take a preference to diamonds with minimum values holding two diamonds and three clubs.

The previous examples are not shown as expected auctions. You should not be proud of bidding as we have suggested in any of those situations. Please understand that we do not like to suggest these auctions, but EVERYTHING ELSE IS WORSE.

Example 16e) opens one of either minor suit. When the response is one heart, many openers will get cold feet and raise hearts rather than correctly rebid one notrump to accurately describe size and shape. When responder holds Example 16f) the correct contract cannot be reached unless opener makes the correct rebid. If the major suits are reversed and opener responds in spades, hearts have probably been denied, and a raise with three good spades is better than a rebid of one notrump with two small hearts.

Opener Jump Rebids a Minor Suit at the Four Level _____

Examine the logic of this auction. Opener starts with one club and receives a one spade response. Opener rebids by jumping to four clubs. What is going on here? Obviously opener has a very good and long club suit, but with such a suit why has opener bypassed the opportunity of playing three notrump? There can be only one reason.

Opener's jump rebid implies not only a very good club suit, but also a fit for responder's major suit in a hand that should have a reasonable play for game with that major as the trump suit. Opener does not need a great deal of high cards but must have values in the two suits shown. Opener should expect that if responder has a typical minimum for the response, the major suit fit and the minor suit trick source will produce ten tricks.

Example 17)

a) ♠ KQ85
   ♥ 7
   ♦ 63
   ♣ AQJ1084

b) ♠ K875
   ♥ A
   ♦ Q3
   ♣ QJ10864

Example 17a) is a typical minimum for the auction. Although opener has only 12 HCP, the concentration of values in the bid suits will produce tricks.

Example 17b) has the same distribution and high cards, but has no expectancy of making game in spades facing a minimum response. This hand simply raises to two spades. Note the importance of honor cards in long suits.

When responder has minimum values, a return to the agreed major suit at the four level will end the auction. When responder has honor cards in both bid suits and another control, the possibility of slam is very strong. Fits and controls take lots of tricks and responder should make a move toward slam.

Example 18)

a) ♠ A962
   ♥ 854
   ♦ K1073
   ♣ 95

b) ♠ A962
   ♥ 854
   ♦ A1073
   ♣ K5

Example 18a) bids one spade in response to an opening bid of one club. When opener rebids four clubs, this minimum hand signs off at four spades.

Example 18b) bids one spade in response to an opening bid of one club. When opener rebids four clubs, this hand should make a try for slam. A cue bid of four diamonds should show the diamond ace as well as working cards in the black suits.

Opener 17a) has a heart control and understands the auction. A bid of six spades should be easy.

Opener Jump Rebids Three Notrump _____

When opener bids a minor suit and jump rebids three notrump after a major suit response, two things are clear:

1. Opener has no desire to play game in a major suit.
2. Opener does not have a balanced hand.

Opener shows these things:

1. The suit of the opening bid is at least six cards long and is a source of tricks.
2. Stoppers in each of the unbid suits.
3. At most a singleton in responder's suit.

Opener expects a stopper in the suit of the response and expects to take nine tricks in notrump.

Example 19)

a) ♠ 5　　　　　　　　　b) ♠ 5
　♥ A3　　　　　　　　　　♥ AJ3
　♦ AKQ10752　　　　　　♦ AKJ1072
　♣ KQ4　　　　　　　　　♣ KQ4

Both hands of Example 19) open one diamond and jump to three notrump after a response of one spade.

Opener 19a) has what figures to be a solid source of seven tricks. When the trick source is solid, opener needs only one stopper in each unbid suit.

Opener 19b) has a trick source but might lose a trick to the queen of diamonds. With a possible loser in the trick source, opener needs more than a single stopper in each of the unbid suits. This opener has the possibility of two stoppers in both hearts and clubs.

With minimum response values and a stopper in the suit that has been bid, responder has the hand that opener needs and can pass. Responder will remove from three notrump with one of two types of hand.

1. When responder's major suit is long and strong, it may win no tricks at all despite the excellent trick source. Rebidding the strong suit usually increases the number of tricks.

2. When responder has no stopper (or a dubious one) in the suit of the response, removal from three notrump is necessary. There is a known place to play since opener has shown a long and strong suit.

   a. When responder is weak and has no stopper in his major suit, three notrump is removed to opener's suit. This auction is the only one in which a removal of three notrump to four of a minor suit is not a slam try.

   b. Without a stopper in the suit of the response but with values that might produce a slam in opener's suit, responder removes to the opposite minor. In some partnerships this removal just describes the nature of responder's hand. Others use this removal to both show values and ask for key cards in opener's hand.

Example 20)

a)
- ♠ KQ103
- ♥ Q76
- ♦ 94
- ♣ 10874

b)
- ♠ KQJ10963
- ♥ 5
- ♦ 93
- ♣ J62

c)
- ♠ 9764
- ♥ KQ5
- ♦ 94
- ♣ J1062

d)
- ♠ 9764
- ♥ KQ5
- ♦ 943
- ♣ AJ2

Example 20a) bids one spade in response to a one diamond opening bid. When opener rebids three notrump, pass confidently.

Example 20b) bids one spade in response to a one diamond opening bid. When opener rebids three notrump, this responder bids four spades. Although spades are stopped for play in notrump, play in spades will produce a better result.

Example 20c) has no spade stopper and poor values. This responder rebids four diamonds. Both Example 19) hands will probably settle for a diamond game which will usually make.

Example 20d) has no spade stopper but good values. Responder removes to four clubs to show this hand. Facing Example 19a) twelve tricks in diamonds are probable and facing 19b) the slam is better than average.

These two auctions should be added to the vocabulary of the growing player. In expert partnerships both rebids by opener will be understood even when there has been no prior discussion.

Opening and Rebid Exercises _____

What opening bid do you make with each of the following hands, and how do you plan to rebid?

1. ♠ K5
   ♥ Q102
   ♦ J863
   ♣ AQJ4

2. ♠ A5
   ♥ 7
   ♦ K9653
   ♣ AKQ104

3. ♠ K83
   ♥ AJ862
   ♦ K10
   ♣ KJ5

4. ♠ J7652
   ♥ AKQ93
   ♦ K6
   ♣ 5

5. ♠ A53
   ♥ 7
   ♦ J1087
   ♣ AKJ63

6. ♠ K6
   ♥ AJ3
   ♦ QJ8542
   ♣ K7

7. ♠ A53
   ♥ 7
   ♦ AKJ5
   ♣ J10876

8. ♠ 7
   ♥ KQ85
   ♦ J976
   ♣ AK82

With the following hands you have opened one diamond and partner has responded one heart. What rebid do you make, and why?

9. ♠ 7
   ♥ AQ104
   ♦ AQJ963
   ♣ 86

10. ♠ 83
    ♥ AQ5
    ♦ K10954
    ♣ A82

11. ♠ K42
    ♥ 6
    ♦ AKQJ853
    ♣ A8

12. ♠ 7
    ♥ AK95
    ♦ AQJ83
    ♣ AQ10

With the following hands you have opened one club and partner has bid one spade. What rebid do you make, and why?

13. ♠ KQ85
    ♥ AQ52
    ♦ —
    ♣ AK1082

14. ♠ KQ83
    ♥ AQ5
    ♦ 104
    ♣ AK82

15. ♠ AQ5
    ♥ KQ83
    ♦ 4
    ♣ AK1082

16. ♠ 6
    ♥ AKJ
    ♦ AKJ
    ♣ QJ10974

With the following hands you have opened one diamond and partner has bid one spade. What rebid do you make, and why?

17. ♠ AJ9
    ♥ KQ104
    ♦ Q10853
    ♣ 7

18. ♠ K
    ♥ AK73
    ♦ J8652
    ♣ Q108

19. ♠ 5
    ♥ AK73
    ♦ J8652
    ♣ KQ10

20. ♠ AJ103
    ♥ A82
    ♦ AQ1083
    ♣ 5

Answers

1. Open one club, not one diamond. You intend to rebid one notrump, but if your side defends you want a club, not a diamond lead.

2. Open one diamond, not one club. You have the strength for a reverse, but you have the wrong pattern. A reverse promises that the first suit is longer than the second suit. You plan to rebid two clubs—not three clubs. This hand is not good enough to force to game facing a minimum responder. However, if partner takes a preference to diamonds showing minimum response values, your extra values entitle you to bid again. You would bid three clubs to show those values and complete the picture of your shape.

3. Open one notrump. This hand passes all tests. It has three cards in the other major. It has no empty doubleton. It has texture and tenaces in all four suits.

4. Open one spade, not one heart. This is similar to problem two. Plan to rebid two hearts.

5. Open one club. You will probably need to rebid two clubs on your good five card suit, but a raise of a one spade response may be best. It would be wrong to open one diamond on such a poor suit.

6. Open one notrump. Yes, you have only fourteen HCP, but you can add for the long suit, and you have tenaces in all of your short suits.

7. Open one diamond. Plan to rebid two clubs. Your excellent four card diamond suit can stand a false preference.

8. Open one diamond. When you have three four card suits, two of which are minors, you have no choice. Suit quality does not enter into your decision. If partner responds one spade or one notrump, you have a prepared rebid of two clubs. If you mistakenly open one club, you will have no adequate rebid. (Some old timers will open one heart!!).

9. Rebid four diamonds. This shows a hand with an excellent six card suit and a good four card heart holding.

10. Rebid one notrump. Describe your balanced minimum. Do not panic just because you have two small spades. Partner may well have excellent spades.

11. Rebid three notrump. You have a classic hand for this auction.

12. Rebid three spades. This **splinter** shows a hand good enough to force to game in hearts.

13. Rebid four diamonds. This shows four card support with values enough for game, and shows a void in diamonds (three diamonds would have shown a singleton).

14. Rebid four spades. This shows four card spade support and a 18 or 19 HCP balanced hand. Failure to **splinter** lets partner know that you are balanced.

15. Rebid two hearts—a natural **reverse**. You show a hand with four hearts, longer clubs, and at least sixteen HCP.

16. Rebid three notrump. Not quite classic, missing the ace and king of your suit. But you do have potential triple stoppers in both unbid suits.

17. Two spades. You would like another spade for this raise, but no other call describes better. Do not rebid your poor five card diamond suit.

18. Rebid one notrump. The best of a poor lot. Do it, but don't like it!!

19. Rebid two clubs. A better choice than one notrump looking at a singleton small spade, or two diamonds on a very bad suit.

20. Rebid three spades. Partner will infer that you are short in clubs. You might have splintered in hearts, but did not, nor did you open one notrump. What did not happen often speaks volumes.

CHAPTER THREE
Is is Forcing?

Synopsis: In Volume I this chapter presented opener's three methods for making the auction forcing—the two club opening bid, the jump shift rebid, and the **reverse**. Responder's tools for making the auction forcing were also introduced—the two over one response, the forcing notrump, and Fourth Suit Forcing.

As Chapter Three continues we continue discussion of **Fourth Suit Forcing**, showing the one jump preference that is forcing, and repeats of and jumps in the **fourth suit**. We then discuss the removal of invitational calls, and auctions after opener bids and rebids clubs. A cameo on X–Y–Z bids is presented by the first of our guest experts, Fred Hamilton.

Fourth Suit Forcing

We need to complete the picture on the use of this tool. **Fourth Suit Forcing** may be used by a passed responder. Although responder does not have the values to force game, the need to make an auction invitational may still exist.

In auctions that have been made game forcing by a two over one response, responder may also need to use **Fourth Suit Forcing**. Responder may have no descriptive call and may need to elicit further information from opener. In such auctions the **fourth suit** should be understood as possibly being artificial.

Jumps in Previously Bid Suits _____

Jumps in previously bid suits are invitational. There is a single exception. When the auction begins with an opening bid of one club and a response of one diamond, opener's rebid will usually be at the one level. If responder continues by jumping to three clubs, this one jump preference is forcing rather than invitational.

When responder has invitational values it will be more important to seek a contract in notrump rather than pursue one in a minor suit. Particularly at match point scoring, game in notrump is far superior to game in a minor suit. The minor suit game is correct only when exactly eleven tricks are taken. If declarer takes either more or fewer tricks, the contract is certainly wrong. And, if notrump makes more than nine tricks when the minor suit game does make eleven, the contract again is wrong.

Most System players use **Walsh Responses** to the opening bid of one club. These responses are detailed in Chapter Six. With all minimum balanced hands opener rebids one notrump after the opening bid of one club and a response of one diamond. In so doing opener does not deny a four card major. Opener knows that responder either does not hold a four card major, or that responder is prepared to **reverse** to show a four card major as a rebid.

Because responder's **reverse** in these auctions is always natural and shape showing, responder can no longer make use of **Fourth Suit Forcing**. Responder therefore gives up the invitational jump when holding both minors with longer diamonds in favor of a forcing jump rebid in clubs. This is the only auction in which a jump preference is forcing rather than invitational.

Example 21)

a)   ♠ 6
       ♥ 95
       ♦ AKJ872
       ♣ KQ104

b)   ♠ 6
       ♥ 95
       ♦ KQ10872
       ♣ KJ104

Responding to an opening bid of one club, Example 21a) bids one diamond. After opener's rebid at the one level this responder makes the forcing jump rebid of three clubs.

**In the same auction responder 21b) is unable to rebid by jumping to
three clubs since that call would be forcing. This responder rebids
invitationally either by jumping to three diamonds or raising to two
notrump.**

Repeats of the Fourth Suit

When responder repeats the fourth suit it will usually be at the three level.
After introducing the **fourth suit**, when responder repeats a previously bid
suit at the three level, the auction is forcing to game. The repeat of the **fourth
suit** is different.

The repeat of the **fourth suit** is natural and shows a very distributional hand
with invitational values. If opener feels that a playable contract has been reached,
a pass is possible. That pass will rarely occur because all suits have been bid
naturally, and the three level has been reached. Three notrump is far more likely.

Example 22)

	a)		b)	
	♠ AJ98		♠ 104	
	♥ 103		♥ AQJ76	
	♦ Q64		♦ KJ1083	
	♣ KQ104		♣ 5	

**With Example 22a) opener bids one club and after a response of one
heart rebids one spade. Responder 22b) continues with two diamonds,
the** fourth suit, **and opener next bids two notrump. Responder continues with three diamonds, rebidding the** fourth suit. **Opener has the
option to pass but with a diamond fit realizes that three notrump
should be viable and makes that call.**

Jumps in the Fourth Suit

When the **fourth suit** is a minor suit, responder may have first bid to show a
four card major. When time comes to rebid, responder jumps in the unbid
minor to describe a six-four hand with minimum values. This jump rebid is
easy when opener has rebid one notrump since that rebid guarantees at

least a doubleton in the unbid minor. Although opener's rebid in a third suit carries no such guarantees, responder needs to describe, and the six card minor suit will nearly always be the best place for the hand to play.

Example 23)

♠ 62
♥ Q974
♦ KJ10862
♣ 5

Example 23 bids one heart (see Walsh responses in Chapter Six) in response to one club. When opener's rebid is one notrump, this hand jumps to three diamonds to show a weak hand with six-four distribution. When opener's rebid is one spade, this hand makes the same rebid, but understands that opener may not have a fit in diamonds.

Removal of Invitational Calls

An invitational call is just that. Invitational. It can be passed. When the invitational call is a jump rebid of a suit, removal to another suit below the level of game is forcing. Opener will have jump rebid to show game invitational values (15+ to 18 HCP), or responder will have jumped invitationally to show a long suit (and 9+ to 12- HCP). When partner bids again, even when that rebid is not in a new suit, the invitation has been accepted and the auction is descriptive and forcing.

However, when the invitational call has been two notrump, acceptance of the invitation is a continuation to three notrump. Simple removal of the invitation to a minor suit indicates that the previous auction has been based on distribution rather than high card values. This removal is a warning that three notrump is not likely to make.

Example 24)

a) ♠ AQ3
♥ J4
♦ AQ109752
♣ K

b) ♠ 7
♥ KQ10973
♦ 86
♣ A1054

c) ♠ AJ94
    ♥ 85
    ♦ Q62
    ♣ AJ102

d) ♠ 3
    ♥ K109
    ♦ AKJ1095
    ♣ 863

e) ♠ J6
    ♥ 4
    ♦ KJ974
    ♣ AQ1053

f) ♠ AK106
    ♥ 8
    ♦ Q109854
    ♣ Q3

Opener with Example 24a) bids one diamond and, after a response of one heart, jump rebids three diamonds to show a good suit and game invitational values.

Responder with Example 24b) bids one heart. After opener jump rebids three diamonds, this responder bids three hearts, which is forcing. Opener 24a) knows not to pass and raises hearts to game.

Opener with Example 24c) bids one club and rebids one spade after a response of one diamond. When responder jump rebids diamonds, opener's fit for diamonds causes opener to bid again. Seeking a heart stopper, opener bids three hearts (opener would bid three notrump holding a stopper in hearts) and responder with Example 24d) bids three notrump. Opener's rebid in hearts was clearly forcing.

With Example 24e) opener bids one diamond and, after a response of one heart, rebids two clubs. When responder next bids two notrump to invite game, this opener bids three clubs to show poor values for the auction and suggest that a contract in notrump would likely fail.

With Example 24f) opener bids one diamond and rebids one spade after a response of one heart. When responder next bids two notrump to invite game, this opener should bid three diamonds to warn responder that a contract in notrump would probably be poor.

Auctions After Opener Bids and Rebids Clubs _____

When responder holds two five card major suits with minimum values (5+ to 9- HCP) and opener bids clubs, responder bids one spade. When opener rebids one notrump, responder can bid two hearts, which is natural and non-forcing.

When opener's rebid is two clubs, a two heart call by responder is forcing and requires at least game invitational values (9+ or more HCP). Responder has no option in standard methods to passing opener's two club rebid. When opener holds three cards in either major suit, the result at the two club contract will leave a lot to be desired.

This problem can be solved if the partnership agrees that after opener's rebid of two clubs, two hearts is natural and non-forcing (alert). Opener can pass when holding four hearts but will take a preference to spades with fewer than four hearts and at least two spades. If this agreement becomes part of the partnership, responder must have an alternate auction when holding five spades and four or more hearts with game invitational or forcing values (9+ HCP or more).

If two hearts is not forcing, the partnership must play that two diamonds after opener's two club rebid is artificial and forcing (alert). Opener continues to bid as naturally as possible. Opener bids two hearts when holding four cards there, or bids two spades holding fewer than four hearts when holding three spades.

When responder holds five-five in the major suits with game forcing values, after opener rebids two clubs responder jumps to three hearts. Opener then knows to raise either major to game with three card support.

Example 25)

a)
- ♠ K9764
- ♥ Q10853
- ♦ 104
- ♣ 2

b)
- ♠ AK764
- ♥ AQ85(3)
- ♦ 104(2)
- ♣ 2

c)
- ♠ Q105
- ♥ 62
- ♦ K3
- ♣ AK10954

d)
- ♠ 3
- ♥ K962
- ♦ K3
- ♣ AQ10763

With the agreement that after opener bids and rebids clubs a one spade responder's second call of two hearts is non-forcing, Example 25a) can make that call.

Example 25b) holding four hearts must make the artificial rebid of two diamonds but with five hearts and an opening bid can instead jump to three hearts.

Example 25c) opens and rebids clubs after a one spade response. If opener rebids either two hearts (natural and non-forcing) or two diamonds (artificial and forcing), this opener bids two spades.

Example 25d) opens and rebids clubs after a one spade response. If responder bids two diamonds (artificial and forcing) opener can bid his four card heart suit. If responder holds either four or five hearts (Example 25b) the correct fit has been found.

If you decide to play this method you will be well placed when you are responder with both majors and minimum values. The frequency with which this problem occurs makes this method one you should consider.

A Modern Alternative

New ideas often appear in modern bidding. Their function is to streamline existing methods. We are quite fortunate that several prominent experts have agreed to present ideas that are the newest thoughts about how to improve various auctions. Following is the first of several cameos from known expert contributors.

THE X-Y-Z CONVENTION (1X-PASS-1Y-PASS, 1Z)
By Fred Hamilton

Much like two way **New Minor Forcing** after a rebid of one notrump, X-Y-Z can be used to advantage over any one level rebid by opener. Four specific auctions exist:

1♣ – pass – 1♦ – pass, 1♥; 1♣ – pass – 1♦ – pass, 1♠; 1♣ – pass – 1♥ – pass, 1♠; and 1♦ – pass – 1♥ – pass, 1♠. This method allows responder to make both low level invitations and **forcing jumps**.

In the early days of bidding all jumps were forcing. Later, most jumps became either weak or invitational. Using X–Y–Z you can have both. This is how it works:

When opener rebids a suit at the one level, responder bids:

Two clubs = a puppet to two diamonds. Responder will pass to play there, or more commonly will bid again which is **invitational**.
Two diamonds = a general game force much like **Fourth Suit Forcing**
Three clubs = **to play**, whether opener's first suit or not.
All other jumps = strong suits and suggest slam possibilities.

Example 26)

a) ♠ AQ63
   ♥ AKJ74
   ♦ 85
   ♣ Q7

b) ♠ Q642
   ♥ AKJ74
   ♦ 85
   ♣ Q7

In the auction: 1♦ – pass – 1♥ – pass, 1♠ – pass:

With Example 26a) jump to three spades which is forcing and invites slam.

With Example 26b) bid two diamonds to establish a game force. Support spades at your next turn.

Example 27)

a) ♠ A4
   ♥ KQJ1084
   ♦ K75
   ♣ Q3

b) ♠ A4
   ♥ KJ8643
   ♦ K75
   ♣ Q3

c) ♠ K64
   ♥ Q109742
   ♦ AJ5
   ♣ 7

In the auction: 1♣ – pass – 1♥ – pass, 1♠ – pass:

With Example 27a) bid three hearts which is forcing and slammish.

With Example 27b) bid two diamonds to force game, then rebid hearts.

With Example 27c) bid two clubs to relay to diamonds, then bid two hearts invitational. Why have to jump to three hearts and go down?

Example 28)

a)   ♠ K5
     ♥ AQJ83
     ♦ KQJ74
     ♣ 5

b)   ♠ A5
     ♥ AQ752
     ♦ KJ764
     ♣ 5

In the auction: 1♣ – pass – 1♥ – pass, 1♠ – pass:

With Example 28a) jump to three diamonds, forcing, showing good suits and slammish.

With Example 28b) bid two diamonds to force to game, then bid three diamonds. Your suits are too weak to jump and invite a slam.

Example 29)

a)   ♠ 72
     ♥ K854
     ♦ 83
     ♣ KJ874

b)   ♠ 72
     ♥ KQ54
     ♦ J98643
     ♣ 6

In the auction: 1♣ – pass – 1♥ – pass, 1♠ – pass:

With Example 29a) bid three clubs to play. If you bid two clubs and then three clubs, the auction would be invitational.

With Example 29b) IF you have responded one heart, continue by bidding two clubs to puppet to diamonds, then pass.

In the auction: 1♣ – pass – 1♦ – pass, 1♥ – pass, a continuation of one spade shows five or more diamonds and four spades, usually with a good hand.

However, if the auction is: 1♣ – pass – 1♦ – pass, 1♥ – pass, a continuation of two clubs is a puppet to two diamonds. Your next call will either be pass or an invitational bid. You can even invite in hearts this way without jumping. This allows a simple raise of opener's major suit rebid to be weak.

Example 30)

a) ♠ K854
    ♥ K7532
    ♦ A4
    ♣ 43

b) ♠ A4
    ♥ AK843
    ♦ KQJ53
    ♣ 3

In the auction: 1♣ – pass – 1♥ – pass, 1♠ – pass:

With Example 30a) why have to jump to three spades to invite? You may be too high. Just bid two clubs to relay to diamonds, then bid two spades—invitational.

With Example 30b) jump to three diamonds which is strong and slammish.

Example 31)

♠ 5
♥ K8
♦ AK654
♣ AQ742

In the auction: 1♣ – pass – 1♦ – pass, one of either major—pass; be careful! Three clubs would be weak. Here you must bid two diamonds, game forcing, then bid three clubs.

Example 32)

♠ 84
♥ KQJ1082
♦ A54
♣ 76

In the auction: 1♦ – pass – 1♥ – pass, 1♠ – pass:

> Here you want to invite in hearts. So, bid two clubs to relay, then three hearts to show a no worry trump suit.

This method makes all jumps strong (except to three clubs which is weak). X-Y-Z is off in competition or by a passed hand.

Opener MAY refuse the two club relay to two diamonds with a very distributional hand. If opener holds:

♠ AJ83
♥ 7
♦ 4
♣ KQJ10754

common sense should prevail. It is probably best to agree that opener can ignore the relay and bid three clubs.

The use of this conventional approach should facilitate both part score and slam auctions.

The reader will find that this presentation closely parallels that of **Grant Baze** in Chapter Seven. The relation is the same as that between **Fourth Suit Forcing** and **New Minor Forcing**. The two way checkback after a rebid of one notrump already has garnered a large following. X-Y-Z bids are relatively new tools at the expert level.

Forcing-Invitational-Non-forcing Auction Exercises _____

The auction has been one club by partner, you have responded one diamond, and partner has rebid one heart. What is your rebid with each of these hands and why?

1.   ♠ 84
     ♥ Q84
     ♦ K7642
     ♣ 1042

2.   ♠ 983
     ♥ Q5
     ♦ AKJ109
     ♣ K75

3.   ♠ KJ4
     ♥ Q5
     ♦ KQ1043
     ♣ 973

4.   ♠ A5
     ♥ 7
     ♦ AK962
     ♣ K10943

5.   ♠ AQ103
     ♥ Q4
     ♦ KQ987
     ♣ 104

6.   ♠ 854
     ♥ 6
     ♦ AQJ954
     ♣ K83

7.   ♠ K82
     ♥ Q4
     ♦ J752
     ♣ J864

8.   ♠ Q4
     ♥ AQ103
     ♦ KQ987
     ♣ 104

With the following hands partner has opened one club, you have responded one heart, and partner has rebid one spade. What is your rebid with each of these hands and why?

9.   ♠ J74
     ♥ AQ1094
     ♦ A83
     ♣ 62

10.   ♠ KJ85
     ♥ AQ103
     ♦ 852
     ♣ J6

11. ♠ 1074
    ♥ AQ10985
    ♦ 3
    ♣ A62

12. ♠ J74
    ♥ AQ109
    ♦ 8532
    ♣ A2

13. ♠ 6
    ♥ AJ52
    ♦ 865
    ♣ KQ1073

14. ♠ K1085
    ♥ AJ103
    ♦ AK4
    ♣ J6

15. ♠ K74
    ♥ AQ10985
    ♦ 3
    ♣ A62

16. ♠ 85
    ♥ J762
    ♦ KQ10973
    ♣ 6

With the following hands partner has opened one club, you have responded one spade, and partner has rebid two clubs. How do you continue and why?

17. ♠ KQ876
    ♥ AJ4
    ♦ 107
    ♣ K92

18. ♠ KQ876
    ♥ AQ43
    ♦ 1042
    ♣ 9

19. ♠ Q765
    ♥ 832
    ♦ KQ10983
    ♣ —

20. ♠ AQ83
    ♥ K104
    ♦ Q962
    ♣ 84

Answers

1. Pass. One heart should be as good a contract as any. And partner has shown an unbalanced hand (see Chapter Six) which means that your diamond king probably faces shortness.

2. One spade. This is **Fourth Suit Forcing**. If partner bids notrump to show a stopper in spades, you will bid game.

3. Two notrump. A natural invitation to game, promising a spade stopper.

4. Three clubs. This is the only jump rebid that is forcing.

5. Two spades. This is natural, showing four spades, five or more diamonds, and game forcing values.

6. Three diamonds. Natural and invitational, showing a good six card suit.

7. One notrump. You did not have the values to respond one notrump originally (8 to 10 HCP), but you have no choice now. You are happy to have a spade stopper.

8. Three hearts. This jump must show four card support, and since you originally bid one diamond you must hold five or more diamonds and game going values.

9. Two diamonds—**Fourth Suit Forcing**. You hope to find a three card heart fit.

10. Three spades. Natural and invitational to game.

11. Three hearts. Invitational, showing a good six card heart suit.

12. Two diamonds. Again, **Fourth Suit Forcing**. You cannot bid two notrump without a stopper in diamonds.

13. Three clubs. Natural and invitational.

14. Two diamonds—**Fourth Suit Forcing**. Your hand is too good to jump to four spades. When you show spade support at your next turn you will have invited a spade slam.

15. Two diamonds—**Fourth Suit Forcing**. You plan to rebid hearts, and when you do your auction will be forcing.

16. Three diamonds. Showing a weak hand with only four hearts and a six card diamond suit.

17. Two diamonds. You must make a forcing call. You cannot force in either clubs or spades, and bidding a three card heart suit is not a good idea. Temporizing in minor suits is safe—in major suits it is dangerous.

18. Two hearts, if your agreements are standard, which is forcing and shows at least game invitational values. If you have agreed to play two hearts as non-forcing in this auction, you would need to bid two diamonds which would be forcing.

19. Three diamonds. Again, this shows a four card major and six diamonds with minimum response values.

20. Two notrump. Natural and game invitational.

CHAPTER FOUR
Responder's Two Over One is Forcing to Game

Synopsis: The fact that a two over one response is now forcing to game rather than possibly just game invitational is the key to modern bidding. When responder makes a two over one there is no doubt about the minimum level that the auction must reach. All of the ambiguities that formerly attended such auctions are gone.

As Chapter Four continues we discuss bidding invitational hands as responder, game forcing free bids, and the **Walsh Negative Double**.

The hands that are most difficult to describe are those with game invitational values and a six card (or longer) suit. When the suit is lower ranking than the suit of the opening bid, responder is unable to bid it immediately. The two over one response would force the auction to game.

In Volume I, there were two instances where responder was able to use an immediate jump response to show a long club suit with game invitational values.

1. In response to the opening bid of one diamond, responder's jump to three clubs shows that hand (see Volume I – Chapter Four – page 48).
2. A passed hand uses a two club response to a major suit opening bid as **Drury.** Holding shortness in opener's major with a six card club suit and game invitational values, responder again jumps to three clubs (see Volume I, Chapter Eight, page 159).

The systemic auction that tries to solve this problem starts with a **Forcing**

Notrump. When opener rebids two clubs, responder can jump in diamonds or in hearts to show an invitational hand with a good suit of at least six cards. When opener rebids in diamonds, responder again can jump to three hearts.

However, when the long suit is lower ranking than the suit of opener's rebid, there is no descriptive call available. A jump in the long suit is no longer possible since that would take the auction to the four level, and a simple call at the three level shows the length of the suit, but not the game invitational strength of the hand (see Chapter Five, page 78). When responder has this problem it is time to improvise. Responder will usually continue by bidding two notrump even though opener will not expect this hand.

One solution is to agree that if responder makes a two over one and then repeats the suit as a rebid, the game force is removed. However, this solution creates another problem. When responder has a very strong hand, the auction to suggest slam and emphasize a long, strong suit is not available. Which of the following hands do you show when the auction is: 1♠ − pass − 2♣ − pass, 2NT − pass − 3♣ ?

Example 33)

a)   ♠ Q5
      ♥ J104
      ♦ 1083
      ♣ AQJ854

b)   ♠ K5
      ♥ AJ4
      ♦ 1083
      ♣ AKQJ84

With Example 33a) after an opening bid of one diamond this responder jumps invitationally to three clubs. However, after an opening bid of one spade or one heart, responder must first use the Forcing Notrump, and plan to rebid two notrump after a two level rebid higher than two clubs. A rebid of three clubs would show the long suit but would promise only minimum response values (5+ to 9- HCP). Some modern bidders solve the problem by agreeing that responder can bid two clubs, then three clubs, to remove the game force and make the auction invitational.

When the partnership has that agreement, it becomes impossible to describe Example 33b). If all two over one responses are uncondi-

tionally forcing to game, this hand can first bid two clubs, then three clubs which is still forcing and often slammish.

Another solution to this problem is for the partnership to agree that all jumps to the three level by responder are invitational with six card or longer suits. However, such agreement may take away other conventional responses which have greater value to the partnership.

Two Over One Responses in Contested Auctions

When an opponent overcalls, a two over one response is known as a free bid (see Volume I, Chapter Eleven, page 219 and 221). The requisites for a free bid are a suit of at least five cards and at least game invitational values (9+HCP). Even though in uncontested auctions the requirements for a two over one response have increased to opening bid strength, the free bid in competition still remains as it was in the dark ages.

Some modern bidders play that free bids must meet the same value minimums as all two over one responses. Partnerships that adopt this more stringent requirement for free bids have easier auctions when a game forcing free bid is made. However, when responder has only game invitational values and cannot make a free bid, auctions become much more difficult.

When the auction begins with one of a minor suit and an opponent overcalls one heart, if responder has five cards in the unbid minor and invitational values, most partnerships will be able to make a free bid. Those who have agreed that the free bid is forcing to game cannot bid freely and need some way to enter the auction.

The Walsh Negative Double

The solution to this problem is known as the **Walsh Negative Double**. Standardly, a **Negative Double** shows length in any unbid major suit. When there has been an overcall of one heart, the **Negative Double** is used to show exactly four spades, and a bid of one spade shows five or more spades.

When the **Walsh Negative Double** is the agreement of the partnership, after the one heart overcall, a bid of one spade shows four or more spades. In that auction a **Negative Double** denies four spades and promises a hand that wanted to make another call, but could not. In most cases, that will express a hand that could not make a free bid in the unbid minor suit because such a free bid would require game forcing values. Most bidders could make a free bid in the unbid minor. Those who require an opening bid are able to show that they most likely have that hand when they make the **Walsh Negative Double**.

Example 34)

a)
♠ 7
♥ A53
♦ AKJ94
♣ J1086

b)
♠ 7
♥ 853
♦ AKJ94
♣ Q1086

Example 34a) is responder in an auction which begins with one club and there is an overcall of one spade. This responder has no trouble making a free bid of two diamonds.

Example 34b) is responder in an auction which begins with one club and there is an overcall of one spade. If the partnership agreement is that the free bid shows invitational values (9+ HCP) this responder makes the free bid of two diamonds. If the partnership agreement is that even in competition the two over one response is game forcing, this responder must be able to make a Walsh Negative Double. **Be sure that your agreements allow some description in competition.**

In rare instances the **Walsh Negative Double** will be used with a hand that does not include five cards in the unbid minor suit. Responder may have a hand with values and no other expressive call.

Example 35)

♠ K52
♥ 973
♦ AQ85
♣ J96

In the auction that begins with an opening bid of one club and an overcall of one heart, the hand of Example 35) is difficult to describe. A bid in notrump would promise a stopper in hearts. A cue bid would imply a fit in clubs. The Walsh Negative Double **suggests five card length in diamonds, but should be made with this hand simply because this responder has values too great not to enter the auction. In this auction, double denies four spades and suggests five or more cards in the unbid minor, but this example must take some action.**

If your partnership adopts this agreement, indicate on your convention card next to **Negative Doubles** that a double "of one heart denies four spades." This use is not standard and requires an alert.

Considering these problems, we recommend that the solution be:

1. All two over one responses be forcing to game. With invitational hands that are problems, use the **Forcing Notrump** and follow with the best available auction.
2. Agree that in competition free bids which are two over one responses conform to the older standard, requiring only that the free bidder have a suit of at least five cards and a minimum of game invitational values.

As you can see, there are some problems relating to two over one auctions which must be considered. Your partnership will have some choices to make. Take the most comfortable path.

All in all the new standard that makes two over one responses forcing to game is a vast improvement over the former standard in which two over one responses were invitational or better. The solution to a problem often brings with it new problems. Having been exposed to the problems which arise when you adopt the new standards, you will need to choose between alternatives. Whatever choices you make, you will find that your bidding is far easier than when you used older methods.

Two Over One Auction Exercises _____

Plan the auction in response to the opening bid of one spade with each of these hands.

1. ♠ K83
   ♥ A5
   ♦ J63
   ♣ AJ987

2. ♠ 75
   ♥ AQ4
   ♦ 93
   ♣ AKQJ86

3. ♠ 4
   ♥ AKJ1073
   ♦ Q1092
   ♣ 64

4. ♠ 64
   ♥ AQ4
   ♦ KJ974
   ♣ J83

5. ♠ 6
   ♥ 875
   ♦ 1063
   ♣ KQJ982

6. ♠ 6
   ♥ J92
   ♦ QJ9763
   ♣ Q42

7. ♠ AK3
   ♥ A5
   ♦ J63
   ♣ AJ987

8. ♠ K83
   ♥ A5
   ♦ 863
   ♣ KJ875

With each of the following hands partner has opened one club and there has been an overcall of one heart. How do you continue and why?

9. ♠ AJ85
   ♥ 62
   ♦ K73
   ♣ 10984

10. ♠ KQ4
    ♥ 62
    ♦ AQ973
    ♣ 1098

11. ♠ 8653
    ♥ KQ4
    ♦ 104
    ♣ KJ97

12. ♠ KQ4
    ♥ 62
    ♦ AQJ73
    ♣ 1098

Answers

1. Respond two clubs. If partner rebids either two spades or two notrump, limiting the values of the opening bid, use **fast arrival** and jump to four spades. If partner bids two of either red suit, bid two spades to show minimum game forcing values with a three card spade fit.

2. Respond two clubs. After any rebid by partner, bid clubs again. The auction is still forcing to game and you are able to show your outstanding club suit.

3. You would love to be able to show your wonderful heart suit right away, but you cannot. A two heart response would be game forcing, and your values do not justify that call. Start by bidding a **Forcing Notrump**. Plan to jump to three hearts if partner rebids in either minor suit.

4. Bid one **Forcing Notrump**. If partner rebids any suit at the two level, bid two notrump to invite game. Your club stopper is suspect, but you have no better description.

5. Start with a **Forcing Notrump**. If partner rebids either two diamonds or two spades, bid three clubs. This shows a hand that has value only if clubs are trumps. If partner rebids two hearts, pass is possible.

6. Aren't you glad that you have a way to get to diamonds? If one notrump were not forcing you might play there. But your bid of one notrump will be forcing and you can correct to diamonds cheaply after any rebid from partner.

7. Bid two clubs. If partner rebids either two spades or two notrump, invite slam by bidding only three spades. If partner rebids a red suit at the two level, you will jump to three spades to show three card support and values that suggest a possible slam.

8. Start with a **Forcing Notrump**. Over any lower ranking two level rebid, jump to three spades to show a **limit raise** with three card support and no ruffing value. If partner's rebid is two spades, jump to four. If partner makes a jump shift rebid in any lower ranking suit, jump to four spades.

9. Using standard methods, make a **Negative Double** to show exactly four spades. If your free bids are game forcing and you are using the **Walsh Negative Double**, double would deny four spades so you need to bid one spade.

10. Using standard methods you can make a free bid of two diamonds. If your free bids are game forcing by agreement, you must make a **Walsh Negative Double**.

11. Although your spades are bad and you have good heart stoppers, it would be wrong to bid one notrump. Make a **Negative Double** if it shows four spades, but otherwise bid one spade.

12. Everybody makes the free bid of two diamonds, regardless of whether it is game forcing or not.

CHAPTER FIVE
Responder's Forcing Notrump

Synopsis: Chapter Five of Volume I (Forcing Notrump) was quite complete. The reader was able to learn about opener's rebids. Responder's rebids in both the minimum range of 5+ to 9- and the invitational range of 9+ to 12- were shown.

Most of opener's rebids were natural. There were two rebids by opener that were new. The first was the rebid in a three card minor suit. The second, the raise of the **Forcing Notrump**, promises a very good hand.

As Chapter Five continues we feature a cameo on the **Bart** convention presented by guest expert Mike Passell, and the **Meckstroth Adjunct** to the **Forcing Notrump** presented by its author, well known expert Jeff Meckstroth. Also included is a presentation on **transfers** after the raise of the **Forcing Notrump**, and notrump responses to a major suit opening bid by a passed hand.

More About the Forcing Notrump

After an opening bid of one spade and a **Forcing Notrump** response, opener will frequently rebid two clubs. If responder then bids either two diamonds or two hearts, it shows a five card or longer suit, shortness in spades, and minimum values (5+ to 9- HCP). When a minimum opening bidder holds a fit of two or more cards for responder's suit, pass will end the auction with no problem. However, when opener holds no fit, pass would usually lead to a bad result. Unless responder holds a six card or longer suit the defense holds more trumps than the declaring side.

With a singleton or void in responder's suit, it is standard for the opening bidder to remove responder's suggested contract and continue with the auction. When responder holds only a five card suit, this action is prudent. However, when responder holds a six card or longer suit, opener has unknowingly made a mistake. A five-one fit is not usually playable, but a six-one fit will usually play reasonably well. Opener has no way to know which action is correct.

This problem has been addressed at the expert level, and a conventional solution has been proposed. The solution was suggested by East Coast expert Les Bart, and the convention that results is named for him. Our presentation of this convention is by guest expert Mike Passell.

THE BART CONVENTION
By Mike Passell

In the auction: 1♠ – pass – 1NT – pass, 2♣ – pass – 2♦, the two diamond call is artificial and shows one of several hands. Opener should expect that responder holds exactly five hearts. Holding minimum values and exactly three hearts, opener will bid two hearts.

Responder will have one of five hand types:

1. Five hearts and two spades. Responder plans to pass opener's rebid (hopefully two hearts).
2. A doubleton spade honor with nine to eleven HCP. Responder plans to correct two hearts to two spades, pass a rebid of two spades, or raise two notrump to three notrump.
3. A game invitational hand with a good diamond suit. Responder plans to bid three diamonds.
4. A good club raise. Responder plans to raise to three clubs over partner's rebid.
5. A raise to two notrump with four clubs. Responder plans to bid two notrump.

Example 33)

a)
- ♠ 104
- ♥ KJ875
- ♦ Q102
- ♣ J73

b)
- ♠ K4
- ♥ AJ73
- ♦ 1096
- ♣ Q743

c)
- ♠ 62
- ♥ Q84
- ♦ AKJ975
- ♣ 85

d)
- ♠ 7
- ♥ AJ3
- ♦ J974
- ♣ KQ1085

e)
- ♠ 76
- ♥ AQ5
- ♦ Q974
- ♣ K1085

In the auction which begins: 1♠ – pass – 1NT – pass, 2♣ – pass – 2♦ – pass, ?

Example 33a) plans to pass either two hearts or two spades by opener.

Example 33b) plans to correct two hearts to two spades, pass if opener rebids two spades, or raise two notrump to three notrump.

Example 33c) plans to bid three diamonds next.

Example 33d) plans to bid three clubs next.

Example 33e) plans to correct either two hearts or two spades to two notrump.

This convention makes many other auctions flow smoothly:

1. 1♠ – pass – 1NT – pass, 2♣ – pass – 3♣ is a courtesy raise to preempt the opponents.
2. 1♠ – pass – 1NT – pass, 2♣ – pass – 2♠ is a very limited hand. It is either a very weak spade raise or more commonly a doubleton spade and less than 8

or 9 HCP. Partner knows not to make a game try with many 16 or 17 HCP hands.

3. 1♠ – pass – 1NT – pass, 2♣ – pass – 2♥ does not ask opener to pass or correct. Responder has six hearts (or five very good hearts) with a singleton spade.

4. 1♠ – pass – 1NT – pass, 2♣ – pass – 3♦ is not invitational. It is preemptive and to play.

All good hands start with two diamonds!!!

Example 34)

	a)		b)
	♠ 7		♠ 95
	♥ 95		♥ K932
	♦ K8543		♦ QJ4
	♣ Q9762		♣ 10987

	c)		d)
	♠ 5		♠ 5
	♥ QJ9862		♥ Q103
	♦ K104		♦ KJ10963
	♣ J52		♣ 852

In the auction: 1♠ – pass – 1NT – pass, 2♣ – pass – ?

Example 34a) raises preemptively to three clubs.
Example 34b) corrects to two spades—a weak preference.
Example 34c) bids two hearts to play.
Example 34d) jumps preemptively to three diamonds.

How does opener continue after responder bids two diamonds? Opener bids two hearts holding three hearts and minimum values, or jumps to three hearts holding three hearts and extra values. This is game forcing since responder has extra values also.

Example 35)

	a)		b)
	♠ AJ1053		♠ AJ1053
	♥ Q92		♥ A92
	♦ J6		♦ 106
	♣ A54		♣ AQ4

In the auction: 1♠ – pass – 1NT – pass, 2♣ – pass – 2♦ – pass, ?

> **Example 35a) bids two hearts holding three cards in that suit and minimum values.**

> **Example 35b) jumps to three hearts to show three cards in that suit and extra values.**

Holding fewer than three hearts and minimum values, opener rebids two spades. Responder will pass with a doubleton spade, bid three clubs with a good club raise, bid three diamonds invitationally, or bid two notrump with four clubs and 10-11 HCP.

Example 36)

> ♠ KQ854
> ♥ Q4
> ♦ AJ3
> ♣ 1095

In the auction: 1♠ – pass – 1NT – pass, 2♣ – pass – 2♦ – pass, ?

> **Example 36) simply rebids two spades.**

If opener continues over two diamonds by bidding two notrump, this shows extra values, denies three hearts, and is forcing. Opener will usually have an open suit. If opener's continuation is a jump to three notrump, this shows extra values, denies three hearts, and promises stoppers in all suits.

Example 37)

	a)		b)
	♠ KQ854		♠ KQ854
	♥ Q6		♥ K6
	♦ 1042		♦ AJ5
	♣ AKJ		♣ Q109

In the auction: 1♠ – pass – 1NT – pass, 2♣ – pass – 2♦ – pass, ?

> **Example 37a) bids two notrump to deny three hearts, show extra values, and imply an unstopped suit.**

Example 37b) jumps to three notrump to deny three hearts, show extra values, and promise stoppers in all suits.

When responder invites by bidding two notrump, opener may pass or accept. When opener accepts this invitation and holds three cards in the heart suit, the acceptance should be a call of three hearts. Remember that responder cannot go through two diamonds and then bid two notrump without holding four clubs.

Example 38)

♠ QJ1054
♥ KQ4
♦ 8
♣ AQJ7

In the auction: 1♠ – pass – 1NT – pass, 2♣ – pass – 2NT – pass, ?

Example 38) accepts the invitation and shows pattern by bidding three hearts.

All told, this is an easy to remember, good, practical convention. Its only downside is that responder is unable to play two diamonds. The advantage is that it limits all other bids at a very early stage. A "must play" convention for all intermediate and up partnerships.

Transfers After the Raise of the Forcing Notrump

Opener's raise of the **Forcing Notrump** promises balanced distribution (usually 5-3-3-2) and 18 or 19 HCP. It is almost forcing to game facing any minimum response. When the eventual contract is in notrump, responder will declare, but if the contract is in responder's long suit, it is right to have opener become declarer. To achieve this end, most experienced partnerships use transfer bids at responder's second turn.

Responder's continuation to three notrump is natural. However, all new suits at the three level transfer to the next higher suit. If responder's new suits were natural they would have to be forcing. The use of transfer continuations allows responder to control the auction and stop in a part score when necessary. It will be advantageous to have the strong balanced hand remain concealed and have the lead come up to its tenaces.

Example 39)

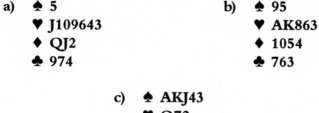

a)
♠ 5
♥ J109643
♦ QJ2
♣ 974

b)
♠ 95
♥ AK863
♦ 1054
♣ 763

c)
♠ AKJ43
♥ Q72
♦ K7
♣ AJ10

Example 39a) responds to the opening bid of one spade, hoping to reach a part score in hearts. Responder uses the Forcing Notrump **intending to sign off at two hearts after opener rebids in a minor suit. However, opener raises to two notrump. If new suits were forcing, responder would need to bid three hearts but opener could not pass. The eventual contract of four hearts would usually have no play. Playing transfers responder bids three diamonds and passes three hearts.**

Example 39b) responds to the opening bid of one spade with a Forcing Notrump, **intending to bid two hearts after a minor suit rebid from opener. When opener raises the** Forcing Notrump, **responder transfers by bidding three diamonds and continues to three notrump to offer a choice of games. Opener 39c) corrects to four hearts. Notice that the lead comes up to opener's tenaces in any suit.**

Example 39c) opens one spade and raises the Forcing Notrump **response. Opener declares three or four hearts facing each of the two responders.**

One of the hands responder will have when the **Forcing Notrump** is used is a three card balanced limit raise of opener's major suit. Responder rebids by jumping in opener's major to show this hand. When the **Forcing Notrump** has been raised and responder has that hand, certain distinctions can be made:

1. Responder can transfer back to opener's major, then bid three notrump. This should show scattered values in the other suits and no ruffing value. Opener can elect to play three notrump rather than the major suit game.
2. Responder can transfer to a suit which includes a concentration of values, then show the major suit fit. This may again allow for a contract of three notrump rather than the major suit game when responder's concentration bolsters opener's weak doubleton.
3. Responder can transfer to opener's major, then show a side source of tricks. This source should be a good five card suit, usually with two of the top three honors. Knowledge of the trick source may be all that opener needs in order to bid a slam.

Example 40)

	a)			b)	
	♠	863		♠	AJ542
	♥	K1054		♥	AJ
	♦	KJ6		♦	Q73
	♣	K98		♣	AQ2

Example 40a) uses the Forcing Notrump **in response to an opening bid of one spade.**

Example 40b) raises to two notrump. Responder then transfers by bidding three hearts and corrects three spades to three notrump. With a spotty spade suit and knowing that there is no ruff in the short trump hand if spades are trumps, opener passes and the superior notrump game becomes the contract.

Example 41)

	a)			b)	
	♠	KQ3		♠	AJ542
	♥	73		♥	AQJ
	♦	AQ1		♦	J6
	♣	98652		♣	KQ10

Example 41a) uses the Forcing Notrump **in response to an opening bid of one spade.**

Example 41b) raises to two notrump. Responder then transfers to diamonds by bidding three clubs, and then corrects to three spades. This gives opener a choice of games. Since responder has shown values where opener is weak, the contract of three notrump is indicated.

Example 42)

a)	♠ KQ3	b)	♠ AJ542
	♥ 95		♥ A73
	♦ KQ842		♦ AJ3
	♣ 862		♣ A4

Example 42a) uses a Forcing Notrump **in response to the opening bid of one spade.**

Example 42b) raises to two notrump. Responder bids three hearts to transfer to spades, then bids four diamonds to show a source of tricks. Opener has the controls and can expect ten tricks in spades and diamonds after asking about responder's spade quality. The slam is cold despite only 28HCP in the combined hands.

The raise of the **Forcing Notrump** can also lead to other descriptive auctions. The following shows how otherwise ambiguous auctions can be clarified. This cameo presentation is by another of our guest experts, Jeff Meckstroth.

THE MECKSTROTH ADJUNCT TO THE FORCING NOTRUMP
By Jeff Meckstroth

The function of the Meckstroth Adjunct is to clarify opener's hands which are worth a game forcing jump shift rebid. Current practices cause responder to wonder about opener's suit lengths. Sometimes the opening bidder will have five cards in his first suit and five cards in the suit of his jump shift as well. If this were always known to be true, responder would have an easy time showing support for either suit in continuing a search for a slam.

Unfortunately, opener's distribution is not always clear. Holding a 7–3–2–1 pattern or a 6–3–3–1 pattern, opener may have made the jump shift in a three card suit. If opener is 7–2–2–2 the jump shift might even have been made in a doubleton. When responder has a fit for opener's first suit there is little or no problem, but when responder has no fit for opener's first suit, the auction becomes difficult.

My solution to the problem is to assign a conventional meaning to opener's raise of a **Forcing Notrump** response. When opener raises the **Forcing Notrump**, responder is next required to bid three clubs with any hand which does not have support for opener's first suit.

If responder instead continues by bidding four of opener's major suit, that shows a weak hand with support for the suit. Responder's plan was to discourage opener by taking a preference to that major suit after a rebid in a lower ranking suit by opener, or to pass if opener simply rebid the first suit at the two level.

If responder continues by bidding three of opener's major suit, this shows a hand with three card support, limit raise values, and no side suit shortness. These are the only two hands with which responder would have used the **Forcing Notrump** while holding a fit for opener's major suit.

When responder does not have a fit for opener's major suit and when opener raises the **Forcing Notrump** response, responder next bids three clubs to allow opener to describe the game forcing hand. Opener's next calls are as follows:

1. If opener repeats the major suit, this shows a single suiter at least six cards long.
2. If opener next bids three diamonds, this shows exactly four cards in diamonds as well as at least five cards in the first suit.
3. If opener next bids three of the other major suit, this shows exactly four cards in that suit as well as five or more cards in the first suit.
4. If opener next bids three notrump, this shows exactly four cards in clubs

and probably only five cards in the major suit. If the major is six long, it is not a suit good enough to play facing a singleton in support.

5. If opener next bids four clubs, this shows exactly four cards in the club suit and six or more in the major suit. This also stipulates that the major suit is good enough to play facing virtually no support in responder's hand.

It follows then that when opener makes a jump shift rebid in a new suit after responder has used the **Forcing Notrump**, this promises at least five cards in each of the suits, thereby allowing responder to support the second suit with confidence when there is no fit for the first suit and three card support for the suit of the jump shift.

Opener's jump rebid of the major suit to the three or four level after the **Forcing Notrump** response remains unchanged. The jump rebid to the three level shows a six card suit and game invitational values, while the jump to the four level shows the desire to play game in the major suit facing minimum values shown by the **Forcing Notrump** response even when responder has no fit.

Any partnership which adopts this conventional addition to the use of the **Forcing Notrump** will need agreements to replace the traditional meaning of the raise of the **Forcing Notrump**. It is suggested that when the opening bidder holds 17 or 18 high card points in addition to the five card major suit, the rebid should be as with a minimum hand, in a three card minor if necessary. With 19 HCP and the appropriate shape (usually 5-3-3-2) opener can instead raise the **Forcing Notrump** to three notrump.

Example 43)

a) ♠ AKQ96　　　　b) ♠ AKJ10953
　　♥ 7　　　　　　　♥ 7
　　♦ AK52　　　　　♦ AQ5
　　♣ A84　　　　　 ♣ A4

c) ♠ AQ52　　　　　d) ♠ AQ9875
　　♥ AKQ964　　　　♥ 7
　　♦ 7　　　　　　　♦ A8
　　♣ A8　　　　　　♣ AKQ7

e)   ♠ 7
    ♥ AKJ975
    ♦ A8
    ♣ AQ106

f)   ♠ AKQ84
    ♥ A6
    ♦ 5
    ♣ AK1092

With Example 43a) opener has bid one spade and received a Forcing Notrump **response**. Opener next conventionally raises to two notrump and responder makes the forced call of three clubs. Opener next bids three diamonds to show a four card diamond holding as well as five or more spades and game forcing values.

With Example 43b) opener has bid one spade and received a Forcing Notrump **response**. Opener continues with a conventional call of two notrump and responder makes the forced call of three clubs. Opener next bids three spades to show a game forcing (and slam interested) single suiter in spades. If the hand had not been so rich in controls and so interested in slam, opener might have rebid by jumping to four spades instead of raising to two notrump.

With Example 43c) opener has bid one heart and received a Forcing Notrump **response**. Opener next bids two notrump and responder makes the forced call of three clubs. Opener then bids three spades to show exactly four cards in that suit as well as at least five hearts and interest in a slam.

With Example 43d) opener has bid one spade and has raised the response of one notrump conventionally to two notrump. When responder makes the forced call of three clubs, opener bids three notrump to show at least five spades and also four clubs. The auction also shows that if opener has more than five spades, the suit is not self sufficient.

With Example 43e) opener has bid one heart and has raised the response of one notrump conventionally to two notrump. When responder makes the forced call of three clubs, opener next bids four clubs to show a four card club holding and to stipulate that the heart suit is at least six cards long and good enough to play as the trump suit without support.

With Example 43f) opener bids one spade and, after a Forcing Notrump response, makes a jump shift to three clubs. Responder knows that this shows five-five in opener's suits, and can raise clubs holding spade shortness and only three card support for clubs.

Example 44)

a) ♠ Q84
   ♥ 7
   ♦ Q9754
   ♣ 10863

b) ♠ J5
   ♥ KJ83
   ♦ Q76
   ♣ 10982

c) ♠ Q84
   ♥ 75
   ♦ KJ97
   ♣ A863

d) ♠ A42
   ♥ —
   ♦ Q9853
   ♣ A9764

e) ♠ 7
   ♥ KQ83
   ♦ Q1094
   ♣ 8542

f) ♠ 7
   ♥ KQ863
   ♦ Q94
   ♣ 8542

Example 44a) is responding to an opening bid of one spade. Rather than raise to two spades, responder has elected to use the Forcing Notrump to slow down the auction. When opener next raises to two notrump, responder jumps to four spades to show support for opener's suit and no interest in bidding further.

Example 44b) has used the Forcing Notrump in response to one spade. When opener next bids two notrump, responder bids three clubs as required. If opener next bids three hearts to show a four card holding, responder will raise hearts to four. Over other rebids from opener, responder will make the most expressive call. In most auctions that call will be three notrump.

Example 44c) has used the Forcing Notrump in response to one spade, preparing to show a balanced three card limit raise. When opener bids two notrump artificially to force game, responder continues by bidding three spades to show this hand.

Example 44d) has used the Forcing Notrump in response to one heart. Opener continues with two notrump and responder bids three clubs as required. If opener's continuation is either three diamonds to show a four card holding or three notrump or four clubs to show a four card club suit, responder should indicate wonderful support by cue bidding the ace of spades. If after the Forcing Notrump opener instead makes a jump shift in either clubs or diamonds, responder again will show wonderful support by cue bidding the spade ace.

Example 44e) has bid a Forcing Notrump in response to one spade. When opener next bids two notrump, responder bids three clubs as required. If opener next bids three diamonds, responder raises to show a four card fit for diamonds, to deny a fit for spades, and to deny interest in reaching a slam.

Example 44f) has bid a Forcing Notrump in response to one spade. When opener next bids two notrump, responder bids three clubs as required. If opener next bids three diamonds, responder bids three hearts. Although opener has shown five spades and four diamonds, there may still be an eight card heart fit.

The One Notrump Response by a Passed Hand

In Volume I mention was made that the one notrump response to a major suit opening bid by a passed hand is no longer forcing, but that its strength range does not change. Particularly in third seat, the opening bid may be on less than usual values. The one notrump responder will never have a fit for opener's major suit because opener might pass and end the auction.

Do not fall victim to the belief that with a near opening hand which you originally chose to pass, you must do something to show your unexpected values. If a passed responder feels the need to jump to two notrump because of eleven or twelve high card points, whenever opener has less than full values the bidding side is probably too high. Why play two notrump with 11 HCP facing 10 HCP when one notrump would be far more comfortable? It is enough for a maximum passed hand to just bid one notrump. When opener has any hand that has game possibilities facing a passed responder, the auction will not end with one notrump. Opener will bid again.

Facing a non-forcing response of one notrump, when opener bids on it is for one of two reasons.

1. When opener has the values that would accept a game invitation (if offered), opener continues as though the response had been forcing. Opener may rebid in a three card minor suit, or even in a two card club suit after opening one heart with 4-5-2-2 distribution. When responder has a maximum pass this still allows game to be reached.
2. Opener may be light in values, but may have a shapely hand that could not afford to pass and play one notrump. Opener continues to bid because of shape, which responder must understand.

A one notrump response to a major suit opening bid by an unpassed responder requires an announcement. Opener must make a visual alert and announce "forcing." When the response of one notrump is by a passed hand it is not forcing, and no announcement or visual alert is required.

Forcing Notrump Exercises _____

Your partnership has agreed to use the **Bart** convention. With each of the following hands the auction has gone one spade by partner, you have used the **Forcing Notrump**, and partner has rebid two clubs. What is your next call and why?

1. ♠ K10
    ♥ J87
    ♦ AQ109
    ♣ J1075

2. ♠ 6
    ♥ 853
    ♦ QJ6
    ♣ K97542

3. ♠ 74
    ♥ KQ6
    ♦ J954
    ♣ AJ72

4. ♠ 4
    ♥ 765
    ♦ AJ8754
    ♣ 1062

5. ♠ J5
    ♥ KQ654
    ♦ J83
    ♣ 965

6. ♠ 86
    ♥ 10854
    ♦ KJ7
    ♣ K1092

7. ♠ 7
    ♥ J109853
    ♦ Q62
    ♣ K84

8. ♠ 8
    ♥ QJ10
    ♦ 7654
    ♣ AQJ94

Playing **Bart,** with the following hands you have opened one spade, partner has used the **Forcing Notrump,** you have bid two clubs, and partner has bid two diamonds. What do you bid next and why?

9. ♠ AJ1065
    ♥ K4
    ♦ AQJ
    ♣ J63

10. ♠ AK976
    ♥ K98
    ♦ 94
    ♣ AJ2

11. ♠ AJ932
     ♥ 64
     ♦ K102
     ♣ A32

12. ♠ A9632
     ♥ Q104
     ♦ 65
     ♣ AQ2

You have agreed to play **transfers** after the raise of a **Forcing Notrump**. You have used the **Forcing Notrump** in response to the opening bid of one spade, and partner has raised to two. What call do you make next and why?

13. ♠ KJ5
     ♥ KQ10
     ♦ J1073
     ♣ 864

14. ♠ 85
     ♥ KQ83
     ♦ Q1072
     ♣ QJ6

15. ♠ 763
     ♥ K105
     ♦ K962
     ♣ KJ4

16. ♠ 7
     ♥ K108743
     ♦ J65
     ♣ 1032

17. ♠ J2
     ♥ AQJ73
     ♦ 954
     ♣ QJ5

18. ♠ AJ5
     ♥ 62
     ♦ 852
     ♣ AQ1095

19. ♠ 6
     ♥ AQ10875
     ♦ J109
     ♣ 932

20. ♠ —
     ♥ 852
     ♦ J64
     ♣ KJ108753

You have agreed to play the **Meckstroth Adjunct** after the raise of a **Forcing Notrump**. With the following hands you have opened one heart and raised your partner's **Forcing Notrump** response. Partner has then bid three clubs as required. What do you do next and why?

21. ♠ AKQ6
     ♥ AKJ103
     ♦ A82
     ♣ 5

22. ♠ 5
     ♥ AKQJ87
     ♦ A3
     ♣ AQ103

23. ♠ AQ2
    ♥ AKQ10975
    ♦ 7
    ♣ A6

24. ♠ 3
    ♥ AKJ93
    ♦ AQ6
    ♣ KQJ10

Answers

1. Two diamonds. You will correct two hearts to two spades to show high honor doubleton and invitational values, pass two spades, or raise two notrump to three.

2. Three clubs. This raise is preemptive. You would first bid two diamonds, then three clubs to make a constructive club raise.

3. Two diamonds. Over two hearts or two spades, bid two notrump. This shows game invitational values with four card club support.

4. Three diamonds. Preemptive.

5. Two diamonds. You hope partner will bid hearts, but have no problem if the rebid is two spades.

6. Two spades. A simple preference.

7. Two hearts. Promising a six card suit and minimum response values.

8. Two diamonds. You will bid three clubs next, which will be invitational.

9. Two notrump. Showing extra values and implying an unstopped suit.

10. Three hearts. If partner has five hearts, as expected, you want to show your fit and extra values.

11. Two spades. Denies three hearts and shows minimum values.

12. Two hearts. Shows three hearts and minimum values.

13. Three diamonds. **Transfer** to hearts (partner will believe that it is a suit), then bid three spades. Partner will understand that you have a balanced limit raise for spades with a concentration of values in hearts.

14. Three notrump. An ordinary hand.

15. Three hearts. **Transfer** to spades, then bid three notrump. You show a completely flat hand with three bad spades. Knowing that there is no ruff in the short trump hand, partner will usually opt to play three notrump rather than in the eight card spade fit.

16. Three diamonds. **Transfer** to hearts, then pass.

17. Three diamonds. **Transfer** to hearts, then bid three notrump to offer a choice of games

18. Three hearts. **Transfer** to spades, then show a trick source – at least five cards including two of the top three honors.

19. Three diamonds. **Transfer** to hearts and raise to game. Partner is balanced and has either two or three hearts.

20. Three spades. **Transfer** to clubs, then pass.

21. Three spades. Shows five or six hearts and four spades.

22. Four clubs. Shows four clubs and a self-sufficient heart suit.

23. Three hearts. Shows a single suited hand with slam interest.

24. Three notrump. Shows five or six hearts that are not self-sufficient plus four clubs.

CHAPTER SIX
Rebids by Responder

Synopsis: Responder's rebids in various ranges and after opener has reversed have been covered.

As Chapter Six continues we examine **Walsh Responses**, the false preference, and **preemptive jump shift** responses.

Walsh Responses

In the opening pages of this Chapter of Volume I **Walsh Responses** were mentioned. The earliest published information on this approach was in **Five Card Majors—Western Style**, which was issued in 1974. In 1985 **Better Bidding with Bergen** presented this method starting on page one. It is not completely essential to modern bidding, but the advantages that accrue from its use have caused many modern experts to adopt the style. In fact, the modern ACBL convention card includes a box to check which says "Frequently bypass 4+ ♦."

Responding to the opening bid of one club, old fashioned methods require that four card suits be bid "up the line." The Walsh approach is to bypass a diamond suit of four, five, or even six cards to bid a four card major suit on all minimum (5+ to 9- HCP) and invitational (9+ to 12- HCP) hands.

With hands of opening bid or greater value, responder will still bypass a four card diamond suit to bid a four card major, but when the diamond suit is longer, responder will bid one diamond, planning to **reverse** to show the four card major as a rebid.

Example 45)

a)
- ♠ QJ84
- ♥ A53
- ♦ J1072
- ♣ 92

b)
- ♠ QJ84
- ♥ 53
- ♦ KJ954
- ♣ 92

c)
- ♠ QJ84
- ♥ 5
- ♦ KJ9542
- ♣ 92

d)
- ♠ AQ84
- ♥ Q5
- ♦ KQ1095
- ♣ 92

With Example 45a) responder to the opening bid of one club does not bid up the line, but bypasses the four card diamond suit to bid one spade. This practice has become reasonably standard among modern bidders.

With Example 45b) responder to the opening bid of one club again bypasses diamonds to bid one spade. This time the diamond suit is five cards long, but responder still does not have opening bid values. Only those playing Walsh Responses will bypass diamonds when the suit is five cards or longer. With both of the previous examples, if opener rebids one notrump, responder will pass.

With Example 45c) those playing Walsh Responses again bypass diamonds even though that suit is six cards long. However, if opener rebids one notrump, responder will jump to three diamonds to show a weak hand that has bypassed a six card diamond suit. Since opener's values have been limited by the one notrump rebid, responder's weak jump ends the auction. Opener is NEVER permitted to take a three card preference in this auction.

With Example 45d) responder to the opening bid of one club has an opening hand and will not bypass diamonds to bid spades. When responder has the values to insist on reaching game, it is imperative that suits be bid in their natural order. Responder

first bids the longer diamond suit, planning to reverse to spades as a rebid. Opener's most probable rebid will be one notrump which may conceal four card major suits. Opener can make this rebid knowing that if responder has a four card major suit it will be shown when responder reverses as a rebid.

After the response of one diamond, opener has no obligation to continue the search for a major suit fit. Opener knows that responder will usually not have a four card major suit. Opener also knows that if responder holds a four card major that hand will also include at least five diamonds and opening bid values. This relieves opener of any need to show a four card major suit as a rebid.

Opener will suppress one or both four card majors to rebid one notrump with any balanced hand (no singleton or void) of minimum (12+ to 15-HCP) values. This conceals from the defenders knowledge which could be vital. In older bidding methods where opener needed to show major suits, the defenders would know a great deal about where to attack against any eventual contract, most particularly in notrump.

When responder does not have a four card major, the contract will probably be in notrump, and the defense may get off to a very favorable lead for the declaring side. Declarer's major suit holdings have been concealed.

When responder does have a four card major, it becomes responder's rebid, and the search for an eight card major suit fit is reinstituted. Opener may have a fit for responder's major suit even after rebidding one notrump. After responder's **reverse**, opener will show the four card major suit which had been concealed. Since responder's **reverse** shows opening bid values, the auction is forcing to game. When opener does not rebid one notrump after the one diamond response, but instead bids a major suit, it denies a balanced minimum hand.

Opener is allowed to use judgement. If the balanced minimum includes a small doubleton in one of the major suits, opener may treat the hand as though it were unbalanced and not rebid one notrump. If notrump does become the final contract, it will be because responder has opener's weak suit under control, and will usually hold a tenace position that the lead should come up to rather than through.

Example 46)

a) ♠ K102
♥ AQ
♦ Q863
♣ K1084

b) ♠ K1092
♥ AQ64
♦ Q8
♣ K108

c) ♠ K1092
♥ 64
♦ Q83
♣ AK108

d) ♠ K1072
♥ AQ64
♦ 8
♣ K1084

With Example 46a) opener bids one club. When responder bids one diamond, opener rebids one notrump. It is clear to protect tenaces in all suits and cause this hand to declare notrump, rather than to raise diamonds.

With Example 46b) opener again bids one club. When responder bids one diamond, opener rebids one notrump. Opener does not show either major suit. Responder will not hold a four card major unless able to reverse as a rebid to show that major as well as longer diamonds and game forcing values.

With Example 46c) opener bids one club. When responder bids one diamond, this opener should judge to rebid one spade rather than one notrump. Responder will expect an unbalanced hand, but opener should not rush to declare notrump with such a weak holding in hearts. If responder has a heart stopper and becomes the notrump declarer the result will probably be better than with opener as declarer and responder's heart stopper subject to attack on the opening lead.

With Example 46d) opener bids one club. When responder bids one diamond, this opener will continue by bidding one heart to describe an unbalanced hand.

We strongly recommend that the reader take careful note of this approach. It integrates well with all of the other modern bidding practices. Note that responder's jump rebid in a minor suit after the initial response in a major and a rebid of one notrump by opener was mentioned in Volume I on page 113. In that presentation responder had not bypassed a minor suit to bid a four card major. Opener had first bid one diamond and responder's six card suit was clubs. The same type of auction occurs when responder has by-passed a six card diamond suit to bid a four card major when **Walsh Responses** are the agreement of the bidding pair.

The False Preference

In some specific auctions responder with minimum values (5+ to 9- HCP) may need to take a **false preference**. This means that responder will take opener back to the first suit opener has bid when holding two cards there and three cards in the suit of opener's rebid.

This happens routinely when opener has bid a major suit, responder has used the **Forcing Notrump**, and opener has rebid in a minor suit. Opener is known to hold five cards in the major suit and will often have rebid in a three card minor suit. In fact, when opener has bid one heart and rebids two clubs, the pattern might be 4-5-2-2. Opener was forced to rebid in a two card suit.

Responder might even hold four cards in the minor suit of opener's rebid, but will still take the preference. The return to opener's major suit shows a doubleton in support, but responder prefers to play in the known five-two major suit fit rather than a three-four fit in a minor suit.

Example 47)

a)   ♠ AQ1074　　　　b)   ♠ J5
      ♥ K3　　　　　　　　　 ♥ 10954
      ♦ 1082　　　　　　　　 ♦ A76
      ♣ AJ5　　　　　　　　　 ♣ Q973

Example 47a) opens one spade and rebids two clubs after responder uses the Forcing Notrump.

Responder with Example 47b) takes a preference back to spades with a doubleton. The five-two fit in a major suit is preferred over a three-four fit in a minor suit.

When opener starts by bidding one spade and rebids two hearts, the minimum suit lengths shown are five spades and four hearts. When a minimum responder holds two spades and three hearts, the **false preference** should be made. In most such auctions opener will play a five-two spade fit rather than a four-three in hearts.

On some occasions opener will have five-five in the major suits. When responder takes the **false preference**, opener will pass and play in the five-two spade fit when the five-three in hearts could have been more comfortable. However, opener might also be six-four in the majors with six bad spades and four better hearts. Play in the six-two spade fit rather than in the four-three heart fit is far superior.

Although in some instances an inferior fit will be reached, more often than not the **false preference** will lead to the best contract (see page 10 in Chapter Two, which discusses opener's rebids when holding both major suits).

Example 48)

a) ♠ AQ1074   b) ♠ J5
   ♥ K983   ♥ J72
   ♦ 8   ♦ A765
   ♣ AJ5   ♣ Q973

c) ♠ AQ1074   d) ♠ A10743
   ♥ K9853   ♥ AK93
   ♦ 8   ♦ 8
   ♣ AJ   ♣ 76

Example 48a) opens one spade and rebids two hearts after a Forcing Notrump **response.**

Responder with Example 48b) takes a false preference **and bids**

two spades rather than pass two hearts. Declarer plays the five-two fit in spades rather than the four-three fit in hearts.

Example 48c) opens one spade and rebids two hearts after a Forcing Notrump **response. When Example 48b) takes the** false preference **back to spades, opener plays the five-two spade fit when the five-three heart fit would have been more comfortable.**

Example 48d) opens one spade and rebids two hearts after a Forcing Notrump **response. When Example 48b) takes the** false preference **back to spades, opener plays the six-two spade fit rather than the four-three heart fit.**

A similar problem might occur when opener bids one diamond and rebids two clubs. There is one small difference. Opener may have generated this auction holding only four diamonds and five clubs (see page 9 in Chapter One). Needing to plan a rebid, opener looks to the relative quality of the two minor suits when holding this pattern. An opening bid of one diamond on a four card holding while holding five clubs needs good diamonds (♠A73 ♥6 ♦AQ104 ♣Q8754).

When opener's diamonds are poor, the opening bid should be one club planning to rebid the five card club suit rather than start with one diamond and play in a four-two fit with a weak diamond suit after responder takes a **false preference**. Also, if the bidding side defends, opener would far rather have a club lead than a diamond.

When opener's four card diamond suit is good and opener bids it first planning a rebid in clubs, the contract will sometimes be played in a four-two diamond fit when a five-three club fit also exists. The extenuating factor will be that opener's diamonds are good when this happens.

Opener also may have bid one diamond holding five, and rebid two clubs on a three card holding (see Example 16d) on page eleven). In this instance the **false preference** gets the bidding side to a five-two fit in diamonds rather than a three-three fit in clubs.

Example 49)

a)　♠ K32
　　♥ 6
　　♦ AJ1062
　　♣ KQ75

b)　♠ Q954
　　♥ KJ103
　　♦ Q7
　　♣ 1082

c)　♠ K3
　　♥ 6
　　♦ AJ1063
　　♣ KQ753

d)　♠ K32
　　♥ 6
　　♦ AJ109
　　♣ KQ753

e)　♠ K3
　　♥ 6
　　♦ AJ10652
　　♣ KQ75

f)　♠ 6
　　♥ Q1083
　　♦ KJ1062
　　♣ AK7

Example 49a) opens one diamond and rebids two clubs after a major suit response. When responder takes a false preference holding two diamonds and three clubs, opener declares in a five-two fit rather than in a four-three fit.

Responder with Example 49b) bids one heart after an opening bid of one diamond. When opener rebids two clubs, this hand takes a false preference by bidding two diamonds.

Example 49c) opens one diamond and rebids two clubs after a major suit response. When responder takes a false preference holding two diamonds and three clubs, opener declares in a five-two fit rather than in a five-three fit.

Example 49d) must plan a suit rebid with this unbalanced hand. The choices are to open one diamond and rebid two clubs, or to open one club and rebid two clubs. The relative quality of the two suits will be the determining factor. Because the diamonds are good and the clubs mediocre, opener opts to start with one diamond and rebid clubs. When responder with Example 49b) takes a false preference, opener declares in a four-two fit when a five-three fit is available (tough luck). Although this may not be best, the good quality in diamonds eases the pain.

Example 49e) opens one diamond and rebids two clubs. The false preference **gets the bidding side to a six-two fit in diamonds instead of a four-three fit in clubs.**

Example 49f) opens one diamond and after a response of one spade rebids two clubs (the least worst bad bid). When responder holds two diamonds and three clubs, the false preference **gets the bidding side to a five-two fit in diamonds rather than a three-three fit in clubs.**

Thus far we have discussed the finding of fits through the **false preference**. On balance there will be more auctions well served when the **false preference** is used, but not just because of the finding of fits. If responder fails to take the **false preference**, the auction ends before opener can show extra values. When the auction continues, opener gets a chance to bid again holding extra values, and a reasonable game might be reached which otherwise could not be bid.

Example 50)

a)
- ♠ J7
- ♥ 1094
- ♦ Q963
- ♣ AJ97

b)
- ♠ AK852
- ♥ AQJ63
- ♦ K8
- ♣ 3

c)
- ♠ AK852
- ♥ AJ63
- ♦ K8
- ♣ Q10

d)
- ♠ AQ10852
- ♥ AK63
- ♦ K8
- ♣ 3

e)
- ♠ K1085
- ♥ Q963
- ♦ Q7
- ♣ J105

f)
- ♠ QJ2
- ♥ K
- ♦ AJ1072
- ♣ KQ73

Example 50a) bids a Forcing Notrump in response to the opening bid of one spade. When opener rebids two hearts, if responder passes - taking a heart preference - the auction ends. If
responder takes the false preference by bidding two spades, when
opener holds extra values a game that should be bid can be bid.

Example 50b) opens one spade and rebids two hearts after a
Forcing Notrump response. When responder prefers hearts by
passing, two hearts becomes the contract. When responder takes
a preference to spades, this opener shows extra values by bidding three hearts. Example 50a) raises hearts to game.

Example 50c) opens one spade and rebids two hearts after a
Forcing Notrump response. When responder prefers hearts by
passing, two hearts becomes the contract. When responder takes
a preference to spades, this opener bids two notrump to show
an otherwise balanced hand with extra values. Example 50a)
accepts the invitation and bids three notrump.

Example 50d) opens one spade and rebids two hearts after a
Forcing Notrump response. When responder prefers hearts by
passing, two hearts becomes the contract. When responder takes
a preference to spades, this opener shows extra values and invites game by bidding three spades. Responder 50a) accepts the
invitation and bids four spades.

Example 50e) responds to an opening bid of one diamond by
bidding one heart. Opener rebids two clubs. If this responder
prefers clubs by passing, the auction is over. If this responder
takes a false preference by bidding two diamonds, opener has a
chance to bid again with extra values.

Example 50f) opens one diamond and rebids two clubs after a
response of one heart. When responder takes a preference to
two diamonds, this opener shows extra values and invites game
by bidding two notrump. Responder 50e) has good values and
accepts the invitation.

Preemptive Jump Shift Responses _____

Keeping with today's philosophy, most modern bidders use jump shift responses not to show strong hands, but to show weak hands. Jump shift responses have traditionally been used to suggest slam, but those slam suggestions can be conveyed in slow moving auctions, and with bidding space conserved there is an easier opportunity to find fits that will produce the needed tricks to make a slam.

Preemptive jump shift responses can be made in higher ranking suits at the two level, or in lower ranking suits at the three level. The requirements change as the level changes.

When the jump shift response is in a higher ranking suit at the two level, only six auctions are possible. In response to one club responder can bid two diamonds, two hearts, or two spades. In response to one diamond responder can jump to two hearts or two spades. In response to one heart responder can jump to two spades. These six auctions present severe restrictions which differ from the requirements for **preemptive jump shifts** that are made to the three level.

Preemptive jump shifts to the two level should indicate that responder's values are less than those for a normal minimum response. Since the value range for a minimum response begins normally at a good five HCP, the jump shift to the two level should show fewer values than a good five HCP and a six or seven card suit.

Responder will rarely be totally broke. The assumed value range for a **preemptive jump shift** to the two level is about two to five HCP. Despite these limitations, responder can have many different hand types. Sometimes responder's values will be in the suit of the jump shift—sometimes they will not. Sometimes responder's pattern will be better than others.

Opener will rarely need to know more about responder's jump shift. With most hands opener will pass and the opponents will have to determine whether or not to continue. In two situations opener will take further action.

When opener has minimum values and a fit of three or four cards for responder, opener will raise the jump shift to the three level. This is not to be construed as a forward going action. Opener knows that the opponents can make some contract at the three level or higher. Opener's raise is an extension of the preemptive action originated by responder's jump shift.

When opener believes that a game is possible facing responder's jump shift, opener will hold a fit and good values. Most often opener will have a hand that had planned a jump rebid to two notrump to show 18 or 19 HCP and a balanced hand. Opener needs to determine as much as possible about the nature of responder's hand in order to know whether or not to continue to game in responder's suit.

Opener can continue by bidding two notrump to ask responder about the nature of the jump shift. Responder must alert this continuation. Opener's bid is an artificial game try rather than an attempt to play two notrump.

The best system available when opener seeks information is the convention known as **Ogust**. Created by the late Harold Ogust, this convention asks for a description in steps. Responder continues as follows:

1. Three clubs shows a bad hand with a bad suit.
2. Three diamonds shows a bad hand with a good suit.
3. Three hearts shows a good hand with a bad suit.
4. Three spades shows a good hand with a good suit.

Hands that are otherwise balanced outside the long suit should be considered bad. Those that have distributional features outside the known long suit should be considered good.

Suit quality is easier to determine. When the limited high cards are in the suit it will be considered good. When they are outside the suit it is obviously bad.

Example 51)

	a)		b)	
	♠	J87543	♠	QJ9875
	♥	85	♥	85
	♦	964	♦	964
	♣	Q2	♣	32

c) ♠ 10976543
    ♥ 2
    ♦ Q96
    ♣ 54

d) ♠ KJ108754
    ♥ 6
    ♦ 8643
    ♣ 2

All Example 51) hands would make a jump shift response of two spades after an opening bid in any of the lower ranking suits. If opener continues by bidding two notrump to ask the quality of the jump shift, these responders, using Ogust, bid as follows:

Example 51a) bids three clubs to show a bad hand with a bad suit. The 6-3-2-2 pattern is the worst that responder might hold. The suit quality is clearly poor.

Example 51b) bids three diamonds to show a bad hand with a good suit. The pattern is bad as before, but all of the high cards and some good spots are in the suit.

Example 51c) bids three hearts to show a good hand with a bad suit. With a seventh card and shape outside the suit this hand has become as good as might be expected, but the suit quality is clearly poor.

Example 51d) bids three spades to show a good hand with a good suit. The shape is wonderfully unbalanced and all of the high cards are in the suit.

Jump shifts to the three level require better hands and better suits, although the nature of the bid does limit responder's values and defensive capability. At the three level, responder's call has no HCP limit and should be regulated by the rule of 2, 3 & 4. Those stipulations were made in Volume I where preemptive bids are discussed. Responder should have a six or seven card suit, and should have winners enough to protect the bidding side against penalties beyond the normal scope.

It will become apparent later that most of responder's jumps to lower ranking suits at the three level will become various types of major suit raises. Chapter Eight discusses responder's conventional raises in great detail.

Responder's Rebid Exercises

Playing **Walsh Responses** what do you bid as responder to the opening bid of one club?

1. ♠ A5
    ♥ KQ103
    ♦ A642
    ♣ J32

2. ♠ Q63
    ♥ KQ103
    ♦ J7542
    ♣ 5

3. ♠ J3
    ♥ A1062
    ♦ QJ9754
    ♣ 5

4. ♠ 62
    ♥ AQ85
    ♦ AK1073
    ♣ 94

Playing **Walsh Responses** you have opened one club and your partner has responded one diamond. What is your rebid?

5. ♠ K85
    ♥ AJ93
    ♦ 84
    ♣ KQ92

6. ♠ A62
    ♥ KJ102
    ♦ 6
    ♣ A10985

7. ♠ AQ85
    ♥ KJ102
    ♦ 84
    ♣ K107

8. ♠ 62
    ♥ AJ92
    ♦ K85
    ♣ KQ92

With the following hands, plan your opening bid and your rebid assuming a response that does not consume space.

9. ♠ K63
    ♥ 5
    ♦ Q642
    ♣ AK1098

10. ♠ K63
    ♥ 5
    ♦ AK109
    ♣ Q8642

11. ♠ Q97543   12. ♠ AJ9762
     ♥ A5   ♥ AKJ3
     ♦ KQJ10   ♦ 65
     ♣ J   ♣ 10

In response to the opening bid of one spade you have used the **Forcing Notrump** and partner has rebid two hearts. What is your next call?

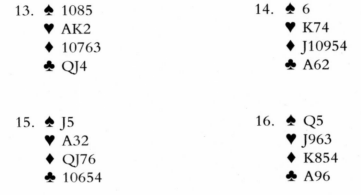

13. ♠ 1085   14. ♠ 6
     ♥ AK2   ♥ K74
     ♦ 10763   ♦ J10954
     ♣ QJ4   ♣ A62

15. ♠ J5   16. ♠ Q5
     ♥ A32   ♥ J963
     ♦ QJ76   ♦ K854
     ♣ 10654   ♣ A96

Playing **preemptive jump shift** responses, you have opened one club and your partner has bid two spades. How do you continue with each of these hands?

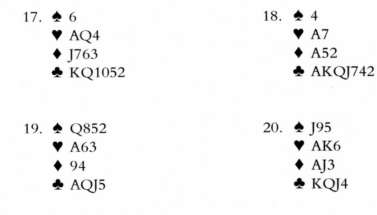

17. ♠ 6   18. ♠ 4
     ♥ AQ4   ♥ A7
     ♦ J763   ♦ A52
     ♣ KQ1052   ♣ AKQJ742

19. ♠ Q852   20. ♠ J95
     ♥ A63   ♥ AK6
     ♦ 94   ♦ AJ3
     ♣ AQJ5   ♣ KQJ4

Playing **preemptive jump shift** responses with **Ogust** continuations after a two notrump rebid, you have bid two hearts in response to an opening bid of one club, and partner has bid two notrump. What call do you make?

21. ♠ 6
    ♥ KJ98742
    ♦ 10954
    ♣ 3

22. ♠ 62
    ♥ 1098765
    ♦ Q3
    ♣ J82

23. ♠ 6
    ♥ J98765
    ♦ K962
    ♣ 104

24. ♠ 62
    ♥ QJ109754
    ♦ 83
    ♣ 92

Answers

1. One heart. Most modern bidders will bypass a four card diamond suit to bid a four card major.

2. One heart. Bypassing a five card diamond suit to bid a four card major is not so common, but it is part of the **Walsh Response** agreement.

3. One heart. Do not dream of bypassing a six card diamond suit to bid a four card major unless your agreement is **Walsh Responses**. If partner rebids either one spade or one notrump, you will jump to three diamonds to show your weak six-four hand.

4. One diamond. Responder with opening bid values should always bid suits in their natural order. The natural response of one diamond prepares a **reverse** as responder's rebid which will paint a picture of suit lengths and show game going values.

5. One notrump. Do not fear missing a four-four heart fit. If partner has four hearts they will be shown by a **reverse** as responder's rebid. After the one diamond response, rebid one notrump with any balanced minimum, feeling free to conceal four card majors (partner should alert and explain, if asked, that you show any balanced minimum and may conceal one or both four card majors).

6. One heart. Your rebid in a major suit after the one diamond response shows an unbalanced hand not suited to a rebid of one notrump.

7. One notrump. If you can conceal one four card major, you can also conceal two. If partner has four in either, a **reverse** at responder's next call will show it.

8. One heart. Yes, we do hold a balanced minimum. But the bad doubleton spade is a "flaw." If we play notrump it should probably be with partner as declarer, protecting our spade stopper on the opening lead.

9. One club. It is likely that we will need to rebid clubs, but better after opening one club than after opening a bad four card diamond suit. A doubleton preference to this bad diamond suit would not be a happy conclusion. Plan to raise if partner bids one spade. A spade raise on king third is better than the rebid of the five card suit.

10. One diamond. Planning a rebid of two clubs. This time we do not fear a doubleton preference to diamonds because of suit quality. With an expressive rebid available it will not be necessary to raise a one spade response on king third.

11. One spade, planning a rebid of two diamonds. The good four card suit should be shown in preference to the terrible six card suit.

12. One spade, planning a rebid of two hearts. Our rule of thumb for this rebid is to bid the four card heart suit when it has as many or more high card points as the six card spade suit.

13. Three spades. A balanced **limit raise**. You prefer your heart quality, but partner is known to hold at least five spades and might have only four hearts.

14. Pass. The contract you have reached is high enough. Even when partner has only four hearts, this will be a useful dummy.

15. Two spades. A classic situation for a **false preference**.

16. Three hearts. Your values warrant a game invitation and you have at least eight hearts between you.

17. Pass. Don't worry about your lack of spade support. If spades are not trumps, partner's hand will have no value.

18. Three notrump. The same call you would have made if partner had responded one spade. Surely partner has spades stopped and knows that you have a trick source for this contract.

19. Three spades. Don't pass and leave an easy balance for the opposition. We don't expect to make three spades, but it is virtually impossible for them to double. They may be cold for a game in hearts or notrump.

20. Two notrump, forcing and asking for further description. If partner has a good hand or a good suit, a spade game should be a favorite.

21. Three spades. Showing a good hand with a good suit. You have an absolute maximum for this auction.

22. Three clubs. Your hand and suit are as bad as they can be.

23. Three hearts. Your shape makes your hand good, even though your suit is bad.

24. Three diamonds. Your suit is excellent, but your shape is terrible.

CHAPTER SEVEN
After Opener Bids Notrump

Synopsis: Chapter Seven of Volume I was presented in sections. The first section showed bidding tools to be used after opener had rebid one notrump. The second section briefly presented auctions in which opener had jump rebid two notrump. The third section presented bidding tools to be used when opener had begun by bidding one notrump. Finally, a brief reference was made to auctions that began with an opening bid of two notrump, and with an opening bid of two clubs and a rebid by opener in notrump.

As Chapter Seven continues we feature a cameo presentation by Grant Baze on an alternative superior to **New Minor Forcing**, the **Wolff Signoff** and **major suit checkbacks** after opener has jump rebid two notrump. We observe **Smolen Transfers**, **Minor Suit Stayman**, and the two notrump relay in response to the opening bid of one notrump, **Puppet Stayman**, and **Roman Gerber**.

The major conventional call presented for responder's use after opener had rebid one notrump in Volume I was **New Minor Forcing**. That tool does a very adequate job when responder needs to build a forcing auction after opener's rebid of one notrump. There is yet a superior approach. Our guest presenter is **Grant Baze**.

MODIFIED TWO-WAY STAYMAN (MTWS) AFTER A
ONE NOTRUMP REBID
By Grant Baze

Modified Two-way Stayman (MTWS) replaces **New Minor Forcing (NMF)** after a one notrump rebid. **MTWS** is much better than **NMF** in

terms of signoff sequences, invitational sequences, and forcing sequences. Additionally, it has a few frill benefits that do not exist using **NMF**. **MTWS** applies any time opener bids one of a suit, responder bids one of a suit, and opener rebids 1NT (1any − pass − 1any − pass; 1NT),
providing responder is not a passed hand.

MTWS does apply if there is one-level competition from the opponents, but for the rest of this discussion we will assume there is no competition and that responder is an unpassed hand. The examples we use will not waste space showing the passes of the opponents.

There are **three important features** to **MTWS.**

Feature one is that 2♣ by responder is a relay to 2♦. Two clubs is an unconditional force upon opener to rebid two diamonds (no exceptions).

Feature two is that 2♦ by responder is **artificial and forcing to game.** It is usually a major suit checkback, although it could be the beginning of a forcing sequence in either minor suit.

Feature three is that **jump rebids** by responder into opener's suit, his own suit, or any lower ranking suit (except to three clubs) are game forcing, describing a "pure" hand type in the suit or suits that responder has bid.

In addition, we will discuss **important inferences, clarifications, passed hand bidding,** and **splinter sequences**.

Feature one: Continuations after the forced relay to two diamonds.

The first possibility is that there may be no continuation. Responder may have a poor hand with diamonds. If so, he will pass and the contract will be two diamonds, unless the opponents balance.

If responder does not pass two diamonds, **any bid he makes is invitational** (except for an obvious splinter, discussed later). Opener may pass, accept the invitation by bidding game, or (in some cases) reinvite.

Example auction: 1♣ − 1♠ − 1NT − 2♣ − 2♦ (forced response). If responder next bids 2♥, 2♠, 2NT, 3♣, 3♦, 3♥, or 3♠, each of these bids is invitational. The value range for all of these bids is 9 to 12 high card points. If responder has only 9 high card points, he has an exceptionally good hand for his bid.

The meanings of the **invitational bids** in this example are:

1. 2♥ shows 5-4 in the majors.
2. 2♠ shows a five (occasionally six) card suit.
3. 2NT invites 3NT, but shows a hand that includes four card support for opener's minor suit. This allows opener to sign off in 3♣ if he wishes. If opener had opened 1♦, then the delayed raise to 2NT would show four card diamond support. Without four card minor support, responder would raise 1NT to 2NT directly.
4. 3♣ shows five card club support.
5. 3♦ shows five-five in spades and diamonds.
6. 3♥ shows five-five in the majors.
7. 3♠ shows a six card suit.

Feature two: Continuations after the artificial 2♦ game force to a 1NT rebid.

2♦ usually shows a junkish game forcing hand, although it can be very strong without the suit lengths or suit quality to make a forcing jump. The 2♦ bid is used to:

1. Find three card support for responder's major.
2. Find a buried 4-4 major suit fit.
3. Create a forcing raise in opener's minor.
4. Create a forcing (and natural) bid in the unbid minor.

In response to 2♦, opener does not jump unless he has an absolute maximum for his 1NT rebid. The important point is that a game force exists, and the auction should proceed slowly unless serious extra values exist. With an absolute maximum, opener may jump into responder's suit with 3 card support, or jump to 3NT if he is exactly 5-3-3-2 with the doubleton in responder's suit. With a maximum and other distributions, opener does not jump; a game force exists and opener gives responder a chance to show the nature of his hand. Opener's extra values (if any) can be shown later.

Feature three: Jump rebids by responder.

A jump by responder to 3♣ is the end of the auction. Responder has some bad hand with lots of clubs. This is the only jump rebid that is not forcing. A typical hand for responder would be: ♠Axxx, ♥x, ♦xx, ♣J10xxxx.

Jumps by responder into his own suit, opener's suit, or a lower ranking suit (other than clubs) are game forcing, "pure," and probably slamish. Responder's hand is **unlimited**, and he could have a hand with which he envisions a grand slam.

Let us assume an auction of 1♥ − 1♠ − 1NT. Following are examples of minimum hands responder will have for his jump bids.

1. A jump in responder's own suit: ♠AKJxxx, ♥AQx, ♦xx, ♣xx.
2. A jump into opener's heart suit: ♠AKxx, ♥AQx, ♦Kxx, ♣xxx.
3. A jump into a lower ranking suit: ♠AKxxx, ♥xx, ♦AQ10xx, ♣x.
4. A jump into clubs: This is the bad hand, end of the auction.

If opener's suit is diamonds, a minimum jump into diamonds would be: ♠AKxx, ♥xx, ♦Axxxx, ♣Ax. Responder must have at least five card support for a jump into opener's diamonds; otherwise he would create a game force by bidding 2♦ and then supporting diamonds.

If opener's suit is clubs, responder must go through the 2♦ game force before he can support clubs, because an immediate jump into clubs is always a bad hand and the end of the auction.

Important inferences:

Opener opens a minor; responder bids 1♠, opener rebids 1NT, responder bids 2♥. Opener has 14 high card points and four hearts; normally he would wonder if he should bid 3♥ or 4♥. Using these methods, he must pass. If responder wanted to invite, he would have used the 2♣ relay. A possible hand for responder is: ♠Qxxxx, ♥Qxxx, ♦Qx, ♣xx. In this sequence, opener is forced to bid 2♠ or pass.

The same reasoning applies if responder rebids his major suit. Opener is not allowed to raise.

The fact that **MTWS** gives definition to these signoff sequences is very important, as these sequences occur quite frequently.

Clarifications:

If the auction is 1♣ − 1♦ − 1NT, 2♦ is still a game force. In this auction, if responder continues with 3♣ or 3♦, he has interest in a minor suit contract, possibly a slam. If responder wanted out in diamonds, he would have used the two club relay.

The use of this convention does not change the meaning of reverses by responder. If the auction is 1♣ − 1♥ − 1NT − 2♠, responder has five or more hearts, presumably four spades, and a game force with likely slam interest.

Passed hand auctions:

When responder is a passed hand and opener has rebid 1NT, 2♣ is still a relay to 2♦, and the entire relay structure applies. Even though responder is a passed hand, he can still have invitational values. If the opening bid was 1♣, you can no longer play 2♣, but the opponents probably were not going to let you play it there anyway.

After opener's rebid of 1NT, a rebid of 2♦ by a passed hand can no longer be game forcing, because a passed hand cannot have a game force. In this case 2♦ is natural and not invitational; it does, however, guarantee five cards in responder's first bid suit. If responder has bypassed a longer diamond suit to bid a four card major, or if he has four card support for opener's diamond suit and only a four card major, he would bid 2♣ to force opener to bid 2♦ and then pass.

Splinter sequences:

Because of the availability of the relay auction, responder has two ways in which to splinter after opener rebids 1NT. An immediate splinter is in support of opener's suit (think of your partner first). A relay followed by an unusual jump is a splinter in support of responder's own suit.

1♣ − 1♥ − 1NT − 3♠ is a splinter raise of clubs. Responder has one spade, four hearts, five or more clubs and a game forcing hand. Responder is not necessarily interested in slam. He may be just describing his hand and warning partner that there may be a spade problem if the final contract is in notrump.

1♣ – 1♥ – 1NT – 2♣ – 2♦ – 3♠ shows one spade, six or more hearts, and a slamish hand. If responder had no interest in slam he would bid 4♥ directly over the 1NT rebid.

Note that responder can splinter in support of either his own suit or responder's suit. The difference is determined by whether he relays first or not. A direct splinter is in support of opener's suit. A relay followed by a splinter is always in support of responder's own suit.

Example 52)

a) ♠ KQ975
    ♥ AJ103
    ♦ 742
    ♣ 9

b) ♠ KQ975
    ♥ A103
    ♦ 72
    ♣ Q74

c) ♠ KQ97
    ♥ 83
    ♦ Q72
    ♣ A1074

d) ♠ KQ95
    ♥ 83
    ♦ Q7
    ♣ A10742

e) ♠ KQ975
    ♥ 8
    ♦ A10742
    ♣ Q7

f) ♠ KQ975
    ♥ A10742
    ♦ 8
    ♣ Q7

g) ♠ KJ9875
    ♥ 8
    ♦ A42
    ♣ Q76

All hands shown are responder's hands. The auction has begun with one club by opener, a response of one spade, and a rebid of one notrump by opener. Responder next relays by bidding two clubs, and after opener makes the forced rebid of two diamonds, responder continues as indicated:

With Example 52a) responder next bids two hearts to show invitational values and a hand with five spades and four hearts.

With Example 52b) responder next bids two spades to show an invitational hand with a five card suit.

With Example 52c) responder next bids two notrump to show a hand which includes four card club support. This allows opener the option to sign off at three clubs as well as to pass or to bid three notrump.

With Example 52d) responder next bids three clubs. This shows a hand with four spades and five or more clubs as well as invitational values.

With Example 52e) responder next bids three diamonds to show a hand with five spades and five diamonds as well as invitational values.

With Example 52f) responder next bids three hearts to show an invitational hand with five spades and five hearts.

With Example 52g) responder next bids three spades to show a game invitation with a six card spade suit.

Example 53 hands show splinter continuations.

Example 53)

a)   ♠ 7   b)   ♠ AQJ974
       ♥ AQJ974   ♥ AQ3
       ♦ AQ3   ♦ 7
       ♣ K84   ♣ K84

c)   ♠ 5
       ♥ AQ73
       ♦ K6
       ♣ AJ10963

With Example 53a) responder has bid one heart after an opening bid of one club and heard opener rebid one notrump. Responder next bids two clubs to relay to two diamonds, then jumps to three spades. This use of the relay followed by an unusual jump shows that responder is splintering in support of his own suit. His suit must be at least six cards long, and his values must suggest a slam.

With Example 53b) responder has bid one spade after an opening bid of one club and heard opener rebid one notrump. Responder next relays with two clubs and after opener bids two diamonds, responder jumps to four diamonds to splinter in support of his own suit. He announces at least six spades, shortness in diamonds, and interest in slam even though opener's values have been limited by the rebid of one notrump.

With Example 53c) responder has bid one heart after an opening bid of one club. After opener rebids one notrump, responder splinters in support of clubs by jumping to three spades. This shows game forcing values, at least five card support for clubs, and warns opener that spades must be under control if the contract is to be played in notrump.

Our thanks to Grant Baze. Notice the similarity between **MTWS** and **X-Y-Z Bids** that were presented by Fred Hamilton in Chapter Three.

Auctions After Opener Has Jump Rebid Two Notrump

In Volume I it was suggested that after a jump rebid of two notrump by opener to show a balanced hand of 18 or 19 HCP, responder could use **New Minor Forcing**. Superior tools are available. Here they are.

The Wolff Signoff

After opener's jump rebid of two notrump, any call made by responder is forcing. This may present a problem when responder does not have the expected values for the original response. If responder has responded with five or a bad six HCP and is reasonably balanced, a pass is in order. When responder's hand is distributional, pass is not an acceptable option. However, responder does not want to correct to a suit and have the auction continue. Any suit continuation is forcing, and holding meager values responder does not want to reach the game level.

The **Wolff Signoff** (created by Texas expert Bobby Wolff) uses a continuation of three clubs as an artificial relay to three diamonds. When responder uses the relay and then bids a suit at the three level, opener is asked to go no higher. This allows responder to get to any suit except clubs and stop at the three level.

Example 54)

a) ♠ KJ10865
    ♥ 873
    ♦ 432
    ♣ 6

b) ♠ Q7642
    ♥ Q9654
    ♦ 52
    ♣ 6

c) ♠ K1095
    ♥ 63
    ♦ J108743
    ♣ 6

All hands of Example 54) respond to an opening bid of one club. Each hand has bid one spade and opener has jump rebid two notrump. Each of these hands wants the auction to end in a suit at the three level.

Example 54a) will not be a problem for most modern bidders. They will have solved the problem in advance by making a preemptive jump shift **to two spades. Those who can not will be happy to have available the** Wolff Signoff. **Responder continues by bidding three clubs. Opener bids three diamonds as required and when responder bids three spades, opener knows to pass.**

Example 54b) bids three clubs and, after opener bids three diamonds as required, continues by bidding three hearts. Opener knows then to either pass or correct to three spades, but to go no higher.

Example 54c) bids three clubs and, when opener bids three diamonds, passes to end the auction.

In its original version, the **Wolff Signoff** allowed opener to take a three card preference to responder's first suit after the three club call instead of relaying to three diamonds. In conjunction with **Walsh Responses** this variation should not be permitted.

The **Wolff Signoff** has one additional facet. When responder uses the three club relay, then corrects to three notrump, this shows mild interest in a slam in opener's minor suit.

Example 55)

♠ 5
♥ AK63
♦ 84
♣ K98652

With Example 55) responder bids one heart after opener bids one club. Opener jump rebids two notrump and responder wants to invite a slam in clubs. Responder bids three clubs, the Wolff Signoff**, then over the forced call of three diamonds bids three notrump. Opener will know that this is an invitation to a slam in clubs. A bid of four clubs after using the** Wolff Signoff **would be a strong slam suggestion. Many use it also as RKC agreeing clubs.**

Major Suit Checkbacks

After opener's jump rebid of two notrump, because three clubs is always the **Wolff Signoff**, three diamonds is used as a checkback for major suit fits. It does not matter in which minor the opening bid has been made. In all cases each minor has been assigned a specific task when bid at the three level after opener's jump rebid of two notrump.

Responder may check back for any of several reasons.

1. Responder may seek a three card fit for a five card major.
2. Responder may have bid one spade holding five spades and four hearts. A rebid of three hearts promises five-five, so responder must use the checkback to find either a four-four fit in hearts (preferred) or a five-three fit in spades.
3. Responder may have bid one heart holding four-four in the majors. Opener's jump rebid of two notrump does not deny holding four spades. Responder may seek a four-four fit in spades.

Regardless of which major responder has bid, when the three diamond checkback is used, opener's first obligation is to bid the other major when holding four cards in that suit. If responder's first bid was in hearts, opener shows four spades after the checkback. If responder's first suit was spades, opener's first priority is to show four hearts after the checkback.

In the auction: 1minor – pass – 1♥ – pass, 2NT – pass – 3♦ – pass, 3♠, when responder was seeking a five-three heart fit, the continuation will be to 3NT. Opener will know that responder's checkback was to find a five-three fit in hearts. Opener will correct to four hearts when holding three hearts or will pass with a heart doubleton.

In the auction: 1minor – pass – 1♠ – pass, 2NT – pass – 3♦ – pass, 3♥, when responder has used the checkback holding five spades and four hearts, the continuation will be to game in hearts or a slam search with hearts agreed. If the continuation is to three notrump, responder indicates that knowledge of opener's four card heart holding had no interest and that responder was simply checking for a five-three fit in spades. Opener will know to pass and play 3NT holding a doubleton spade, or to correct to four spades when holding three.

Example 56)

a) ♠ KJ1054
    ♥ AJ95
    ♦ 75
    ♣ 94

b) ♠ KJ104
    ♥ AJ95
    ♦ 753
    ♣ 94

c)   ♠ KJ1054   d)   ♠ KJ104
     ♥ AJ5   ♥ AJ965
     ♦ 75   ♦ 753
     ♣ 943   ♣ 4

Example 56a) bids one spade in response to a minor suit opening bid and opener jump rebids two notrump. Responder then bids three diamonds to check back for major suit fits. If opener bids three hearts to show four, responder raises to four hearts. If opener bids three spades to show three and deny four hearts, responder raises to four. If opener bids three notrump to deny four hearts or three spades, responder passes.

Example 56b) bids one heart in response to a minor suit opening bid and opener jump rebids two notrump. Responder then bids three diamonds to check back for a spade fit. If opener bids three hearts to show three, responder bids three notrump to indicate holding only four hearts and imply that the checkback was to find a spade fit. Opener will then know to correct to four spades when the four-four fit exists. If opener bids three spades to show four and deny three hearts, responder raises to four spades. If opener bids three notrump to deny three hearts or four spades, responder passes.

Example 56c) bids one spade in response to a minor suit opening bid and opener jump rebids two notrump. Responder then bids three diamonds to check back for a five-three spade fit. If opener bids three hearts to show four, responder bids three notrump and opener knows that the checkback was to find a five-three fit in spades. Opener will correct to four spades holding three cards or will pass with a doubleton spade.

Example 56d) bids one heart in response to a minor suit opening bid and opener jump rebids two notrump. Responder bids three diamonds to checkback and opener will show four spades as a first option or will show three hearts secondly. Responder raises either major to game or passes 3NT.

Upgraded Responses to One Notrump _____

Smolen Transfers _____

Holding both majors, one of four cards and the other longer (five or six cards), responder begins by using **Stayman**. With minimum values (about 0 to 7 HCP) responder will pass a major suit rebid by opener. If opener's rebid is two diamonds, responder corrects to the longer major to end the auction.

With better values (about 8+ HCP) responder will see that game is reached. When opener shows a major suit in response to **Stayman**, responder raises that major to game. When opener bids two diamonds to deny holding a four card major, responder will then seek game in the longer (five or six card) major. In order to cause opener to declare the eventual contract, responder's continuation will be a **Smolen Transfer** (created by deceased California expert Mike Smolen).

Responder's continuation is a jump to the three level in the four card major. This jump identifies the unbid major as being five cards or longer. Opener bids that suit holding three cards, and declares in the five-three fit from the three card side.

With a doubleton in the unbid major, opener bids three notrump. Holding five cards in the unbid major, responder will know that there is no eight card fit, and will pass. Holding six cards in the unbid major, responder continues by bidding the suit that ranks below the major as a **transfer** to the unbid six card major, again causing opener to declare in the six-two fit.

This extended auction in which responder transfers to six card major carries overtones of slam interest. The reason is that responder also is able to **transfer** to the six card major immediately after opener's two diamond response to **Stayman**. The **transfer** at that point in the auction denies slam interest, while the extended auction ending with a **transfer** implies slam interest. When opener shares slam interest in the extended auction, the final **transfer** is noted but not accepted. Opener instead makes a call that indicates acceptance of the slam invitation.

Example 57)

a)   ♠ K9754
         ♥ J1063
         ♦ 5
         ♣ 852

b)   ♠ AJ97
         ♥ KJ1084
         ♦ 5
         ♣ 852

c)   ♠ AJ97
         ♥ KJ10874
         ♦ 5
         ♣ 82

d)   ♠ AQ107
         ♥ KQJ874
         ♦ 5
         ♣ 82

All Example 57) hands respond to an opening bid of one notrump by bidding two clubs—Stayman. Opener rebids two diamonds.

Example 57a) ends the auction by bidding two spades.

Example 57b) jumps to three spades to show four spades and longer hearts, and passes opener's call of either three notrump or four hearts.

Example 57c) jumps to four diamonds to transfer to hearts, then passes.

Example 57d) jumps to three spades to show four spades and longer hearts. If opener bids four hearts, responder continues by bidding four spades which is RKC when hearts are agreed (see Chapter Twelve). If opener bids three notrump, showing a doubleton heart, responder bids four diamonds to transfer to hearts and show interest in reaching a slam.

Minor Suit Stayman

In Volume I simple transfers to minor suits were presented. Other methods are available. Instead of being a transfer to clubs, two spades is best used as **Minor Suit Stayman**. A response of two spades to an opening bid of one notrump asks opener the question, "Do you have a four card minor suit?"

Opener bids either three clubs or three diamonds to show four cards in that suit. With four cards in each minor suit, opener bids the better one. To deny holding a four card suit, opener bids two notrump.

Responder will have one of three hand types.

1. A diamond bust. Responder may hold six or more diamonds and a very weak hand. A contract in diamonds will be better than one notrump. It is not possible to reach and stop at two diamonds, but even three diamonds will be easier to make than one notrump. Responder bids two spades—**Minor Suit Stayman**. If opener bids three diamonds to show four cards there, responder passes. If opener bids either two notrump or three clubs, responder corrects to three diamonds and opener must pass.

2. A two suited minor bust. Responder may hold five-five (or longer) in the minor suits and a very weak hand. A contract in either minor suit, even at the three level, will be easier to make than one notrump. Responder bids two spades—**Minor Suit Stayman**. If opener bids three of either minor to show four cards, responder passes. If opener bids two notrump to deny a four card minor, responder corrects to three clubs. Opener can either pass or correct to three diamonds.

3. A two suited minor hand with interest in slam. Responder's continuation beyond the level of three diamonds will further describe the nature of the slam interested hand that has at least five-four in the minors. A continuation in notrump expresses a hand that has doubletons in both major suits. Three notrump shows only slight interest in reaching slam. Four notrump (quantitative) indicates strong interest in reaching slam. A continuation of three of either major suit shows shortness—a singleton or a void—in the major suit bid.

When responder shows shortness in a major suit, opener will know how to continue. Holding a concentration of honor cards facing responder's shortness, opener bids three notrump. With no wasted values facing responder's shortness, opener makes a move toward slam in a minor suit. If opener has shown a four card minor, a repeat of that minor at the four level becomes RKC with six key cards—both minor suit kings are important because responder is two suited. If opener has denied a four card minor by bidding two notrump, a three card minor will be shown as opener indicates interest in reaching a minor suit contract rather than playing in notrump.

Example 58)

a) ♠ 752   b) ♠ 75
    ♥ 863   ♥ 3
    ♦ Q109753   ♦ Q10973
    ♣ 6   ♣ J8654

c) ♠ A5   d) ♠ A5
    ♥ 63   ♥ 3
    ♦ KQ103   ♦ KQ1073
    ♣ AJ962   ♣ AJ962

All Example 58) hands use Minor Suit Stayman **in response to the opening bid of one notrump.**

Example 58a) passes if opener bids three diamonds, or corrects either two notrump or three clubs to three diamonds. Opener is required to pass.

Example 58b) passes if opener bids either minor suit. If opener bids two notrump to deny a four card minor, responder corrects to three clubs. Opener then knows to either pass or correct to three diamonds to end the auction.

Example 58c) continues over any rebid by opener by bidding three notrump. This shows doubletons in both major suits and only mild interest in slam.

Example 58d) continues over any rebid by opener by bidding three hearts. This shows slam interest and shortness in hearts.

Example 59)

a) ♠ KQ103   b) ♠ KJ6
    ♥ AQ72   ♥ AQJ2
    ♦ A8   ♦ 84
    ♣ 1054   ♣ KQ103

c) ♠ KQ103
   ♥ J72
   ♦ AJ
   ♣ KQ103

d) ♠ KQ3
   ♥ J732
   ♦ AJ4
   ♣ KQ10

All Example 59) hands have opened one notrump. Responder has bid two spades—Minor Suit Stayman.

Example 59a) bids two notrump to deny a four card minor suit. If responder then bids three or four notrump, opener passes. If responder shows shortness in either major, this opener bids three notrump.

Example 59b) bids three clubs to show a four card suit. If responder shows shortness in either major suit, bid three notrump.

Example 59c) bids three clubs to show a four card suit. If responder shows shortness in hearts, continue by bidding four clubs which will be RKC. Facing Example 58d) a club slam will be easy.

Example 59d) bids two notrump to deny a four card minor. If responder shows shortness in hearts, bid four clubs to deny heart values and show a three card club holding.

Reaching minor suit slams holding single suiters can be done by using Stayman, then showing the minor suit (see Volume I, page 124), or through the use of **Walsh Relays** (see Chapter Twelve). Without the availability of **Minor Suit Stayman**, responder has difficulty finding minor suit slams when holding both minors.

The Two Notrump Relay

In conjunction with **Minor Suit Stayman**, responder's call of two notrump is best used as a relay to three clubs. Opener is not offered alternatives. A response of two notrump requires that opener bid three clubs. Responder will have one of two hand types.

1. A club bust. Responder will have six or more clubs and a very weak hand. When opener bids three clubs as required, responder passes.
2. A slam interested three suiter. Responder identifies this hand type by next bidding to show a singleton or a void. Responder's pattern will be 4-4-4-1 or 5-4-4-0 (the five card suit will always be a minor—never a major. With a five card major responder will start with **Stayman** when holding four in the other major as well, planning on using the **Smolen convention**, or will **transfer** to the five card major and show the better of the four card minor suits).

To show shortness in spades, hearts or diamonds, responder bids that suit after opener has been forced to bid three clubs. Club shortness with only mild slam interest is shown by a rebid of three notrump. With club shortness and strong slam interest, responder bids four clubs.

Example 60)

a) ♠ 852
    ♥ 7
    ♦ J64
    ♣ Q109763

b) ♠ A1098
    ♥ 5
    ♦ KQJ3
    ♣ KJ72

c) ♠ A1098
    ♥ KJ72
    ♦ KQJ3
    ♣ 5

d) ♠ AQ108
    ♥ KJ72
    ♦ KQJ32
    ♣ —

All Example 60) hands respond to the opening bid of one notrump. Each hand bids two notrump to relay to three clubs.

Example 60a) passes to end the auction.

Example 60b) bids three hearts to show short hearts and at least four cards in each other suit, as well as interest in reaching a slam.

Example 60c) bids three notrump to show short clubs and only mild interest in slam.

Example 60d) bids four clubs to show short clubs and strong interest in slam.

Once responder has described a slam interested three suiter, opener has the option to sign off at game in a four-four major suit fit, or at three notrump when holding plentiful values in responder's short suit. If responder has bid four clubs, with wasted values in the club suit opener's signoff is four notrump.

Opener's continuation to four of a minor suit, which is one of the suits responder has shown, sets the trump suit and also serves as RKC. If opener has adequate controls and a suitable hand, a jump to slam is possible.

Responding to Two Notrump

An opening bid of two notrump shows a balanced hand of 20 or 21 high card points. Balanced hands of 22 or more HCP are shown by an opening bid of two clubs followed by a rebid in notrump.

When responder to the opening bid of two clubs is able to make an immediate response that is either positive or negative, opener's rebid in notrump may be affected. When responder shows values enough that game should be reached, opener will rebid two notrump with values that have no top limit as the auction is forcing. When responder shows negative values, opener will need to bid notrump at the level that shows those values.

The normal range for the rebid of two notrump will be 22 to 24 HCP. Facing a negative response opener will need to jump to three notrump to show 25 to 27 HCP. When opener must jump to show more than 24 HCP, the chance to use **Stayman** and **Jacoby** disappears. Having the three level available makes auctions easier.

Balanced hands of 20 HCP or more that include a five card major suit present a problem. If opener bids the major suit, the auction may die at the one level when responder passes, and the tricks for game may be available. If opener instead starts with two notrump or rebids two notrump holding a five card major, the best contract in a five-three major suit fit may be impossible to find.

Example 61)

a)   ♠ AJ5
      ♥ KQ1074
      ♦ AQ
      ♣ KJ3

b)   ♠ AK53
      ♥ KQJ74
      ♦ AK
      ♣ 83

c)   ♠ AK5
      ♥ QJ983
      ♦ AQ
      ♣ AKJ

d)   ♠ AKJ
      ♥ KQJ95
      ♦ AQ
      ♣ AKQ

Example 61a) should open two notrump rather than one heart. This will allow opener to declare whether the contract is in hearts or in notrump. If responder uses Puppet Stayman this hand may declare in a five-three heart fit. Otherwise the hand has been right-sided when the ultimate contract is in notrump.

Example 61b) should open one heart. With nine major suit cards, an opening bid of two notrump would make the auction quite difficult if a major suit contract was to be reached. After an opening bid of one heart a game might be missed, but if responder is able to bid there is a far better chance of reaching the right game than after an opening bid of two notrump.

Example 61c) opens with two clubs. If responder shows positive values, opener can rebid only two notrump to enable the use of Puppet Stayman or a Jacoby Transfer. If responder shows negative values, this hand must jump to three notrump. This makes conventions difficult, but enables the bidding side to reach game when the negative responder has some sparse values. Jacoby Transfers are no longer available, but responder can still Texas at the four level.

Example 61d) opens with two clubs. If responder shows positive values, opener can rebid only two notrump to enable the use of Pupet Stayman or a Jacoby Transfer. If responder shows negative values, this hand must jump to four notrump. Conven-

tions will no longer be available, but if the negative responder has sparse values a slam can still be bid.

Puppet Stayman

A variation of the **Stayman** convention is used by many to solve this problem. Instead of asking for four card majors only, **Puppet Stayman** after opener's call of two notrump asks for either five or four card major suits in opener's hand. In response to three clubs, opener bids as follows:

1. Three notrump denies that opener has either a four or five card major suit.
2. Three of a major suit by opener shows five cards.
3. Three diamonds by opener denies a five card major and promises one or both four card majors.

Responder needs to know to use **Puppet Stayman** not only when he holds four card majors, but also when he holds three card majors and a singleton or doubleton in some other suit. When the five-three major suit fit is found, responder can produce additional trump tricks only when it is possible to ruff something in the hand that holds three trumps.

When opener shows a five card major suit in response to **Puppet Stayman** and responder bids three notrump, responder is known to have been seeking a four-four fit or five in the other major and does not have three cards in opener's five card major.

Similarly, when opener announces possession of a four card major by bidding three diamonds and responder continues by bidding three notrump, it is clear that responder was seeking a five-three major suit fit and has no interest in opener's four card majors.

When opener announces possession of a four card major suit by bidding three diamonds and responder wants to pursue the possibility of a four-four fit, responder proceeds as follows:

1. Holding one four card major, responder bids the one that he does not

hold. When opener learns of a four-four fit in such an auction, it is opener who bids the major suit and become declarer.

2. When responder has four cards in each major suit, a continuation of four diamonds announces that fact. It also stipulates that responder has no interest in reaching a slam.

3. When responder has four cards in each major suit and is also interested in reaching a slam, a continuation of four clubs rather than four diamonds makes that announcement. Over responder's call of four clubs, opener can sign off by bidding four in a known major suit fit, or can pursue slam by bidding four diamonds. The four diamond call becomes RKC with six key cards (both major suit kings become key cards).

Stayman is so commonly used that it is assumed to apply when responder to two notrump bids three clubs. **Puppet Stayman** is not so common, and requires an alert.

Although this convention solves the problem of finding five-three major suit fits when opener has bid two notrump, if you adopt it you will be unable to also use **Smolen Transfers**. The structures of the two auctions overlap. Your partnership will need to decide which of the two bidding methods it prefers to have available.

Example 62)

a)	♠ Q85		b)	♠ J109	
	♥ K84			♥ K10874	
	♦ J10754			♦ 63	
	♣ 83			♣ Q75	
c)	♠ K1096		d)	♠ K1096	
	♥ 84			♥ Q853	
	♦ K8543			♦ 42	
	♣ 62			♣ 765	
e)	♠ J1095		f)	♠ A1074	
	♥ K10874			♥ KJ63	
	♦ 63			♦ 543	
	♣ Q5			♣ K2	

Example 62) hands are responders. The auction has been either

an opening bid of two notrump or opener has bid two clubs, and each responder has shown positive values by bidding two diamonds (see Chapter Nine) before opener has rebid two notrump to show 22 or more high card points with no upper limit.

Example 62a) bids three clubs—Puppet Stayman. **Responder is seeking a five-three major suit fit. If opener shows five cards in either major, responder will bid game in that major. If opener denies both a five or four card major by bidding three notrump, this responder will pass. If opener bids three diamonds to show a four card major, this responder has no interest and will bid three notrump.**

Example 62b) has a choice of actions. Puppet Stayman **might uncover a five-three fit in spades. However the chances of a heart fit are far greater, so responder bids three diamonds to** transfer, **showing five hearts.**

Example 62c) bids three clubs—Puppet Stayman. **If opener bids three hearts to show a five card suit, this responder bids three notrump. If opener bids three diamonds to show a four card major, this responder bids three hearts to show a four card spade suit.**

Example 62d) bids three clubs—Puppet Stayman. **If opener bids three diamonds to show a four card major this responder bids four diamonds to indicate four cards in each major without interest in slam.**

Example 62e) has a choice of actions. **Since** Smolen Transfers **are not available, this responder must decide either to make a** Jacoby Transfer **to the heart suit or to use** Puppet Stayman. **If the latter and opener shows a four card major, responder will bid four diamonds to show both majors and no slam interest.**

Example 62f) bids three clubs—Puppet Stayman. **If opener bids three diamonds to show a four card major, this responder bids four clubs to show both majors and interest in slam.**

Gerber _____

In Volume I the **Gerber** convention was presented quite simply. The key to understanding the convention was to know that it requires a jump from notrump to clubs. Discussion included jumps from one or two notrump to four clubs.

When three notrump has been reached, if a bidder needs to use **Gerber** the same requirement exists. A removal of three notrump to four clubs IS NOT GERBER. To use **Gerber** from three notrump, there must be a jump to five clubs.

The removal of three notrump to four clubs is virtually always a slam try (but see **Example 20** in Chapter Two). It will reemphasize a previously bid club suit or show a fit for partner's club suit, or it will show the ace of clubs in support of a previously bid suit.

The use of this convention can be amplified if **Roman Responses** are used. There is no trump suit agreed in notrump auctions, but the response structure can be similar to that of RKC. In response to four clubs as **Gerber**:

1. Four diamonds shows zero or three aces.
2. Four hearts shows one or four aces.
3. Four spades shows two aces, but denies interest in slam.
4. Four notrump shows two aces and affirms interest in slam.

If the originator of **Gerber** continues by bidding five clubs, the same schedule applies in showing kings. However, if two aces have been shown either with or without interest in slam, that interest or lack of interest can be reinforced or modified at the five level.

If opener has shown interest by bidding four notrump in response to four clubs, over five clubs opener can reinforce that interest by bidding five notrump, or can modify that interest by bidding five spades. Or if opener has bid four spades to deny interest over four clubs, it is possible to bid five notrump over five clubs to upgrade the level of interest, or to bid five spades to continue to show lack of interest.

*Notrump Response Exercises*_____

You have agreed to play **Modified Two Way Stayman** after partner rebids one notrump. You have responded one spade to an opening bid of one diamond and partner has rebid one notrump. What do you bid with each of these hands?

1. ♠ A854
    ♥ 6
    ♦ 3
    ♣ QJ107543

2. ♠ KQ1074
    ♥ AJ4
    ♦ 62
    ♣ A76

3. ♠ K10743
    ♥ Q9642
    ♦ 8
    ♣ 54

4. ♠ KQ1074
    ♥ 54
    ♦ A106
    ♣ Q54

5. ♠ AKJ8
    ♥ 62
    ♦ KQ1083
    ♣ A3

6. ♠ A854
    ♥ 6
    ♦ KQJ73
    ♣ J64

7. ♠ KQJ1094
    ♥ 6
    ♦ A63
    ♣ 754

8. ♠ A654
    ♥ 6
    ♦ Q10762
    ♣ J63

9. ♠ AKJ854
    ♥ AQ6
    ♦ 85
    ♣ 93

10. ♠ AK83
    ♥ 6
    ♦ KQ10832
    ♣ K5

11. ♠ AJ954
    ♥ KQ1062
    ♦ 85
    ♣ 2

12. ♠ AQJ954
    ♥ 6
    ♦ A64
    ♣ K53

You have agreed to play the **Wolff Signoff** after partner's jump rebid of two notrump. Partner has opened one club and has jump rebid two notrump after your response of one spade. What continuation do you plan?

13. ♠ Q875
    ♥ 6
    ♦ QJ9543
    ♣ 104

14. ♠ AK62
    ♥ 75
    ♦ 8
    ♣ K108754

15. ♠ J8762
    ♥ K9543
    ♦ 6
    ♣ 84

16. ♠ KJ76
    ♥ 1093
    ♦ J842
    ♣ 62

You have agreed to play that after jump rebids of two notrump, three diamonds is a **major suit checkback**. Partner has opened one diamond and has jump rebid two notrump after your response of one heart. What continuation do you plan?

17. ♠ A54
    ♥ KJ1073
    ♦ 6
    ♣ J752

18. ♠ A954
    ♥ KJ103
    ♦ 6
    ♣ 9852

19. ♠ 6
    ♥ AKJ954
    ♦ 962
    ♣ A63

20. ♠ A954
    ♥ KJ1073
    ♦ 6
    ♣ J75

You have agreed to play **Smolen transfers** after **Stayman**. Partner has opened one notrump and has bid two diamonds in response to **Stayman**. Plan the continuation.

21. ♠ A854
    ♥ QJ963
    ♦ K42
    ♣ 6

22. ♠ A854
    ♥ QJ9643
    ♦ J3
    ♣ 8

23. ♠ AQ10754
    ♥ AK53
    ♦ 6
    ♣ 72

24. ♠ A854
    ♥ J9632
    ♦ 854
    ♣ 2

You have agreed to play **Minor Suit Stayman** in response to an opening bid in notrump. You have bid two spades in response to partner's opening bid of one notrump and received a two notrump call which denies possession of a four card minor. How do you continue?

25. ♠ 73
    ♥ 2
    ♦ Q9743
    ♣ J10865

26. ♠ A4
    ♥ 86
    ♦ KQ104
    ♣ AQ1062

27. ♠ 73
    ♥ 2
    ♦ QJ9743
    ♣ J865

28. ♠ A42
    ♥ 6
    ♦ AK74
    ♣ KJ1053

You have agreed to use a two notrump response to an opening bid of one notrump as a relay to three clubs. You have used that auction. What continuation do you plan with each of these hands?

29. ♠ AJ62
    ♥ KQ75
    ♦ K1092
    ♣ 4

30. ♠ 86
    ♥ 5
    ♦ 943
    ♣ Q985432

31. ♠ AJ106
    ♥ —
    ♦ KQ843
    ♣ K954

32. ♠ AK62
    ♥ KJ75
    ♦ A963
    ♣ 4

You have agreed to use **Puppet Stayman** after the opening bid of two notrump or after the rebid of two notrump by a two club opening bidder.

With these hands partner has opened two notrump and has rebid three diamonds after your response of three clubs. How do you continue?

33. ♠ A54
    ♥ Q92
    ♦ J10642
    ♣ 86

34. ♠ AJ54
    ♥ 92
    ♦ Q1063
    ♣ 854

35. ♠ AJ54
    ♥ KQ1063
    ♦ 5
    ♣ Q83

36. ♠ AJ54
    ♥ K1093
    ♦ 54
    ♣ J62

Answers

1. Three clubs. The only jump that is weak.

2. Two diamonds. Start by forcing game. Partner will show a three card spade fit and maximum or minimum values.

3. Two hearts. Partner will know to pass or correct to two spades, but to go no higher.

4. Two clubs, then two spades over two diamonds to show the five card suit and invite game.

5. Three diamonds. Jump to show a powerful hand with primary diamonds and imply only four spades.

6. Two clubs, then invite by raising diamonds to three.

7. Two clubs. Limit values, then jump to three spades to show this excellent suit.

8. Two clubs, and pass two diamonds.

9. Three spades. Forcing. Show a "prime" hand with a good suit.

10. Three hearts. A **splinter** in support of diamonds.

11. Two clubs, then jump to three hearts to invite and show five-five in the majors.

12. Two clubs, then jump to three hearts to **splinter** in support of your own good spade suit.

13. Three clubs, to force three diamonds, then pass.

14. Three clubs, then bid three notrump over three diamonds. This is an invitation to a club slam.

15. Three clubs, then over three diamonds bid three hearts. Partner will know to pass or correct to spades, but to go no higher.

16. Pass. No reason to bid any further.

17. Three diamonds. Checking back for a five-three heart fit.

18. Three diamonds. Checking back for a four-four fit in spades.

19. Three hearts. A natural slam try. With a six card suit and only game interest, you would bid four hearts instead.

20. Three spades. A natural **reverse** showing four spades and longer hearts. The three diamond checkback would be wasted motion since if partner bid three hearts, showing three, there would be no way to find a four-four fit in spades.

21. Three spades, showing only four spades and longer hearts.

22. Four diamonds. When **Stayman** finds no fit, it is time to **Texas** holding limited values.

23. Three hearts, showing exactly four hearts and longer spades. If partner bids three spades, cue bid the heart ace as a slam try. If partner bids three notrump to show a doubleton spade, you must show that you hold six spades. You now **transfer** by bidding four hearts. Since you did not **Texas** after two diamonds, partner will know that you have made a mild slam try.

24. Two hearts. Signing off.

25. Three clubs, showing a bad hand with five-five in the minors.

26. Four notrump, showing a hand with no major suit splinter and strong interest in reaching a slam.

27. Three diamonds. A signoff.

28. Three hearts. A **splinter**. Pass three notrump. If partner bids again in a minor suit, that will show bad hearts and a three card minor suit holding.

29. Three notrump. A mild slam try with three suits and shortness in clubs.

30. Pass. One of the functions of the relay is escape to clubs.

31. Three hearts. A slam interested three suiter with heart shortness.

32. Four clubs. A slam interested three suiter with club shortness. Shows greater interest than if you had bid three notrump.

33. Three notrump. You tried to find a major suit five-three fit, but did not.

34. Three hearts. You show a four card spade suit.

35. Four clubs. You show four cards in both majors with interest in reaching a slam.

36. Four diamonds. You show four cards in both majors with no slam interest.

CHAPTER EIGHT
Raising Partner's Suit

Synopsis: Chapter Eight of Volume I reviewed bidding priorities. This chapter discussed raises of partner's minor suit opening bid with hands of various values including **splinter** raises. The presentation on major suit raises included jumps to game, limit raises, **splinter** raises, the **Jacoby Two Notrump**, and **Drury**. Simple game tries after the raise of opener's major were also presented.

All of the raise structures were the simplest possible in modern bidding. As promised, substantial upgrades are detailed in this volume.

As Chapter Eight continues you will learn about **Inverted Minor Raises**, major suit raise complexes created by both **Bergen** and **Hardy**, and modern game try methods.

Inverted Minor Raises

Instead of having single raises be weak and jump raises strong, **Inverted Minor Raises** do just the opposite. Jump raises become weak and preemptive while single raises become strong and forcing. Single raises by unpassed responders have at least game invitational values and are unlimited in strength. Single raises by passed responders show game invitational (limit raise) values.

The Preemptive Raise

The preemptive jump raise requires almost no values. The greater the number of trumps responder holds, the fewer values are needed. On a practical basis the jump raise shows about two to eight high card points. If maximum, the raise will include soft cards rather than defensive values.

Responder must beware of making the preemptive jump raise with a hand that is balanced. Holding 5-3-3-2 with five card support for opener's minor suit, responder should not jump raise to the three level. Opener may have only three cards in the suit of the opening bid and be otherwise balanced. It makes no sense for two balanced hands to play a minor suit part score at the three level when one notrump is the preferred contract.

If the requirement of the partnership is that a one notrump response to the opening bid of one club shows 8 to 10 HCP, when responder holds a five card fit for clubs and only minimum values of 5+ to 7 HCP, it may be necessary for responder to temporize by bidding one diamond on a three (or even two) card holding. Temporizing in minor suits should never create problems since partner knows full well to first seek a major suit fit, then settle for notrump, rather than try to reach a contract in a minor suit.

Example 63)

<table>
<tr><td>a)</td><td>♠ Q82
♥ 53
♦ K9654
♣ J75</td><td>b)</td><td>♠ Q82
♥ 53
♦ J75
♣ K9654</td></tr>
<tr><td>c)</td><td>♠ Q2
♥ 104
♦ K873
♣ Q9653</td><td>d)</td><td>♠ Q2
♥ 4
♦ J986532
♣ 975</td></tr>
</table>

All Example 63) hands are responders.

If the opening bid is one club, Example 63a) should bid one diamond. Despite tenaces in three suits this hand is not big enough for an unpassed hand to respond 1NT which promises

8 to 10 HCP. As a passed hand this responder could bid one notrump (6 to 10 HCP). Over one club it is possible for responder to temporize in diamonds, but over one diamond that is not possible.

If the opening bid is one diamond, this hand should not make the preemptive jump raise to three diamonds. It is a balanced hand with some values, and if opener is also balanced the contract should be one notrump rather than in a minor suit at the three level.

The same thoughts should apply to Example 63b). Responder should bid one notrump in response to an opening bid of one diamond, but should temporize by bidding one diamond if the opening bid is one club. It would be wrong to jump raise clubs to the three level with this balanced hand.

Example 63c) should bid one notrump after an opening bid of one diamond. If the opening bid is one club, one notrump is also best. If the opponents compete, this hand can show the club fit later.

When the opening bid is one diamond, Example 63d) has a clear jump raise to three diamonds. If the opening bid is one club, a preemptive jump shift to two diamonds is best if available.

The Single Raise

The single raise of a minor suit opening bid denies a four card major, promises at least a four card fit for the opening bid, has values that are at least game invitational (9+ HCP), and is forcing for one round if made by an unpassed responder. If responder is a passed hand, the single raise shows a limit raise (9+ to 12- HCP) for the opening bid, usually with a distributional feature, and opener can either pass or continue to bid as the hand indicates.

Opener does not know how much responder has, but must rebid as descriptively as possible. Opener has four possible rebids:

1. Opener's rebid of two notrump shows a balanced hand with minimum values (12 or a bad 13 HCP) and promises stoppers in both major suits.

2. Opener's jump rebid of three notrump promises a balanced hand of 18 or 19 HCP.

3. Opener's rebid in a new suit at the three level is a **splinter**. In all auctions except one this rebid will be a jump. Opener promises more than minimum opening bid values—at least a sound 14 HCP.

4. With all other hands opener rebids to show "stoppers up the line." Opener's new suit bid promises a stopper for a possible notrump contract. Opener will not bypass any suit containing a stopper.

Example 64)

a) ♠ AJ4   b) ♠ AQ4
   ♥ K973   ♥ KJ73
   ♦ KJ102   ♦ KJ102
   ♣ 86   ♣ A6

c) ♠ AQ4   d) ♠ 6
   ♥ K973   ♥ KJ73
   ♦ KJ102   ♦ KJ1052
   ♣ 86   ♣ AQ4

e) ♠ 6   f) ♠ AQ4
   ♥ K973   ♥ KJ73
   ♦ KJ1052   ♦ KJ1052
   ♣ AJ4   ♣ 6

All Example 64) hands have opened one diamond and responder has raised to two diamonds (alert).

Example 64a) bids two notrump to show a balanced hand with minimum values (12 or 13- HCP) and stoppers in both major suits.

Example 64b) jumps to three notrump to show a balanced hand of 18 or 19 HCP.

Example 64c) is balanced and has stoppers in both major suits but has too much in values to bid two notrump and not enough

to bid three notrump. The only alternative is to bid "stoppers up the line," so opener's rebid is two hearts.

Example 64d) has good values and makes a splinter jump to three spades.

Example 64e) has the same pattern as 64d) but does not have enough in values to splinter. Opener rebids two hearts to show "stoppers up the line."

Example 64f) splinters by bidding three clubs. This is the only rebid at the three level that is not a jump. Nevertheless, it does show a splinter.

Responder's Obligations

Responder is the only member of the partnership who knows whether the single raise was made on game invitational values (9+ to 12- HCP) or on game forcing values (12+ HCP). When opener shows probable minimum values (either bidding two notrump or "stoppers up the line"), responder has the responsibility of making sure that the auction does not go awry.

When responder's values are game invitational (9+ to 12- HCP), no call can be made that takes the auction beyond the three level in the original minor. When responder's values are enough for game (12+ HCP) no call can be made below the three level in the agreed minor that opener might be able to pass.

For example, in the auction: 1♦ – pass – 2♦ – pass, 2♥ – pass – ? a bid of two notrump or of three diamonds would be non-forcing. With values that are enough for game (12+ HCP) responder cannot make either of those calls.

In the same auction a bid of two spades or three clubs would be forcing. Responder can make either of those calls regardless of values.

With game forcing values (12+ HCP) responder cannot bid either two notrump or three diamonds. Opener could pass. However, responder with game values can bid either two spades or three clubs, or make a call beyond three diamonds. Any such call would be justified.

Example 65)

a) ♠ J84
    ♥ 93
    ♦ AKJ95
    ♣ A65

b) ♠ 85
    ♥ K106
    ♦ 764
    ♣ AQJ85

Example 65a) raises one diamond to two. If opener continues by bidding two hearts, two spades, or two notrump, responder can bid three clubs which is forcing and the best available descriptive call. If opener jumps to three notrump to show a balanced 18 or 19 HCP, responder should make an invitational raise to 4NT.

Example 65b) raises one club to two. If opener bids two diamonds, responder can bid two hearts which is forcing and descriptive. If opener bids two notrump to show minimum values with stoppers in both majors, responder can pass and hope that the defense does not have too many diamond tricks, or can bid three clubs. If opener bids two spades, responder can bid two notrump—again hoping that diamonds are not a problem—or can bid three clubs. In no case can this responder bid beyond three clubs voluntarily.

Responder should be sure that the raise of opener's minor suit is the most descriptive bid possible. Sometimes responder should bid notrump despite having a fit for opener's minor suit. This will be true with stoppers and tenaces in unbid suits.

Example 66)

a) ♠ K7
    ♥ AJ4
    ♦ Q9632
    ♣ J85

b) ♠ AQ5
    ♥ K6
    ♦ K105
    ♣ Q10984

With Example 66a) in response to an opening bid in either minor suit, bid two notrump (invitational). Do not make the error of

raising an opening bid of one diamond. You have tenaces in every suit and need to be declarer at any contract, particularly one in notrump.

With Example 66b) in response to an opening bid in either minor suit, bid three notrump. With tenaces in every suit do not make the error of raising clubs.

When there has been an overcall the jump raise remains preemptive, but the single raise changes. All good raises are shown by a cue bid of the over-call. The single raise reverts to the older standard of minimum response values (5+ to 9– HCP).

Example 67)

a) ♠ J64
    ♥ 853
    ♦ KQ85
    ♣ 1092

b) ♠ K83
    ♥ 106
    ♦ Q64
    ♣ KQJ75

In response to the opening bid of one diamond Example 67a) would bid one notrump. However, after an overcall in either ma-jor suit, this responder makes a simple raise to two diamonds.

In response to the opening bid of one club Example 67b) would make a single (limit or better) raise. However, after an overcall of one heart, cue bid two hearts to show a good club raise.

Major Suit Raises

In Volume I major suit raises were discussed in their simplest form. Now we need to look at several facets of the major suit raise spectrum and deter-mine what the best possible methods might be.

Constructive Major Raises

Those who play **constructive major raises** require that single raise of an opening major show 7+ to 10 HCP. An advantage does accrue when opener has more than minimum values and can try for game knowing that responder has sound values.

1. The use of this agreement requires responder with a three card or longer fit and a good five to a bad seven HCP to start by using the **forcing notrump,** then return to opener's major at the two level. This opens the door to disaster for several reasons. When opener has a good hand and needs only to find a fit in the trump suit to bid game, it's a guess whether to try or not. When responder returns to opener's suit at the two level, does that show or deny a fit? Opener cannot tell. If opener assumes a probable fit and bids on, with no fit opener will get too high. When opener decides to be conservative and assume no fit, the game bonus available because of the fit will not accrue.

2. When responder conceals a fit to use the **forcing notrump**, the opponents are given free access to the two level. A great many opponents will be able to overcall at the two level, thank you, but would be shut out of the auction if a single raise required entry into the auction at the three level. When responder conceals a fit for opener's major and allows an opponent to enter at the two level, if the other opponent raises the overcall should responder now show the concealed fit at the three level? No! If responder first bids a **forcing notrump** and then shows a fit at the three level, that hand must include game invitational values (9+ to 12-HCP).

3. Knowledge of a fit often will enable opener to compete when the opponents enter the auction. When responder conceals a fit **for any reason**, opener is rendered helpless.

Example 68)

a) ♠ J87542
    ♥ 6
    ♦ AK
    ♣ AKJ5

Example 68a) opens one spade. Responder uses the forcing notrump. **Opener rebids two clubs and responder bids two spades. What does opener do next?**

b) ♠ 93
    ♥ KJ85
    ♦ 9872
    ♣ Q4

c) ♠ KQ3
    ♥ 8543
    ♦ 8764
    ♣ 104

Example 68b) is a classic hand for the auction. Responder takes a preference to opener's major suit with a doubleton.

If Constructive major raises **have been agreed, responder 68c) would produce the same auction. The fact that responder has a true fit for opener's major makes all the difference. If responder raises to two spades opener can try for game by asking for good trumps, and responder will bid four spades.**

The plus side of the use of **Constructive major raises** is the facilitation of game tries on marginal hands. But opener can still make game tries with knowledge that the single raise might have been made with very minimum values. The minus side, however, is so devastating that this bidding method should be set aside entirely. Concealing fits from partner will usually create the worst possible result. When you can raise partner because you have a fit, DO IT. And in competition don't be afraid to stretch a bit to show that important fit.

Example 69)

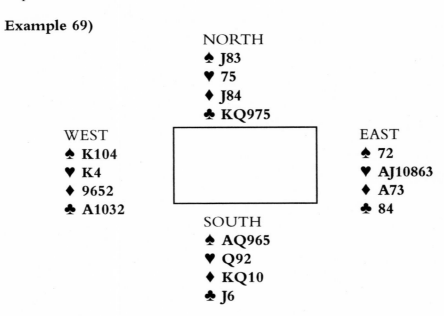

NORTH
♠ J83
♥ 75
♦ J84
♣ KQ975

WEST
♠ K104
♥ K4
♦ 9652
♣ A1032

EAST
♠ 72
♥ AJ10863
♦ A73
♣ 84

SOUTH
♠ AQ965
♥ Q92
♦ KQ10
♣ J6

When this hand was dealt in actual play South opened one spade and West passed. North should have raised to two spades, which would have been followed by three passes. South would have made two spades easily.

North, however, made the error of bidding one notrump. This allowed East to overcall two hearts. South passed and West had no better call than to raise to three hearts. North now bid three spades. Expecting a game invitational hand, South continued to four spades. West was quick to double and lead the heart king. The difference to North–South was minus 500 rather than plus 110.

Enough on this topic. Avoid disaster. Do not agree to play **constructive major raises**.

Bergen Raises

A very popular major suit raise complex has been created by bidding theorist **Marty Bergen**. This complex is based on the application of "The Law of Total Tricks" (see Chapter Eleven). Bergen suggests that when opener has bid a major suit, promising at least five cards in the suit, whenever responder holds a four card fit, the auction should immediately reach the three level.

Here are the main facets to **Bergen Raises**.

1. The single raise shows minimum response values and exactly three card support.
2. The minimum raise with four card support is shown by a jump to three clubs.
3. Jump raises to three in opener's major show four card support and are strictly preemptive (0 to 6 HCP).
4. Limit raises with four card support are shown by a jump to three diamonds.

Example 70)

a) ♠ 94
   ♥ QJ106
   ♦ 97432
   ♣ 85

b) ♠ K53
   ♥ K1096
   ♦ 92
   ♣ 10742

c) ♠ A7
   ♥ KQJ6
   ♦ 9543
   ♣ 872

d) ♠ K65
   ♥ Q1065
   ♦ 943
   ♣ 872

e) ♠ A43
   ♥ J95
   ♦ K874
   ♣ 1054

f) ♠ Q74
   ♥ J9643
   ♦ 85
   ♣ J74

All Example 70) hands are responding to the opening bid of one heart.

Example 70a) jumps to three hearts preemptively.

Example 70b) jumps to three clubs to show a minimum raise with four card support.

Example 70c) jumps to three diamonds to show a limit raise with four card support.

Example 70d) is a maximum preemptive jump raise to three hearts.

Example 70e) makes a single raise to two hearts. This shows exactly three card support.

Example 70f) jumps to three hearts. Although the bidding side has ten trumps, Bergen considers the preemptive jump to the three level with five card support to be even better than with four trumps.

The Jacoby Two Notrump

Bergen Raises also include use of the **Jacoby Two Notrump** when responder holds four card support with opening bid values and a relatively balanced hand.

The **Jacoby Two Notrump** response to a major suit opening bid asks opener to describe the nature of the opening bid. These are opener's rebids.

1. Minimum hands that do not contain a singleton or void use **fast arrival** and jump to game in the agreed major suit.
2. Opener shows shortness (a singleton or void) by bidding that suit at the three level. When the shortness is a void opener will repeat the suit of the shortness at the next opportunity.
3. Opener shows a sound opening bid without shortness (14+ HCP) and exactly five cards in the major suit by bidding three notrump.
4. Opener shows a sound opening bid without shortness (14+ HCP) and a six or seven card suit by repeating the opening bid major at the three level.
5. Opener shows a second five card suit by jumping to that suit at the four level. This promises that the second suit is very good—headed by two of the top three honors. With a lesser suit, opener instead shows the short suit at the three level.

Concealed Splinters

Another facet of **Bergen Raises** is the use of **concealed splinters**. Direct **splinter** bids, which are used by the masses, divulge far too much information to the defenders when the bidding side stops at game. The information conveyed by the **splinter** has value to the bidding side only when knowledge of responder's shortness allows opener to evaluate how well the two hands fit together for a possible slam. When information regarding responder's shortness has no value to opener, the beneficiaries are the defenders.

The opening leader against a game contract has been told where the defense will NOT have tricks coming. The defense will waste a tempo on the opening lead if it starts by leading the **splinter** suit. It is a far better idea for the defense to attack where there may be more than one defensive trick.

Sophisticated defenders will capitalize even further when direct **splinters** are used. They have the partnership agreement that "double" calls for the lead of the higher ranking of the remaining suits, and that "pass" suggests that a lead in the lower ranking of the remaining suits may be best for the defense.

Playing **Bergen Raises** a jump to the three level in the opposite major shows that responder holds four card support for opener's major, the values to reach a game, and shortness in one of the three suits other than the agreed major. When opener has no need to know the location of responder's short-ness, game is bid in the agreed major suit.

If a slam should be reached when responder's shortness is in the right place, opener continues by making the cheapest call. This asks responder to show the location of the **splinter**.

When the auction is: 1♠ – pass – 3♥ – pass, 3♠ asks the location of responder's shortness. Responder uses the next three steps to show where. Step 1, 3NT shows shortness in clubs; step 2, 4♣ shows shortness in diamonds; and step 3, 4♦ shows shortness in hearts.

When the auction is: 1♥ – pass – 3♠ – pass, 3NT asks the location of responder's shortness. Responder uses the next three steps to show where. Step 1, 4♣ shows shortness in clubs; step 2, 4♦ shows shortness in diamonds; and step 3, 4♥ shows shortness in spades.

Example 71)

a) ♠ KQ1064
   ♥ AK4
   ♦ 8732
   ♣ 8

b) ♠ Q8743
   ♥ KJ8
   ♦ K104
   ♣ A6

c) ♠ Q87432
   ♥ KQ65
   ♦ AK7
   ♣ —

All Example 71) openers have bid one spade and received a three heart response which shows game forcing values with four card spade support and shortness somewhere.

Example 71a) bids three spades to ask for the location of the short-ness. If responder shows short diamonds by bidding four clubs, opener uses RKC to find out about controls. If responder's short-ness is in either hearts or clubs, opener signs off at four spades.

Example 71b) has no interest in slam no matter where responder's shortness is. Opener does not ask for the location of the known splinter but just bids four spades.

Example 71c) has interest in slam, but does not need to know about responder's shortness. A cue bid of four diamonds is the best continuation.

Strong Raises

A response of three notrump shows a balanced three card raise and offers a choice of contracts. Opener can pass, play game in the known major suit fit, or cue bid to suggest slam. Responder virtually always will be 4-3-3-3.

Example 72)

	a)			b)	
	♠	KQ5		♠	A64
	♥	Q74		♥	743
	♦	A1064		♦	Q972
	♣	K43		♣	AK9

Both hands of Example 72) would bid three notrump as a response to the opening bid of one heart.

Because of the use of **concealed splinters,** jumps to four in a minor suit are not necessary for that purpose and are available for further description.

Four clubs is used as a big balanced **Swiss** raise with at least good three card support. It definitely shows a hand too big for the response of three notrump.

Example 73)

	a)			b)	
	♠	KJ72		♠	AK9
	♥	KQ		♥	QJ7
	♦	K74		♦	AQ5
	♣	KJ73		♣	Q1074

Both hands of Example 73) would bid four clubs in response to an opening bid of one spade.

Four diamonds is used to show five card support for the opening major and distinguish between the hand that is purely preemptive, which bids four of the major, and this hand which has some constructive value.

Example 74)

a)
♠ 9
♥ KQ743
♦ K1054
♣ 843

b)
♠ 9
♥ K10743
♦ 10743
♣ 854

Responding to the opening bid of one heart, Example 74a) would bid four diamonds; Example 74b) would bid four hearts.

Most practitioners of **Bergen Raises** today incorporate the first features which include the single raise and jumps to the three level. Many invert the meaning of the jumps to three of a minor suit—using three clubs as a **limit raise** and three diamonds as the four card single raise. Very few use the entire system. Little do they realize how much they are missing by not using **concealed splinters** and some form of **Swiss**.

Bergen Raises—Summary

Here is a summary of responder's calls when **Bergen Raises** are agreed:

1. The single raise of opener's major shows minimum response values (5+ to 9- HCP) and **exactly** three card support.
2. A **limit raise** with three card support is shown after responder uses the **forcing notrump**. Responder's rebid is a jump in opener's major suit.
3. The cheapest call in the unbid major suit is natural.
4. 2NT is the **Jacoby Two Notrump**.
5. Three clubs is a constructive single raise (7+ to 10- HCP) with four card support.
6. Three diamonds is a limit raise (10+ to 12- HCP) with four card support.
7. Three of opener's major is preemptive showing 0 to 6 HCP and four card support.
8. Three of the other major shows four card support with game values and a **concealed splinter**.

9. Three notrump is a balanced non-forcing raise with three card support.
10. Four clubs is a big balanced raise with either three or four card support.
11. Four diamonds is a constructive five card raise of the opening major.
12. Four of opener's major is a five card preemptive raise.

Two Way Reverse Drury

When responder is a passed hand major suit raises must take into account two things:

1. Opener may have opened light, particularly in third seat.
2. Opener may have bid a four card major.

For these reasons it is important that **limit raises** be shown at the two level. If responder needed to reach the three level to show a **limit raise**, the auction would often be out of control. The simplest version of **Drury** was presented in Volume I, page 158.

Bergen suggests that when a passed responder uses **Drury** to show a **limit raise** for the opening major suit bid, it is far easier to reach or stay out of game when opener knows how many trumps responder holds. This suggestion has led to the creation of the modification which allows responder to show how many trumps are held as the **limit raise** is announced.

Original **Drury** was simply a range finder. When a passed responder used the convention by bidding two clubs, a simple question was being asked: "Partner, do you have a real opening bid, or have you opened light?" Opener was asked to bid two diamonds (artificial) to deny a real opening bid, or to make any other descriptive call to announce possession of a real opening hand. There was no suggestion of a fit for the opening bid—only interest in finding out whether the opening bid was real or not.

It did not take long for the realization to set in that there could be only one reason for responder to need this information. A passed responder would only need to know about the opening bid when there was reason to believe that game was possible. What could cause responder to feel that game was still possible? Two things—near opening bid values and A FIT FOR OPENER'S MAJOR SUIT.

The modern use of **Drury**, then, is based on the assumption that responder must hold a **limit raise** for opener's major suit.

The first refinement was made to allow more space for exploration. Instead of showing a non-opening bid with two diamonds, it made far more sense to have opener rebid the major with less than an opening hand. Two diamonds was reassigned the task of showing a hand that was a true opening bid (therefore promising five cards in the major suit), but without enough information to bid a game facing a known **limit raise**. This refinement is called **Reverse Drury** since it reverses the meaning of the two diamond call and the repeat of opener's major suit.

The second refinement, **Bergen's** improvement, was to stipulate that a **Drury** call of two clubs promises a **limit raise** with three card support, and that a call of two diamonds promises a **limit raise** with four card (or longer) support.

When any **Drury** call is made:
1. Opener will jump to game with a hand that feels a **limit raise** is adequate to produce game.
2. Opener will repeat the major suit cheaply facing any **Drury** call to deny holding an opening bid.
3. When responder has bid two clubs to show a **limit raise** with three card support, a rebid of two diamonds shows that opener has a real opening bid but is not sure what to do.
4. When responder bids two diamonds to show a **limit raise** with four card (or longer) support, opener's call to show indecision is two notrump.

Game Tries After Drury

Since the key to reaching game in marginal situations is the degree of fit between two hands, we recommend short suit game tries in **Drury** auctions where opener has a real opening bid but has doubts about game.

When responder bids two clubs to show a three card **limit raise** and opener bids two diamonds, responder's next call in a new suit should show a singleton or void. This will allow opener to determine how well the two hands fit, and either bid game or sign off cheaply. Responder's return to the agreed major at the two level denies a singleton or void. If opener then continues by bidding a new suit, it is opener's short suit. When neither opener nor responder can show a short suit, the two relatively balanced hands are not likely to produce ten tricks. When responder bids two of the agreed major, opener passes to deny a short suit.

Example 75)

a) ♠ KQ875
♥ A6
♦ K104
♣ 873

b) ♠ A103
♥ Q853
♦ 7
♣ K10952

c) ♠ A103
♥ Q853
♦ A9532
♣ 7

Example 75a) opens one spade in third seat and after a Drury **two club response bids two diamonds to show an opening bid with inability to bid game facing a three card** limit raise.

After opener shows full values by bidding two diamonds, Example 75b) bids three diamonds to show shortness. This shortness fits badly facing secondary honor cards, so opener signs off at three spades.

After opener shows full values by bidding two diamonds, Example 75c) bids three clubs to show shortness. This fits well facing opener's losers, so opener bids four spades.

Example 76)

a) ♠ KQ875
♥ A63
♦ 7
♣ K1042

b) ♠ A103   c) ♠ A103
     ♥ KJ2   ♥ 8643
     ♦ 8643   ♦ KJ2
     ♣ QJ7   ♣ QJ7

Example 76a) opens one spade in third seat and after a Drury **two club response bids two diamonds to show an opening bid with inability to bid game facing a three card** limit raise.

Examples 76b) and 76c) do not have shortness to show and return to two spades.

Example 76a) continues by bidding three diamonds as a short suit game try.

Example 76b) knows that the hands fit well and jumps to four spades.

Example 76c) knows that the hands fit poorly and signs off at three spades.

Game will be easier to reach when responder uses two diamonds as **Drury** to show a four card **limit raise**. The comfort of knowing about the fourth trump will cause opener to jump to game on most shapely minimums. Still, opener can express doubts by a rebid of two notrump.

When opener bids two notrump to confirm a real opening bid, any four card **limit raise** that is distributional will bid game in the agreed major. Responder has a hand that would have made a **splinter** raise facing an unpassed opening bidder.

Hardy Raises

Belief in many of the concepts embraced in **Bergen Raises** is shared by this author. There are some areas in which I believe that a different approach will achieve better results. Over the years I have organized an approach to major suit raises that I believe is superior to other methods. I claim credit for very few of them, but I can claim credit for organizing them into a complete and interactive approach. These methods are expressed in Part Three of *The Problems With Major Suit Raises and How to Fix Them,* which was published by Devyn Press in 1998.

The Single Raise

You know my opinion of **Constructive major raises.** When responder has a fit for opener's major suit and minimum response values (5+ to 9-HCP), it is important to express that fit immediately. Responder's raise not only allows opener to know of the fit which is the essence of partnership need, it also serves to preempt the auction against intrusion by the opposition. Does not "The Law of Total Tricks" suggest that the eight card fit be expressed immediately by raising to the two level?

I have reservations about reaching the three level prematurely when the bidding side holds a nine card fit. Often the bidding side can stop at the two level and take eight tricks on hands that produce minus scores if a nine card fit causes the three level to be reached immediately. Discretion should be used when responder has minimum raise values. If the single raise is made with either three or four card support, the bidding side will often be allowed to play at the two level.

If the opposition balances against this attempt to stop at the two level and responder has a fourth trump, it is clearly right to "take the push" and compete to the next level. If one opponent bids all of the values of the opposition by balancing, when responder bids again that will probably end the auction. If a minus score is generated by this further competition, that cannot be avoided. Frequently the auction will end at the two level.

Example 77)

a)   ♠ 85   b)   ♠ 85
         ♥ Q93   ♥ Q953
         ♦ K862   ♦ K82
         ♣ J1054   ♣ J1054

Both hands of Example 77) are responding to the opening bid

of one heart. **Both hands raise to two hearts. If opener passes and the opponents balance, Example 77a) will pass—Example 77b) will continue to three hearts.** The Law of Total Tricks **is responder's guide to further competition.**

The Raise to Game

Responder's jump raise to game in opener's major suit shows meager values and five card trump support. **Bergen Raises** did well to provide for the hand with some extra value. Responder's jump raise to the four level should deny possession of an outside ace or king. If responder holds such a card, a distributional opener may be able to take twelve tricks far too often.

Our agreement when responder has five card trump support and meager values and also has an ace or king outside the trump suit is to have responder use the **forcing notrump**. Responder then jumps to game in the agreed major as a rebid. If opener can visualize slam and needs to know where that key card is located, the cheapest call asks and responder bids the suit of the outside value.

Example 78)

a) ♠ Q9763   b) ♠ Q9753
    ♥ 85   ♥ 85
    ♦ J962   ♦ K962
    ♣ 104   ♣ 104

Both hands of Example 78) are responding to the opening bid of one spade. Example 78a) jumps to four spades, in keeping with The Law of Total Tricks.

Example 78b) holds a control card which might be all that opener needs to make a slam. Responder starts by bidding a forcing notrump, **then jumps to four spades. This auction tells opener that responder holds five card support and that the hand also includes a control card that might facilitate a slam contract. If opener continues by bidding four notrump, this responder bids five diamonds to show the location of the control card.**

The Limit Raise

The **Walsh System**, which was created in the 1960's by Richard Walsh, John Swanson, and Paul Soloway, gave credence to a certain **limit raise** which is largely ignored today by disciples of **The Law of Total Tricks**. When responder has game invitational values (9+ to 12- HCP) with three card support for opener's known five card or longer major suit, possession of a ruffing value (a side singleton or void) makes the hand far more valuable.

The power of such a hand caused **Walsh System** users to classify this three card **limit raise** as good enough for a jump to the three level. Although the three card **limit raise** without a ruffing value was shown after the use of the **forcing notrump**, the **good limit raise** was determined to be either a hand with four card support or with three card support and a side singleton or void. Loss of this distinction by disciples of **The Law** regarding **limit raises** with three card support certainly must deter proper hand evaluation.

It is clear that all **limit raises** are not created equal. Although they have the same high card values of a good nine to a bad twelve in high cards, the number of trumps and the structure of the hand have caused us to categorize **limit raises** into three groups.

1. The **bad limit raise** has three card trump support and no ruffing value.
2. The **good limit raise** has either four card trump support or three card support with a ruffing value.
3. The **game forcing limit raise** has four card support and also has a ruffing value.

There is complete agreement that the **bad limit raise** is shown by the use of the **forcing notrump**, followed by a jump in opener's major suit. The common auction is one in which opener's rebid is in a lower ranking suit at the two level. Responder then jumps to the three level to show this specific raise.

There are two auctions in which showing support for opener's major suit at the three level does not express this hand.

1. When opener's rebid is a repeat of the original major at the two level,

showing a six card (or longer) suit, responder must jump to the four level to describe the hand with game invitational values and a true fit. Responder's raise to the three level describes the hand with invitational values but shows only a doubleton in support of the major suit. Two card support becomes adequate when opener has shown a six card suit, so when responder has a three card fit, that should be enough extra for game.

2. When opener's rebid is a jump shift in a lower ranking suit, the auction becomes game forcing. Responder's return to opener's major at the three level is a simple preference showing minimum response values and a doubleton in opener's major. In order to confirm a true fit responder must jump to four in the major suit in this auction.

Example 79)

a)   ♠ Q107
     ♥ 96
     ♦ J853
     ♣ AK62

b)   ♠ J853
     ♥ Q107
     ♦ 96
     ♣ AK62

Both hands of Example 79) have game invitational values (9+ to 12− HCP).

If the opening bid is one spade, Example 79a) is a bad limit raise **containing three card support and no ruffing value (singleton or void). Responder bids a** forcing notrump, **then makes a jump raise in spades.**

Example 79b) is a good limit raise **when the opening bid is one spade. When the opening bid is one heart, responder bids one spade (it would be wrong to use the** forcing notrump **holding four card spade length), then makes a jump raise in hearts to show the** bad limit raise.

Much of the improvement in the structure of major suit raises should be credited to Marty Bergen. He led the way years ago when the change was made from forcing jump raises to limit jumps. He again was the pioneer when jump raises in major suits were changed to preemptive. The preemptive jump raise is a powerful weapon which is included in our structure.

Example 80)

a) ♠ 85   b) ♠ QJ73
    ♥ QJ73   ♥ 85
    ♦ 654   ♦ 654
    ♣ 9862   ♣ 9862

Example 80a) would pass any other opening bid, but if the opening bid is one heart, this responder makes a jump raise to three hearts.

Example 80b) would pass any other opening bid but would jump raise the opening bid of one spade to three spades.

It follows that the **good limit raise** must be shown by some artificial means. The jump response of three clubs shows this hand. When responder makes that call, opener knows to expect one of two configurations—four trumps and no side shortness or three trumps with a ruffing value.

Holding a bare minimum, opener may continue by signing off at three of the agreed major. Or opener can sign off by bidding game in the agreed major suit. Opener's hand will be reasonably substantial, but there will be no interest in reaching a slam.

When opener visualizes the possibility of a slam, it will be helpful to learn the nature of responder's hand. Opener's continuation will be three diamonds, the **Mathe Asking Bid**. This adaptation comes from the era when jump raises of major suits to the three level were limit. Opener's cheapest call asked responder to show shortness or to deny shortness by returning to the agreed suit as cheaply as possible. When three clubs shows the **good limit raise**, the cheapest call is three diamonds, and responder can show not only whether or not the hand contains shortness, but also can show whether shortness is a singleton or a void and in what suit it is.

When opener bids three diamonds to ask, responder's next call of three of the agreed major denies shortness, thereby confirming four card trump support. If responder bids three of the opposite major suit, that announces a void in some suit. Responder's bid of four of either minor suit shows a singleton in the suit bid, and three notrump shows a singleton in the opposite major.

If responder bids three of the opposite major to announce a void (and thereby confirm three card trump support), opener can bid the cheapest call to ask the location of the void.

Once opener receives such a complete description of responder's hand and is still below the game level, it should be easy for opener to know whether +-or not to pursue the slam search.

Example 81)

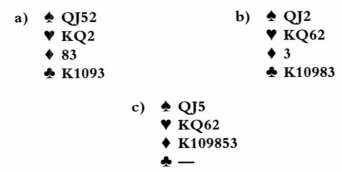

a) ♠ QJ52
   ♥ KQ2
   ♦ 83
   ♣ K1093

b) ♠ QJ2
   ♥ KQ62
   ♦ 3
   ♣ K10983

c) ♠ QJ5
   ♥ KQ62
   ♦ K109853
   ♣ —

Example 81) hands are responding to the opening bid of one spade. All three bid three clubs to show a good limit raise **containing either four trumps or three trumps with a ruffing value (singleton or void) in some side suit.**

If opener bids three diamonds, the Mathe Asking Bid**, to ask about shortness, Example 81a) bids three spades to show four trumps and no ruffing value.**

Example 81b) bids four diamonds to show a singleton diamond.

Example 81c) bids three hearts to announce that the shortness held is a void.

Opener then bids three spades to ask the location of the void, and responder bids four clubs to announce a void in that suit.

The Game Forcing Limit Raise _____

When responder holds four card support for opener's major, game invitational values, and shortness in some side suit, game should be reached. The
nature of the fit in responder's hand replaces the high card values usually
sought for game. Remember that fits take tricks.

In Volume I we showed that responder could **splinter** to show this hand.
Earlier in this chapter we made the case for **concealed splinters** rather
than direct **splinters**. Giving the opponents the location of responder's short
suit will serve the bidding side only when slam is to be pursued. When the
auction stops at game, the information conveyed by a direct **splinter** is of
more use to the opponents than to the bidding side.

Our approach to **concealed splinters** is more thorough than the ones
previously shown. We know that showing shortness is important, but we
can also indicate various high card ranges and show the nature of the shortness when responder has the values of 9+ to 12- HCP.

Responder makes an **under jump shift** to show this hand. When the opening bid has been one spade, this is a jump to three hearts. When the opening
bid is one heart, this is a jump to three diamonds.

With no interest in slam, opener simply bids game in the agreed major suit.
When opener does feel that slam is possible, the continuation is to three of
the agreed major suit. This sounds as though opener is backing away, but
that is not at all what opener has done. Opener's repeat of the agreed major
suit at the three level is a slam try which asks responder to describe both
the nature and the location of the shortness which has been promised.

Responder's cheapest call promises that the shortness is a void. Opener then
makes the cheapest call to ask the location of the void, and responder shows
where the void is.

In the auction: 1♠ – pass – 3♥ – pass, 3♠ – pass – 3NT, opener bids four
clubs to ask the location of the void. Responder bids four diamonds to
show a diamond void, four hearts to show a heart void, or four spades (the
agreed suit) to show a club void.

In the auction: 1♥ – pass – 3♦ – pass, 3♥ – pass – 3♠, opener bids three notrump to ask for the location of the void. Responder bids four clubs to show a club void, four diamonds to show a diamond void, or four hearts (the agreed suit) to show a spade void.

After opener asks about shortness, responder's call beyond the cheapest (which is void showing) shows and locates a singleton. When opener asks by bidding three spades, a four level call in any other suit locates the singleton. When opener asks by bidding three hearts, three notrump shows a spade singleton and four of a minor locates a singleton there. Note that in all auctions opener receives the desired information and is not required to go beyond the level of game in the agreed major.

Example 82)

a)　♠ AJ84　　　　　　b)　♠ AJ84
　　♥ KQ63　　　　　　　♥ J10982
　　♦ 6　　　　　　　　　♦ KQ63
　　♣ 10982　　　　　　　♣ —

In response to an opening bid in either major suit, Example 82a) would make an under jump shift. **If the opening bid is one spade, responder bids three hearts; if the opening bid is one heart, responder bids three diamonds. If opener then rebids cheaply in the suit of the opening bid to ask for a description of responder's shortness, responder bids four diamonds to show a singleton in that suit.**

In response to an opening bid in either major suit, Example 82b) would make an under jump shift. **If the opening bid is one spade, responder bids three hearts. If opener then rebids three spades to ask for a description of the shortness, responder bids three notrump to announce a void. Opener then bids four clubs to ask the location of the void, and responder bids four spades (the agreed suit) to show a void in clubs.**

If the opening bid is one heart, responder bids three diamonds. If opener then bids three hearts to ask for a description of the shortness, responder bids three spades to announce a void. Opener then bids three notrump to ask for the location of the void, and responder bids four clubs.

The Jacoby Two Notrump

The **Jacoby Two Notrump** is an excellent convention. Unfortunately it is not put to best advantage in most partnerships. When responder uses this convention and holds only the values of an opening bid, if slam is to be reached it must be opener who has considerable extra values. Usually this is not the case, and the auction stops at game after opener has told the defenders things which will not help the bidding side at all, but will aid the defense.

When opener does have the extra values which might lead to a slam contract, the captaincy has been assumed by the wrong hand. The lesser hand of the responder is asking about the better hand of opener. The tail is wagging the dog. Surely this cannot be the right way for the auction to unfold. The hand that has extra values should be the captain, with the lesser hand describing. This can only happen when responder's requirements to use the **Jacoby Two Notrump** are far greater than those of an opening bid. Responder's values should be 16+ HCP, which is the agreement in the **Hardy Raise** complex.

Even when responder values good enough to use the **Jacoby Two Notrump**, making a slam still depends upon the degree of fit between the two hands.

Example 83)

	a)		b)	
	♠	K93	♠	A6
	♥	KQ1073	♥	A852
	♦	5	♦	A1098
	♣	AJ92	♣	KQ3

Example 83a) shows a good minimum opening bid facing Example 83b) which holds values good enough to use the Jacoby Two Notrump **in response to the opening bid of one heart. Opener would rebid three diamonds to show shortness and responder would mark time by bidding three hearts. Then would follow a series of cue bids and the good grand slam might be reached.**

Example 84)

	a)		b)	
	♠	KJ1073	♠	KJ1073
	♥	K106	♥	K106
	♦	AJ532	♦	—
	♣	—	♣	AJ532

c) ♠ AQ85
    ♥ AJ7
    ♦ KQ10
    ♣ 874

Example 84a) bids one spade and rebids three clubs when responder uses the Jacoby Two Notrump. **Responder cue bids three hearts and opener bids four clubs to show that the shortness is a void. If responder next bids four diamonds to show values there, opener might bid five notrump—the** grand slam force. **The excellent grand slam would be reached in this auction or many other possible auctions.**

Example 84b) bids one spade and rebids three diamonds when responder uses the Jacoby Two Notrump. **Responder cue bids three hearts and opener bids four diamonds to show that the shortness is a void. Responder signs off by bidding four spades.**

Example 84c) is responder in both auctions. **Note that opener's hand is the same in both auctions except for the different suits. When the hands fit together as with Example 84a) thirteen tricks are extremely likely. When the hands fit poorly as with Example 84b) any slam is likely to fail.**

With responder needing 16+ HCP to use the **Jacoby Two Notrump,** there is a gap that needs to be filled. When responder has a four card fit for opener's major and 12+ to 15 HCP, two tools are provided.

The Over Jump Shift _____

The **over jump shift** is a jump to the three level in the denomination ranking just above opener's major. In response to one spade, this is a jump to three notrump. In response to one heart, this is a jump to three spades. Responder announces 12+ to 15 HCP, four card support for opener's major suit, and a **concealed splinter.**

Opener can sign off at game with minimum values. With any thought of slam, opener makes the cheapest call to ask responder the location of the shortness.

In the auction: 1♠ – pass – 3NT, opener bids four clubs to ask. Responder bids four diamonds or four hearts to show shortness in the suit bid, or four spades (the agreed suit) to show shortness in clubs.

In the auction: 1♥ – pass – 3♠, opener bids 3NT to ask. Responder bids four clubs or four diamonds to show shortness in the suit bid, or four hearts (the agreed suit) to show shortness in spades.

The **over jump shift** does not leave enough space for the nature of the shortness to be shown. Again, opener receives the needed information and is below the level of game.

Example 85)

a) ♠ A95
♥ KQ63
♦ 5
♣ A10972

b) ♠ KQ63
♥ A95
♦ A109762
♣ —

In response to one spade, Example 85a) would bid two clubs and show support for spades as a rebid. In response to one heart, this hand would make an over jump shift by jumping to three spades. This shows four card support for hearts, 12+ to 15- HCP, and some shortness. If opener bids three notrump to ask the location of the shortness, this hand bids four diamonds to show shortness in that suit.

In response to one heart, Example 85b) would bid two diamonds (NOT one spade) and show heart support as a rebid. In response to one spade, this hand would make an over jump shift by jumping to three notrump. This shows four card support for spades, 12+ to 15- HCP, and some shortness. If opener bids four clubs to ask the location of the shortness, this hand bids four spades (the agreed suit) to show club shortness. Note that unlike under jump shift auctions responder does not have enough room to distinguish between singletons and voids.

Inverted Trump Swiss _____

Holding 12+ to 15 HCP, four card trump support, and a balanced hand, responder uses **Inverted Trump Swiss**. A jump to four clubs promises good trump support—either four headed by two of the top three honors or five headed by the ace or king. With any lesser trump holding responder jumps to four diamonds.

Example 86)

a) ♠ A95
   ♥ KQ63
   ♦ J2
   ♣ A1097

b) ♠ AQ5
   ♥ K1063
   ♦ J2
   ♣ A1097

In response to the opening bid of one heart, both of these responders would use Inverted Trump Swiss.

Example 86a) would jump to four clubs to show a balanced hand, 12+ to 15- HCP, and good trumps (two of the top three honors with four, or ace or king with five).

Example 86b) would jump to four diamonds to show the same hand with lesser trumps.

Hardy Raises—Summary _____

Preemptive (0-5- HCP)
1. Jump raises to the three level show four card support and less than the value of a single raise (0 to 5- HCP).
2. The jump raise to game promises five trumps, 0 to 6 HCP, and no outside ace or king. Holding an outside ace or king, responder uses the **forcing notrump**, then jumps to game in the major suit. If opener continues with the cheapest call, responder bids the suit of the outside value.

Simple (5+ to 9- HCP)
3. The single raise shows 5+ to 9- HCP and three or four card trump sup-

port. If opponents balance, responder carries on to the three level holding four card support.

Limit (9+ to 12- HCP)

4. The **bad limit raise** (9+ to 12- HCP) with three card support and no ruffing value is shown by use of the **forcing notrump**. Responder jumps in opener's major as a rebid.

5. The **good limit raise** (9+ to 12- HCP) has three trumps and a ruffing value, or four trumps without. It is shown by a jump to three clubs. Opener can sign off at three or four of the major suit. With thoughts of slam, opener bids three diamonds—the **Mathe Asking Bid**. Responder bids three of the major holding four trumps. Responder bids three of the opposite major to announce possession of a void. Opener's cheapest continuation asks the location of that void. Responder bids three notrump to show a singleton in the opposite major, or four of a minor suit to show a singleton there.

6. The **game forcing limit raise** (9+ to 12- HCP) has four trumps and a ruffing value. Responder shows this hand as a **concealed splinter** by making an **under jump shift**. Responder to one spade bids three hearts—responder to one heart bids three diamonds. Opener can sign off by bidding game in the agreed major. Opener's continuation of three in the agreed major asks about responder's shortness. Responder's cheapest call announces a void and opener's cheapest call asks where the void is. Responder's non-cheapest continuation locates a singleton.

Forcing (12+ HCP)

7. Responder shows 12+ to 15- HCP, four card support, and a **concealed splinter** by making an **over jump shift**. Opener can sign off at game or make the cheapest call to determine the location of responder's shortness.

8. Responder shows 12+ to 15-, four card support, and a balanced hand by using **Inverted Trump Swiss**. A jump to four clubs shows two of the top three honors with four cards, or five cards to the ace or king. A jump to four diamonds shows any lesser trump holding.

Slammish (15+ HCP)

9. Responder uses the **Jacoby Two Notrump** with four card support and 15+ HCP. Only then should responder assume the captaincy. The components of this convention were presented in the discussion of **Bergen Raises**. They may differ slightly from other presentations, but are as played by this author in partnership with the late Jim Jacoby.

Let us give credit where it is due. The single raise with minimum values has been a long time crusade. The jump raise to game denying an outside ace or king, the **forcing notrump** followed by a jump to game to show an outside ace or king, and the cheapest continuation to locate that outside value are other suggestions of this writer. The jump raise as preemptive originates with Marty Bergen. The jump to three clubs to show a **good limit raise** was inspired by **Bergen Raises**. Inclusion of the three card raise with a ruffing value originated with the **Walsh System**. The **Mathe Asking Bid** was created by deceased California expert Lew Mathe. The **over** and **under jump shifts** were suggested by Los Angeles expert Bill Schreiber. **Inverted Trump Swiss** was also part of the **Walsh System**. The **Jacoby Two Notrump** was created by the late Texas expert Oswald Jacoby. The modifications presented here were made by the late Jim Jacoby.

Game Tries

Natural game tries were presented in Volume I. In the presentation of **Drury** in this chapter short suit game tries were also presented. Clearly, showing shortness when possible is the most complete method of allowing accurate hand evaluation. With this knowledge there has been an expert attempt to promulgate short suit game tries. There is a simple problem with this approach. After a single raise if opener does not have a singleton or void, a short suit game try is not possible. If the partnership has agreed to use short suit game tries, opener has only the omnibus try of two notrump available. This does not allow for the exchange of vital information and is extremely ineffective. Given the choice of agreeing short suit game tries and living with the scenario when opener does not have an appropriate hand, most experts have abandoned this convention.

There is much misunderstanding as to what makes a "help suit game try." In this standard approach the game try is made in a side suit of at least three cards containing an honor holding. It is ludicrous to make a game try on three or four small cards. The purpose of "help suit game tries" is that of finding secondary honor card fits. The game try is made with an honor holding, and will be accepted holding a high honor which will mesh with the honor cards in the hand making the game try. Shortness facing a "help suit game try" is not an asset. Facing shortness, secondary honor cards lose value.

When the game try is made on three or more small cards, it is not a "help suit game try." It is a "weak suit game try." "Weak suit game tries" can be effective when agreed by the partnership, but their use is not standard and requires an alert. The holding sought facing a "help suit game try" is one or more high honor cards. But facing a "weak suit game try," who wants to find queen third or king third? A single honor card does not solve the problem. Facing a "weak suit game try," the ideal fit is shortness. This is the opposite of what is desired facing a "help suit game try."

To summarize:

1. A "help suit game try" is made with three or more cards including an honor card holding. The ideal fit is one or more high honor cards. Shortness facing a help suit game try is a poor fit, since honor cards are wasted facing shortness.
2. A "weak suit game try" is non-standard but playable. It consists of three or more small cards. The ideal fit is shortness or a concentration of honor cards. Single honor cards facing a weak suit holding are of little value.

Two-way Game Tries

The next expert consideration was the attempt to play both short suit game tries and natural game tries at the same time. Opener's new suit after a single raise becomes a short suit game try. In order to make a natural game try after the single raise, opener must use a relay. Following a spade raise, the relay is a rebid of two notrump. Following a heart raise, the relay is an artificial bid of two spades.

After either relay responder is asked to make the cheapest call. Opener then bids the suit in which help is needed. The problem with the approach is that the use of bidding space often leaves responder unable to make a counter offer.

In the auction: 1♠ – pass – 2♠ – pass, 2NT – pass – 3♣, opener can make a natural game try of three diamonds or three hearts, or bid three spades to show a natural game try in clubs. Responder's only possible counter offer is in hearts after a game try in diamonds.

In the auction: 1♥ – pass – 2♥ – pass, 2♠ – pass – 2NT, opener can make a natural game try of three clubs or three diamonds, or bid three hearts to show a natural game try in spades. Responder's only possible counter offer is in diamonds after a game try in clubs.

Kokish Game Tries

Canadian expert Eric Kokish suggested that rather than ask for help in a specific suit, opener might ask responder to show where help existed. After the single raise, opener's cheapest continuation asked responder to bid the nearest suit in which help was available. Responder would bypass suits with no values or could bid three in the agreed major to reject all tries or jump to game to accept all tries.

When responder shows help in the cheapest suit, opener can make a further inquiry in one of the two remaining suits before the agreed major at the three level is reached. When responder bypasses the cheapest suit to show help in the next suit, opener still has the opportunity to ask in the last remaining suit.

In the auction: 1♠ – pass – 2♠ – pass, 2NT – pass, if responder shows help in clubs, opener can ask in either diamonds or hearts. If responder shows help in diamonds, opener can ask in hearts. No side suit is left out of the loop.

In the auction: 1♥ – pass – 2♥ – pass, 2♠ asks and 2NT shows help in spades. If responder shows help in spades, opener can ask in clubs or diamonds. If responder shows help in clubs, opener can still ask in diamonds. Again, help can be shown or denied in all side suits after the single raise.

Because opener uses the cheapest call to ask responder to show help, opener can call in any of the other three suits to send other messages. It again becomes possible to play short suit game tries by opener

Our modification is to have opener show short suits in the minors, but also to allow a search for a four-four fit in the other major suit.

In the auction: 1♠ – pass – 2♠ – pass, two notrump asks responder to show the suit in which help (a high honor holding) can be found. However, three of either minor suit by opener shows shortness (a singleton or void), and three hearts is natural—usually a four card suit. Responder can bid three spades to reject or can accept by jumping to four spades or by raising hearts when holding four cards there.

In the auction: 1♥ – pass – 2♥ – pass, if opener bids two spades responder can bid two notrump with spade values or show help in either minor suit. However, opener's continuation of three of either minor shows shortness in the suit bid. Opener bids two notrump to show a holding of four spades. Responder can reject by returning to three hearts or can bid three spades holding four cards with minimum values. Responder can accept by jumping to four hearts or can jump to four spades holding four cards there with maximum values.

To summarize our modified **Kokish Game Tries**:

1. After a single raise, opener's cheapest call asks responder to show the nearest suit in which help can be provided.
2. Continuation to three of the agreed major asks for good trumps.
3. Continuation to three of a minor suit is a **short suit game try**.
4. After a spade raise, a game try of three hearts is natural showing four cards. After a heart raise, a game try of two notrump shows four spades.

Example 87)

a) ♠ AQJ73
    ♥ 104
    ♦ KQ2
    ♣ AJ5

b) ♠ AQJ73
    ♥ KQ104
    ♦ A5
    ♣ J2

c) ♠ AQJ73
    ♥ AJ5
    ♦ 4
    ♣ KQ62

d) ♠ A5
    ♥ J8762
    ♦ AQ103
    ♣ AK

e) ♠ AJ5
    ♥ AQJ73
    ♦ KJ62
    ♣ 4

f) ♠ AK102
    ♥ KQ1074
    ♦ A5
    ♣ J2

Example 87a) opens one spade and is raised to two. Opener continues by bidding two notrump to ask responder where help exists. If responder bids either clubs or diamonds, a jump to game is reasonable. If responder bids hearts, opener should sign off at three spades.

Example 87b) opens one spade and is raised to two. Opener continues by bidding three hearts which is a natural game try. Responder can reject by returning to three spades. Responder can accept by bidding game in hearts when holding four hearts and maximum values or can accept by jumping to four spades.

Example 87c) opens one spade and is raised to two. Opener continues by bidding three diamonds as a short suit game try.

Example 87d) opens one heart and is raised to two. Opener continues by bidding three hearts to ask for good trumps.

Example 87e) opens one heart and is raised to two. Opener continues by bidding three clubs as a short suit game try.

Example 87f) opens one heart and is raised to two. Opener continues by bidding two notrump to make a game try showing four spades.

Suit Raise Exercises

Opener has bid one club. What is your response with each of the following hands?

1.   ♠ AJ5
    ♥ 6
    ♦ AQ42
    ♣ KQ1073

2.   ♠ KJ8
    ♥ AJ4
    ♦ Q95
    ♣ 10762

3.   ♠ K74
    ♥ 3
    ♦ J86
    ♣ Q108752

4.   ♠ A92
    ♥ J84
    ♦ A6
    ♣ KQ953

You have opened one diamond and partner has made a forcing raise to two diamonds. What is your rebid?

5.   ♠ AJ5
    ♥ 6
    ♦ KQ1073
    ♣ AQ42

6.   ♠ AJ3
    ♥ KJ2
    ♦ QJ1054
    ♣ 103

7.   ♠ 107
    ♥ AK3
    ♦ KQJ82
    ♣ J74

8.   ♠ KJ84
    ♥ AQ6
    ♦ Q1093
    ♣ AQ

Partner has opened one club and you have made a forcing raise to two. Partner continues by bidding two diamonds. What is your rebid?

9.   ♠ 84
    ♥ 72
    ♦ AQ85
    ♣ AK1063

10.   ♠ AQ5
    ♥ K93
    ♦ 62
    ♣ KJ1054

11. ♠ AQ5
    ♥ KJ4
    ♦ 62
    ♣ J10754

12. ♠ AK5
    ♥ 1073
    ♦ 85
    ♣ KQ973

Partner has opened one spade. What response do you make playing **Bergen Raises**? What response do you make playing **Hardy Raises**?

13. ♠ Q83
    ♥ 65
    ♦ KQ74
    ♣ 9762

14. ♠ Q853
    ♥ A5
    ♦ KQ74
    ♣ 962

15. ♠ Q83
    ♥ A5
    ♦ KQ74
    ♣ 9762

16. ♠ Q853
    ♥ 65
    ♦ KQ74
    ♣ 962

17. ♠ AK92
    ♥ K93
    ♦ 85
    ♣ A974

18. ♠ QJ83
    ♥ 54
    ♦ 10972
    ♣ J86

19. ♠ AK92
    ♥ KQ3
    ♦ 85
    ♣ A974

20. ♠ A1092
    ♥ KQ3
    ♦ 5
    ♣ KJ984

Partner has opened one heart. What response do you make playing **Bergen Raises**? What response do you make playing **Hardy Raises**?

21. ♠ 5
    ♥ Q83
    ♦ KQ74
    ♣ A9762

22. ♠ 5
    ♥ Q853
    ♦ KQ74
    ♣ A962

23. ♠ A8
 ♥ K1084
 ♦ KQ74
 ♣ J92

24. ♠ 83
 ♥ K10842
 ♦ K743
 ♣ 92

25. ♠ 65
 ♥ Q853
 ♦ KJ74
 ♣ 962

26. ♠ 6
 ♥ Q83
 ♦ A742
 ♣ A10863

27. ♠ 854
 ♥ K9754
 ♦ 7
 ♣ 10862

28. ♠ AJ2
 ♥ AJ84
 ♦ —
 ♣ J109632

With the next four hands you have opened one heart and partner has raised to two. How do you continue 1) using help suit game tries; 2) using short suit game tries; 3) using modified **Kokish Game Tries**?

29. ♠ 6
 ♥ AQ853
 ♦ KQ1062
 ♣ A5

30. ♠ A2
 ♥ AKJ853
 ♦ 7
 ♣ AQ74

31. ♠ AJ3
 ♥ J7642
 ♦ AKQ6
 ♣ 6

32. ♠ KQ103
 ♥ AQJ76
 ♦ 5
 ♣ A94

Answers _____

1. Three hearts. A **splinter** in support of clubs. If partner bids three notrump to show heart values, pass. If partner makes any other call, make a move toward a club slam.

2. Two notrump. Natural and invitational.

3. Three clubs. Up the ante with a preemptive raise.

4. Two clubs—Inverted. Forcing one round, showing a limit raise or better for clubs.

5. Three hearts. This good hand best defines by making a **splinter** bid.

6. Two notrump. This promises bare minimum values and that both majors are stopped.

7. Two hearts. Start showing "stoppers up the line."

8. Three notrump. This promises a balanced 18 or 19 HCP.

9. Three diamonds. This shows diamond values, tends to deny values in either major suit, and indicates values enough to insist on reaching game.

10. Three notrump. Values for game and stoppers where needed.

11. Two notrump. Stoppers in the unbid suits but not as much in values.

12. Two spades. Partner has shown a diamond stopper but has not denied heart values. We continue showing stoppers.

13. Two spades playing either raise method.

14. Three diamonds playing **Bergen** to show a limit raise with four card support. Three clubs playing **Hardy** to show a good limit raise with either four cards or three cards with a ruffing value.

15. Bid a **forcing notrump** playing either method. You will jump in spades at your next turn to show a three card limit raise (**Bergen**) without a ruffing value (**Hardy**).

16. Three clubs—**Bergen**—to show a good single raise with four card support. Two spades—**Hardy**—to show a single raise intending to carry forward to three if the opponents balance.

17. Playing **Bergen** use the **Jacoby Two Notrump**. Playing **Hardy** you are not good enough for **Jacoby**. Bid four clubs—**Inverted Trump Swiss** to show 12+ to 15- HCP, a balanced hand, and good four card support (two of the top three honors).

18. Jump to three spades playing either. Strictly preemptive.

19. Four clubs—a big **Swiss** raise playing **Bergen**. Playing **Hardy** this hand is good enough for the **Jacoby Two Notrump**.

20. Three hearts playing **Bergen** to show four card support, values for game, and a **concealed splinter**. Three notrump playing **Hardy** to show four card support, 12+ to 15- HCP, and a **concealed splinter**.

21. One notrump—**forcing**—playing **Bergen**, preparing to show a three card limit raise by jumping in hearts as a rebid. Three clubs playing **Hardy** to show a good limit raise with either four card support or three card support with a ruffing value.

22. Three spades playing **Bergen** to show a **concealed splinter** and values enough for game. Three diamonds, an **under jump shift** playing **Hardy** which is a game forcing **limit raise (9+ to 12- HCP)**, including a **concealed splinter**. If partner asks you will be able to show that it specifically is a singleton (rather than a void) in spades.

23. Playing **Bergen** this hand should use the **Jacoby Two Notrump**. Playing **Hardy** this hand is not good enough for **Jacoby**. Make the **Inverted Trump Swiss** call of four diamonds to show 12+ to 15- HCP, a balanced hand, and four not-so-good trumps.

24. Four diamonds playing **Bergen**. This shows a good raise to four hearts. Playing **Hardy** start with the **forcing notrump**. Jump to four hearts at your rebid and partner will know that you hold an outside ace or king.

25. Three hearts playing **Bergen**. Not good enough for the jump to three clubs and cannot raise to the two level with four card support. The best possible preemptive jump raise. Two hearts playing **Hardy**. A minimum single raise, still willing to bid to the three level against a balance.

26. One notrump playing **Bergen**. You will jump in hearts at your rebid to show a three card limit raise. Three clubs playing **Hardy** to show a good **limit raise** with either four trumps or three trumps and a ruffing value.

27. Four hearts no matter what you play.

28. Three spades playing **Bergen** to show a **concealed splinter** with four card support and values enough for game. If partner asks you will be able to tell when where your shortness is, but you will not be able to indicate a void. Three diamonds playing **Hardy**. After your **under jump shift**, if partner asks you will not only be able to tell where the shortness is—you will be able to identify it as a void.

29. Jump to four hearts. Do not make a game try with a good two-suiter. With two trick sources you expect to take ten tricks.

30. You could just jump to four hearts, but you might miss a slam. Check for secondary fits by making what appears to be a game try. Bid three clubs playing help suit tries. Bid three diamonds playing short suit tries. Bid two spades playing **Kokish**. If partner likes your club try or shows clubs, you will know about the valuable club king and slam will start to look very good. If partner denies diamond values, the situation is not quite so clear, but you should still make another slam try. If partner's response to whatever try you use is to say no, carry on to game anyway.

31. Three hearts. No matter what king of game tries you use, this should ask for good trumps, and that is where your crying need is.

32. Bid two spades using help suit game tries. Bid three diamonds using short suit game tries. Bid two notrump playing modified **Kokish** to show four spades.

CHAPTER NINE
High Level Opening Bids

Synopsis: Thus far in Chapter Nine you have learned about preemptive and descriptive opening bids. Weak two bids were presented in the simplest context, as were opening bids of two clubs, and subsequent auctions in each case.

As Chapter Nine continues you will learn about opening bids of three notrump, the **Namyats** convention, upgraded responses to weak two bids, and modern responses to the opening bid of two clubs.

Opening Bids of Three Notrump _____

The advent of the opening bid of two clubs to show all very strong hands released the opening bid of three notrump. Instead of showing a strong balanced hand of 25 to 27 HCP, three notrump can serve a conventional purpose. The strong balanced hand is expressed after a two club opening. One of three different meanings is usually assigned to three notrump. It can be **Gambling**, **Acol**, or **Namyats**.

The Gambling Three Notrump Opening Bid _____

Many notrump game contracts are bid and fulfilled when the bidding side does not have a major suit of sufficient length to be the trump suit. Rather than consider a minor suit contract, the bidding side next looks to a contract in notrump because of the nature of the scoring system. Major suits pay thirty points per trick as opposed to twenty points per trick for minor suits. However, notrump also pays thirty points a trick with the bonus that the first trick pays forty points. This means that game in notrump can be reached at the nine trick level, which is usually a better idea than a minor suit game at the eleven trick level.

Most notrump contracts come about because two reasonably balanced hands have the values to produce tricks in several suits and are able to keep the opposition from running off several tricks in a suit in which only one offensive trick exists. This one offensive trick is called a stopper. The two assets needed to produce the game in notrump are trick sources and stoppers. When both hands are balanced each of several suits must produce two, three or four tricks. This plus a stopper in the fourth suit will do the job.

Sometimes a player will pick up a hand which includes a solid seven card minor suit. If the suit were a major, this player would attempt to play game with the solid major suit as the trump suit, furnishing seven of the ten needed tricks. But when the solid suit is a minor, a source of tricks is present for the nine trick game in notrump. All that is needed in partner's hand is stoppers in the other suits.

The **Gambling** opening bid of three notrump announces a solid seven card minor suit with no outside strength. When responder holds stoppers in three suits (two of them will be major suits), the one suit in which a stopper is missing must be partner's completely solid minor. Responder knows that the necessary trick source is available, and has the stoppers which will also furnish the last two tricks necessary to make game in notrump. Responder knows to pass and expect the contract to make.

Sometimes responder will hold stoppers in only two suits. Clearly, the opponents might lead the only unstopped suit and beat the notrump game. If responder has length in that unstopped suit, the defenders may not have enough tricks to beat the game contract. Responder is free to gamble further that with nine tricks available the defense will not find five first.

But, when there is no reason for responder to believe that three notrump is a viable contract, opener's long suit is a better place to play. Responder removes from three notrump. When opener holds one or more honor cards in a minor suit, it is clear that the other minor is partner's solid suit. But when it is not clear, opener removes to four clubs. Responder is asked to pass if clubs is the long, solid suit, but if the suit is diamonds, opener is asked to correct rather than pass.

There will be times when responder is willing to play at a higher level than four. Responder might have four top tricks in the major suits and shortness in one minor with length in the other. For example, if responder holds: ♠KQJ62 ♥AK54 ♦853 ♣7, if opener's suit is diamonds, one club ruff will yield eleven tricks, but if opener's suit is clubs, the defense might cash a spade and two diamond tricks. Responder bids four clubs, and if opener corrects to diamonds, responder raises to five.

But if responder holds: ♠AK653 ♥KQ84 ♦7 ♣853 the maximum contract in diamonds is probably at the four level, but clubs will take eleven tricks. So instead of removing three notrump to four clubs, responder removes to four diamonds. Again, opener cannot pass unless diamonds is the solid suit. If the suit is clubs, opener must correct to five clubs, and responder will be happy to have reached game.

Example 87)

a) ♠ 7　　　　　　　　b) ♠ A62
   ♥ J5　　　　　　　　 ♥ A9643
   ♦ 963　　　　　　　　 ♦ K104
   ♣ AKQJ642　　　　　 ♣ 73

c) ♠ AK62　　　　　　　d) ♠ Q652
   ♥ AK963　　　　　　　 ♥ AK62
   ♦ 85　　　　　　　　　 ♦ 854
   ♣ 93　　　　　　　　　 ♣ 93

Example 87a) is a classic hand for the Gambling three notrump **opening bid.**

Example 87b) knows that opener's solid suit is clubs and can provide stoppers in all other suits. Pass is clearly indicated.

Example 87c) can count eleven tricks no matter which minor

partner holds. Responder jumps to five clubs, expecting opener to correct if the long suit is diamonds.

Example 87d) has no reason to believe that any game will make and removes to four clubs, knowing that opener will pass or correct.

*The Acol Three Notrump Opening Bid*_____

The **Acol three notrump** opening bid is similar. The difference is that opener, in addition to the solid seven card minor, will hold a stopper in one side suit and at least a half stopper in another. Obviously, opener is s stronger favorite to make three notrump since responder needs to furnish much less in the way of stoppers.

The problem is simple. When responder holds one or even two stoppers, it is not clear whether or not all suits are stopped. The defense may have the first five or more tricks in one suit, and there is no way for responder to know if the stoppers held are the needed ones.

Best is to use **Gambling three notrump** opening bids in the first three seats, and **Acol** in the fourth seat. It makes no sense in fourth seat to open three notrump without a strong chance to make.

Example 88)

a) ♠ A7
♥ Q83
♦ AKQJ953
♣ 7

b) ♠ KQ54
♥ A1062
♦ 72
♣ J85

c) ♠ 95432
♥ J102
♦ 72
♣ A65

d) ♠ KQ52
♥ J1062
♦ 72
♣ 865

e) ♠ A
♥ 5
♦ 973
♣ AKQJ8652

f) ♠ K6
♥ K73
♦ AJ85
♣ 10943

Example 88a) is a **classic** Acol three notrump **opening bid.**

Example 88b) has stoppers in both majors and a partial stopper in clubs. If responder elects to pass, the defense may cash at least five club tricks.

Example 88c) is not nearly so well endowed as 88b) and will probably run to diamonds, the known long suit. However, this responder has the right stopper and the right half-stopper to make three notrump iron clad.

Example 88d) has no hopes of making three notrump and runs to four clubs knowing that partner will pass or correct.

Examples 88e) and 88f) were facing hands in a Regional Knock-out match. In fourth position 88e) opened with an Acol three notrump. Yes, the half stopper is missing, but the eighth club was deemed adequate compensation. The passed hand of 88e) was held by World Champion John Swanson. After some consideration John leaped to six clubs. When dummy appeared John smiled and announced that from his side the slam was cold, but from the other side it would go down. The opening lead was the ace of hearts. Declarer's two major suit kings provided discards for dummy's two diamond losers. If the heart had not been led, John would have unblocked spades and pitched dummy's heart on the spade king, then played on diamonds. The diamond high honors were divided and the ten was on side.

The Namyats Three Notrump Opening Bid _____

The **Namyats** convention uses the opening bid of four clubs to show a strong preempt in hearts, and the opening bid of four diamonds to show a strong preempt in spades. When this agreement exists, opener needs to replace the natural meaning of those opening bids. Holding a broken eight card minor suit, opener will often need to preempt to a greater level than the three level, but not be able to preempt at the five level. Three notrump is used artificially to show the hand that would otherwise have opened with a natural preempt in a minor suit at the four level.

With this agreement, when opener bids three notrump in first or second seat, responder (who has not yet passed) could have a very good hand—one that would like to pass and play three notrump assuming that opener's eight card minor suit will furnish many tricks. Unlike the **Gambling** or **Acol** opening bids of three notrump, the **Namyats** opening of three notrump does not guarantee a solid trick source.

An agreement to make this pass possible is that when opener in first or second seat makes the opening bid of three notrump to show a broken eight card minor suit, the suit must be headed by either the ace or the king (but not both). With that agreement, when responder holds stoppers in both major suits and the ace or king in each of the minor suits (along with at least one small card in the suit), responder can pass knowing that the bidding side holds ten cards in the minor suit including both the ace and the king, therefore guaranteeing a sure trick source.

Third seat preempts need no such guarantee. Responder has passed and game is remote. Regardless of agreement for the first three seats, the fourth seat agreement should be **Acol**.

Example 89)

a) ♠ 7
    ♥ 65
    ♦ KJ1097642
    ♣ 103

b) ♠ A632
    ♥ J1094
    ♦ A5
    ♣ K92

Example 89a) would ordinarily open by preempting four diamonds at most vulnerabilities. However, if the Namyats **convention has been agreed, that opening bid would promise a good preempt in spades. Opener substitutes the artificial opening bid of three notrump.**

With the agreement that the opening bid of three notrump holds a broken eight card suit but that the suit must be headed by the ace or king, Example 89b) will pass expecting to make three notrump no matter which minor opener holds. Virtually all other hand types would remove and play in the known long, broken minor.

The Namyats Convention

Often conventions are spawned and named in humorous fashion. The story of this convention happens at lunch where a group of New York experts was gathered. The conversation turned to the infrequent use of the opening preemptive bids of four in a minor suit. Someone suggested that a conventional use could be developed in which an opening bid of four clubs showed hearts and an opening bid of four diamonds showed spades, and that there could be a distinction made between the qualities of the two hands when opener elected to open with the artificial bid rather than a natural major suit bid at the four level.

Sam Stayman spoke up and said, "Yes, four hearts could be the stronger one and four clubs the weaker one." All eyes turned to Sam, and as if with one voice the group said, "Sam, you've got it backwards." Thus was the name of the convention born. Namyats is Stayman spelled backwards.

The conventional opening bid of four in a minor suit in this context shows a hand worth exactly eight, or eight and one half tricks. Opening bids of four in a major suit have fewer than eight tricks.

The matter of suit quality is subject to partnership agreement. The two agreements that are most popular are:

1. The bid promises a solid suit.
2. The bid promises a suit that is missing one top honor card—either the king or the queen, but not the ace.

Of course, some partnerships are fast and loose, and have no firm agreement regarding suit quality—only the number of tricks that have been promised.

Based on frequency, we suggest the second listed agreement—that the suit be missing either the king or the queen, but not the ace. Obviously, such a suit will occur twice as often as a completely solid suit.

When opener holds a completely solid suit with eight or eight and one half tricks, we suggest that the auction begin with two clubs. No matter what the response, opener next jumps to four in the major suit to describe the nature of the hand.

Example 90)

a) ♠ AQJ10875
   ♥ 8
   ♦ KQJ
   ♣ 42

b) ♠ AKQJ973
   ♥ 6
   ♦ 542
   ♣ 63

c) ♠ 7
   ♥ AKQJ9873
   ♦ J104
   ♣ 3

d) ♠ 62
   ♥ AKJ10753
   ♦ —
   ♣ AJ103

Example 90a) has the required suit quality and a spade suit that should furnish six and one half tricks. With two more tricks in diamonds, opener makes the Namyats **opening bid of four diamonds.**

Example 90b) has a solid suit but only seven winners. Using the rule of two, three, and four, opener would bid three spades if vulnerable vs. not, but at any other vulnerability would open four spades.

Example 90c) has a solid suit and eight winners. Open two clubs and jump rebid four hearts to show this hand.

Example 90d) has eight plus winners and a suit of the expected quality. Open four clubs.

When the opening bidder starts with four of a minor suit, responder is able to determine which of the two hands should become declarer. If no contract higher than game seems likely, responder can bid the indicated major suit and opener is asked to pass. Or, responder can bid the suit that ranks between the suit of the opening bid and the suit shown as a relay, causing opener to become declarer.

Responder's decision will be based on whether or not there are tenaces that need protection on the opening lead. Holding one or more tenaces, responder will bid the known anchor suit and become declarer. Holding no such tenaces, responder will relay.

When the opening bid causes responder to believe that slam is possible, there are two possible courses of action:

1. Responder can use the relay, then continue to bid.
2. Responder can immediately make a call beyond the anchor suit.

These two auctions should be assigned specific meanings. We suggest that an immediate call beyond the anchor (four notrump over four diamonds, or four spades over four clubs) be **Roman Key Card** in the anchor suit. After the relay, a continuation in a new suit should be an **Asking Bid** (see Chapter Twelve).

Example 91)

a)
- ♠ A962
- ♥ 85
- ♦ AK83
- ♣ 654

b)
- ♠ K962
- ♥ 85
- ♦ AQ83
- ♣ J54

c)
- ♠ A632
- ♥ 852
- ♦ A
- ♣ AKQ53

d)
- ♠ A6
- ♥ Q542
- ♦ AKQJ
- ♣ 832

All Example 91) hands are responding to a four club Namyats **opening bid.**

Example 91a) has no tenaces to protect and wants opener to declare. Responder bids four diamonds to relay to four hearts.

Example 91b) is rich in tenaces and wants to protect them on the opening lead. Responder bids four hearts to become declarer.

Example 91c) needs to know the quality of opener's long suit

and bids **four spades** which is Roman Key Card. **If the king is missing, a small slam will be adequate. But if the queen is the missing honor, responder will bid seven hearts.**

Example 91d) relays by bidding four diamonds, then makes the Asking Bid **of five clubs. If opener has second round club control it will be safe to bid a slam.**

Responses to Weak Two Bids

In Volume I you learned to raise a weak two bid preemptively and to bid two notrump to seek further information about the nature of the weak two bid. You learned that opener should return to the suit with minimum values, but should show a feature in another suit when the weak two bid was maximum. You also learned how opener should show or deny a fit for responder's two level major suit response. Those methods are the oldest and simplest available, but better methods have emerged in later years.

In Chapter Six you learned the **Ogust** convention to be used in auctions in which responder made a preemptive jump shift response. This convention was created for auctions beginning with weak two bids. Responder to the opening weak two bid uses two notrump to seek information which is expressed by the opening bidder using step rebids. Reviewing those steps:

1. Three clubs shows a bad hand with a bad suit.
2. Three diamonds shows a bad hand with a good suit.
3. Three hearts shows a good hand with a bad suit.
4. Three spades shows a good hand with a good suit.
5. Three notrump shows a solid suit.

The fifth item was not included earlier because the preemptive jump shift response shows the values of about 2 to a bad 5 HCP. However, the weak two bid is descriptive and not preemptive and normally in the range of 5 to 11 HCP. That makes it possible for opener to hold a suit including all four top honor cards.

Bear in mind that the number of high card points in a hand is not the factor that determines whether the hand is bad or good. Hands that are 6-3-2-2 have the worst possible distribution and are generally considered bad. Hands with better shape can be classified as good.

We recommend the use of **Ogust** facing a first or second seat weak two bid. In those two positions the gamut of possible hands is extensive. Using **Ogust** to determine qualities will enable the bidding side to know whether or not to bid game or seek slam. Opener is able to express far more easily than through the older method of showing a feature with a maximum and repeating the suit with a minimum.

One advantage of **Ogust** is that opener does not need as robust a suit to open with a weak two bid. Responder has a quality control that relates to the nature of the suit. Older weak two bids virtually promised two of the top three, or three of the top five honors. When **Ogust** is available, the suit quality can be considerably less impressive.

The one concern about quality is that the weak two bidder must be happy to have the suit led on defense, virtually regardless of partner's holding. If the weak two bid is made on a headless suit, it would be disastrous for partner to be on lead with doubleton king and place the king on the table. To forestall that possibility, agreement should be that in first or second seat the minimum quality for the suit should be that it is headed by the queen. When the queen is the only face card in the suit, prudence suggests that it be fortified by excellent spot cards. Queen-ten-nine sixth is a far safer holding than queen empty sixth.

We believe that the suit shown by an opening weak two bid should be the prime candidate to be the trump suit. Certain distributional patterns have more than one true trump candidate. If opener has a six-five pattern and opens a weak two bid, when responder has no fit for the six card suit but an excellent fit for the five card suit, opener will often languish in a poor contract. A far better one may be available but cannot be reached. When opener holds a six-four-three pattern, the problem is similar. Responder may have a five card or longer fit for one of opener's side suits. After the weak two bid is made, the chance of reaching a contract in the superior fit is reduced drastically. If opener does hold a second four card suit, it should be a minor.

So, our rules for a weak two bid in first and second seat are these:

1. The suit will usually be six cards. The requirements for seven card and five card weak two bids were spelled out in Volume I.
2. The suit will be headed at least by the queen. If only the queen, the suit will include good spot cards.
3. Six-five hands and hands that are six-four-three are not included as acceptable weak two bid patterns because of the good chance of better trump fits.
4. A side four card suit is permitted if it is a minor suit. Hands that include a superb six card major and a poor four card holding in the other major are allowable exceptions.

Example 92)

a)
- ♠ KQ10953
- ♥ 62
- ♦ Q94
- ♣ Q6

b)
- ♠ 7
- ♥ AJ8632
- ♦ K1052
- ♣ 83

c)
- ♠ 63
- ♥ J863
- ♦ KQ10943
- ♣ 8

d)
- ♠ 9753
- ♥ KQJ1082
- ♦ K4
- ♣ 7

e)
- ♠ 54
- ♥ 96
- ♦ AKQJ83
- ♣ 852

f)
- ♠ J63
- ♥ AQJ106
- ♦ 1054
- ♣ J10

g)
- ♠ QJ9863
- ♥ 102
- ♦ K75
- ♣ QJ

h)
- ♠ 6
- ♥ KJ10742
- ♦ K7632
- ♣ 8

Example 92a) is a classic weak two spade bid. If partner bids two notrump to get an Ogust rebid, three diamonds will show your bad hand with a good suit. Do not count nine high card points and believe that makes this a good hand in the range of five

to eleven. The shape is as bad as it can be, and the two minor suit queens might be entirely useless.

Example 92b) is a clear two heart bid. The shape makes this a good hand, but the suit is obviously poor. Your Ogust rebid will be three hearts to show a good hand with a bad suit. Note that the presence of one and one half plus defensive tricks does not preclude the weak two bid which is descriptive, not preemptive.

Example 92c) should not be opened with a weak two bid in first or second seat. Even though the diamond suit is wonderful, major suits are too important and you might miss a heart fit. In third seat, anything goes, so two diamonds is acceptable.

Example 92d) is a weak two bid despite the four card spade holding. A heart suit that good should be trumps. If partner bids two notrump, bid three spades to show a good hand with a good suit.

Example 92e) opens two diamonds and, if partner bids two notrump, rebids three notrump to show a solid suit.

Example 92f) is fine for a weak two heart bid in first, second, or third seat because of the good suit. If partner asks this is a bad hand with a good suit.

Example 92g) should open two spades in any seat except fourth. Despite nine high card points, this is a bad hand with a bad suit.

Example 92h) should not open with a weak two bid in first or second seat because of the two possible trump suits. However, in third seat do what you must and bid two hearts.

All hands of Example 92) should pass in fourth seat. None has adequate values to believe that a plus score is likely opposite a passed partner.

When weak two bids were introduced, the only forcing response was two notrump, and all new suits were non-forcing. Progress does change things. The standard today is that all new suits are forcing and assumed to be natural. We believe that it is important for a response in a major suit to be forcing for obvious reasons. We cannot find many reasons for a new minor suit to be forcing. Our preferred approach—new majors forcing and new minors non-forcing—must be expressed on the convention card, and when a non-forcing call in a new minor occurs, it must be alerted since in standard the call is forcing.

Remember that when responder bids a higher ranking suit at the two level in response to an opening weak two bid, opener is required to show a fit for the suit of the response when possible. Holding ace, king, or queen third, opener will raise the suit of the response to the three level. With a lesser three card holding or doubleton ace, king, or queen, opener bids two notrump to show a marginal fit for responder's suit. The new major response is forcing and assumed to be natural, but opener has the obligation to rebid to show or deny a fit.

When **Ogust** has been agreed, it still applies after responder bids a higher ranking suit at the two level. Holding two small cards or less in responder's suit, opener makes an **Ogust** rebid. The minor suit rebids retain their meanings, but one major suit step is lost. The major suit rebid that would raise responder's suit is removed from the **Ogust** steps. Opener must rebid in the other major to show any good hand.

Following an opening bid of two diamonds, responder may use a new suit to ask for opener's holding not to discover a fit for the major as a possible trump suit, but rather to find stoppers for play in notrump. When opener shows a good fit for responder's major suit and responder then bids three notrump, opener may not remove. Responder has placed the contract and opener has no power of override. The probe may have been for the purpose of determining stoppers for notrump rather than to try to play in the major suit that was bid in response to the weak two bid.

Example 93)

a)	♠ 863		b)	♠ KJ963
	♥ —			♥ AQ5
	♦ K42			♦ Q92
	♣ AQJ9763			♣ K10

c) ♠ QJ6
   ♥ Q3
   ♦ A842
   ♣ J854

d) ♠ J85
   ♥ AK2
   ♦ A853
   ♣ AQ4

With Example 93a) you are responding to an opening bid of two hearts. You are pleased that when you respond three clubs your call is non-forcing (alert).

With Example 93b) you are responding to an opening bid of two diamonds. Do not make the error of bidding two notrump. Your best game contract could be in spades. Respond two spades, and if partner shows a spade fit by bidding either three spades or two notrump, play four spades. If partner denies a spade fit and shows a bad hand, play three diamonds. If partner denies a spade fit but shows a good hand by bidding three hearts, you can gamble three notrump or play five diamonds.

With Example 93c) you are responding to an opening bid of two spades. Bid three spades to try to steal the hand by shutting out your opponents. They can probably make some number of hearts, but may not be able to find a heart contract after your raise.

With Example 93d) you are responding to an opening bid of two diamonds. Bid two spades to find out what partner's spade holding is. If partner shows some spades by either raising to three spades or bidding two notrump, play three notrump. If partner shows short spades and a bad hand and a bad suit by bidding three clubs, settle for three diamonds. If partner shows a good suit by bidding three diamonds, you can gamble three notrump hoping that the defense has no more than four spade tricks, or (less attractive) can gamble five diamonds playing partner for a stiff spade and a secondary card in either hearts or clubs. If partner bids three hearts to deny spades and show a good hand, five diamonds is clear.

Example 94)

a)
- ♠ 106
- ♥ Q85
- ♦ AK10972
- ♣ 54

b)
- ♠ J106
- ♥ K3
- ♦ QJ9765
- ♣ Q6

c)
- ♠ 6
- ♥ AQJ954
- ♦ K62
- ♣ 854

d)
- ♠ KJ10962
- ♥ 85
- ♦ K6
- ♣ 843

With Example 94a) you have opened two diamonds. If partner bids two spades or two notrump, bid three diamonds to show a bad hand with a good suit. If partner bids two hearts, raise to show a top honor.

With Example 94b) you have opened two diamonds. If partner bids two notrump, bid three clubs to show a bad hand with a bad suit. If partner bids either major suit, bid two notrump to show a partial fit—either high honor doubleton or three cards without a high honor.

With Example 94c) you have opened two hearts. If partner bids two notrump, bid three spades to show a good hand with a good suit. If partner bids two spades, bid three hearts. You cannot show both a good hand and a good suit by bidding three spades. That would promise three spades to a high honor.

With Example 94d) you have bid two spades. If partner bids two notrump, you will show a bad hand by rebidding in a minor suit. If vulnerable bid three clubs to show a bad suit. If not vulnerable it is reasonable to bid three diamonds to show a good suit. If partner bids three of a minor suit, alert, because it is non-forcing, and pass. If partner bids three hearts, bid three spades. Partner's response is forcing, and you have no other expressive rebid.

This structuring of weak two bids applies only when the weak two bid is made in first or second seat. In third and fourth seats there are entirely different considerations that apply.

Third seat weak two bids are left to the imagination of the bidder. If partner has passed and you have a poor hand in third seat, it is reasonably clear that the opponents have the values to make at least a game, maybe even a slam. The discipline that applies in the first two seats is completely set aside in third. Don't be unreasonable, but make a weak two bid on any holding that seems right.

Fourth position has yet another face. After three passes you can also pass to end the auction, knowing that you will not get a minus score on the hand. You should only keep the auction alive if you believe that your side will achieve a plus score. This means that there are no minimum weak two bids. A weak two bid in fourth seat should be very substantial. In fact, often it will be made with a hand that might have opened with a one bid in an earlier position.

In fourth position the high card point range changes. It is no longer 5 to 11—it becomes about 10 to 13 HCP. It is expected that after this fourth seat weak two bid, neither opponent will be able to compete. On some occasions partner will seek game, but **Ogust** serves no purpose. The fourth seat weak two bid is always a good hand and a good suit.

When partner has a fit and a near opening bid, if game is to be bid and made there must be good fits in the rest of the hand. For this reason we suggest that facing a weak two bid in fourth seat, when responder bids two notrump as a try for game, opener is asked to show shortness. We have learned that evaluation is facilitated when one partner can show shortness. That is very true in this instance.

Game is less likely when the opening weak two bid has been made in third seat. Therefore, facing a weak two bid in either third or fourth seat, two notrump is not **Ogust**. It asks if the weak two bidder holds shortness in any suit. If opener does show shortness that fits with the hand of the passed responder, a fitting game may easily be bid.

Example 95)

a) ♠ AQJ965
    ♥ 6
    ♦ K94
    ♣ 1083

b) ♠ AQJ965
    ♥ 6
    ♦ A104
    ♣ 1083

c) ♠ 63
    ♥ AQJ965
    ♦ J1054
    ♣ 4

d) ♠ K2
    ♥ KQJ854
    ♦ A102
    ♣ 105

With Example 95a) open two spades in any seat. If you have opened in first or second seat and partner bids two notrump to ask for an Ogust rebid, bid three spades to show a good hand with a good suit. If you have opened in third or fourth seat and partner bids two notrump to ask for shortness, bid three hearts to show your singleton.

With Example 95b) open one spade in first, second, or third seat. In fourth seat open two spades, and if partner bids two notrump to ask for shortness, bid three hearts to show your singleton.

With Example 95c) open two hearts in first, second, or third seat. If you have opened in first or second seat and partner bids two notrump to ask for an Ogust rebid, bid three spades to show a good hand with a good suit. If you are in third seat and partner bids two notrump to ask for shortness, bid three clubs to show your singleton. In fourth seat, be grateful that the opponents have not found their spade fit, and pass. If you open two hearts, the door is opened for them once again. Don't do it!

With Example 95d) open one heart in first, second or third seat. In fourth seat open two hearts and if partner bids two notrump to ask for shortness, bid three notrump. You want to be in some game, and this should show no singleton and sound opening bid values. Partner knows to pass with scattered values or convert to four hearts with a distributional hand.

Modern Responses to the Opening Bid of Two Clubs _____

The opening bid of two clubs is used by the opening bidder to create a force. Unless responder has a specific message to send, such as a good suit to show, responder marks time by bidding two diamonds. Responder is permitted to bid a five card or longer suit headed by two of the top three honors, but otherwise must bid two diamonds. This has been the approach adopted since the advent of the forcing two club opening bid.

Responder makes the waiting bid of two diamonds to allow opener to describe the nature of the strong hand. Only at responder's second turn is information about the nature of the responding hand available. Responder's second call shows positive values and a fit for opener, or positive values without a fit, or negative values. Opener's rebid to show the nature of the forcing opening bid is made without knowledge of responder's values, or lack of them. This often creates a problem.

It is clear that if responder can show positive or negative values in response to the opening bid of two clubs, opener will be better placed to evaluate the hand and the continuing auction. This gives rise to the modern improvement in responding to two clubs. Two diamonds is a positive response. To show a negative response, responder artificially bids two hearts. With two hearts as an artificial negative, responder bids two notrump to show a positive response with a good heart suit containing two of the top three honors.

If responder's first call gives no expression of values and opener has a balanced hand of twenty-two or more high card points, opener rebids two notrump. With 25 to 27 HCP opener rebids three notrump. With 28 to 30 HCP opener bids four notrump. With 31 or 32 HCP opener bids five notrump. With 33 to 35 HCP opener bids six notrump. With more than 35 HCP opener just opens seven notrump. This is as expressive as possible.

There is a major problem when opener must bid more than two notrump. The best contract is often not in notrump despite opener's balanced hand. When **Stayman** and **transfer bids** are available, better contracts can often be reached. If opener must jump to three notrump or higher to express the values of the opening hand, it becomes virtually impossible to put these useful conventions to work. By jumping and taking up space, opener has effectively preempted his partner.

When responder's first call after opener has bid two clubs expresses positive values, a game force is established. It is no longer necessary to jump to some high level just to express values. Opener can rebid two notrump regardless of values. This leaves room for responder to use **Stayman** or to **transfer** at either the three or four level. Opener can then later show any extra values that have been concealed.

Consider the wasted motion in the older method. Responder first had to make a bid with no meaning so that opener could start to describe the strong hand that had bid two clubs. Responder was then required to select the call to express negative values and was not able to either show or deny a fit until the third call. When responder's first call expresses either positive or negative values, the descriptive portion of the auction is permitted to take place without further delay. An entire round of bidding is saved, as well as several steps of bidding space.

Far too often exuberant bidders open two clubs simply because they like the hand they hold. There is also a psychological force in effect. Opening two clubs gives the bidder a feeling of power. It provides a rush of adrenaline that makes the bidder feel that something special has been accomplished. Far too often this is not the case. Hands that are opened two clubs are, in fact, pretty good hands, but the use of the convention distorts what should be a simple and straight forward auction that begins with an opening one bid. All this happens so that the bidder can bask in euphoria.

In real life, when you pick up a good hand you should find any excuse not to open two clubs. With a balanced hand of 22 or more HCP, you have no choice. When the hand is unbalanced with nine or more tricks, you will sometimes need to open two clubs, but more often than not opening a one bid will do just fine. Bear in mind that if the good hand you wish to describe is two suited, or if it is a minor single suiter, opening two clubs may be your downfall.

Suppose you are two suited and open two clubs. Left hand opponent overcalls. Partner passes and right hand opponent makes a preemptive raise of the overcall to the four or five level. There you sit with egg on your face. Do you now show one of your suits? At this high level your call will not be forcing. Sometimes you will be lucky and be in the right suit, but Murphy's Law will usually prevail and you will find yourself in the suit for which partner has no fit. Your contract will fail. If there is a fit in your other suit, you might have made a slam if you had been able to find that fit.

How much easier it would be if you opened at the one level by bidding one of your suits. Let them preempt all they wish. When you introduce your second suit at a high level, partner knows you have a very good hand and will be able to be sure that the right contract, the one where a fit exists, is reached.

There is a rule for opening two clubs. Do so only when absolutely necessary. Do not stretch to open two clubs just so you can feel powerful. Holding a great number of high card points, there may be danger that an opening one bid would be passed out. You might miss a certain game. Do not let that happen. When your hand is so rich that not much in values is left for others at the table to bid, open two clubs because you need to—not because you want to.

Knowledge that a real two club opening bid must truly have "the goods" makes life easier for responder. Responder should believe that the opening two club bidder's values are so close to making game that one working card in responder's hand is all that might be needed to assure that game. It is on this basis that we establish what constitutes a positive or negative response. To make a positive response, we require responder to hold one working card.

An ace is a working card. A king will usually be a working card. A queen that fits opener's hand is a working card. If responder holds only one queen, however, it might be in one of opener's short suits. So for a positive response, we establish responder's minimum as an ace, a king, or two queens. With these values or more, responder makes the waiting positive response of two diamonds. With less, responder makes the negative response of two hearts.

Often your opponents will get in your way after the opening bid of two

clubs. When this occurs it is important that responder be able to show positive or negative values so that opener will know what to do. When there is
interference, responder uses pass to show positive values. If the interference
is an overcall, double is used to deny values. If the interference is double,
redouble denies values. The bid of a suit no longer guarantees two top honor
cards. Responder will show any five card or longer suit headed by the ace
or king.

Bear in mind that the ACBL has a regulation which prohibits the psychic
use of the opening bid of two clubs. A definitive article which was published in *The Bulletin* (the official organ of the ACBL) states, "Opening a
strong two-bid (artificial and forcing) without the requisite high card values is acceptable under the following circumstances: *if, in the view of the
opening bidder, there is a reasonable chance for game in hand with little help from
partner.*" The article then presents two acceptable hands. See **Example 96c)**
below.

Example 96)

a) ♠ AQ4
    ♥ AK93
    ♦ A6
    ♣ AKJ5

b) ♠ 6
    ♥ AKQJ1075
    ♦ AK5
    ♣ 83

c) ♠ AKQ1098
    ♥ J109876
    ♦ 4
    ♣ —

d) ♠ A5
    ♥ AK73
    ♦ AKQ1064
    ♣ 6

e) ♠ 6
    ♥ AKQ952
    ♦ AKQ1064
    ♣ —

f) ♠ A
    ♥ AKQJ5
    ♦ AKQ2
    ♣ 854

g) ♠ A62
    ♥ 6
    ♦ AKQJ9874
    ♣ 3

h) ♠ AKQJ9853
    ♥ 6
    ♦ J102
    ♣ 4

Example 96a) opens two clubs and rebids in notrump. If two diamonds is undefined, opener must jump to three notrump with these values. If responder holds length in either major suit, a superior contract in that major can no longer be reached. When responder can make a positive response of two diamonds, opener needs only rebid two notrump. This allows responder to use Stayman or a transfer bid, and the major suit contract can be reached.

Example 96b) has nine winners and only seventeen high card points. There is no reason to believe that an opening bid of one heart would be passed out. So you might believe that there is no reason to open two clubs. However, there is an overriding reason to open two clubs, and that is that opener can give a complete description by opening two clubs, then jumping in hearts. Any time opener bids two clubs, then jumps in a major suit to the three level, it shows nine or more tricks and a completely solid suit. It establishes the trump suit. This auction asks responder to show controls. After the suit jump responder is asked to bid an ace, or to bid three notrump without aces but with a hand that has other controls. This understanding leads the way to auctions that may produce slams when responder holds the controls needed by opener. These auctions are best served when the agreement of the partnership is the use of Asking Bids, which are detailed in Chapter Twelve.

Example 96c) is the minimum hand example presented by the ACBL for the use of the opening bid of two clubs as acceptable and not subject to penalty.

Example 96d) should be opened one diamond, with a planned reverse in hearts. There is no need to open two clubs even though the trick count is reasonably close to nine. I include this as a poor example of what random hands two club bids are made with. However, on OKBridge someone opened two clubs against me with this hand WITHOUT THE KING OF HEARTS. I am happy to report that this bit of terrible judgment met with an appropriate fate. In a competitive auction the bidding side reached six hearts which had no play because responder had the temerity to believe that opener really had a two club bid.

Example 96e) has only eighteen high card points, but it has twelve winners if partner has a fit for either suit. Do NOT open two clubs!!! Open one heart and plan a rebid of six diamonds. If you open two clubs and there is a black suit overcall which is preemptively raised to the four or five level, you will not be able to show both of your suits.

Example 96f) probably has ten tricks at a heart contract, assuming normal suit distributions. But if you open two clubs you might face preemption in spades and not find the right fit if partner has short hearts and long diamonds. Still, if you open one heart holding 23 HCP, everyone might pass. Open two clubs, but do not be happy about it.

Example 96g) has nine winners either with diamonds as trumps or in notrump. The temptation to open with two clubs will overwhelm many. But if you open two clubs, you must rebid three diamonds, an unappetizing auction, and you might not get that chance if there is any bid by the opponents. With only fourteen high card points, you can open one diamond without fear that everyone will pass. What happens next depends on the auction, but you should be able to convey the fact that you have a remarkable source of tricks and a spade stopper if you do not preempt your own auction by opening two clubs.

Example 96h) was mentioned in the discussion of Namyats. We suggested there that an opening bid of two clubs followed by a jump to four spades should show a solid eight card major suit.

Example 97)

a)
- ♠ J73
- ♥ J62
- ♦ J94
- ♣ QJ87

b)
- ♠ AQ983
- ♥ 62
- ♦ Q84
- ♣ J107

c) ♠ 1042
   ♥ Q83
   ♦ 963
   ♣ Q762

d) ♠ 965
   ♥ 8
   ♦ KQ10975
   ♣ J109

e) ♠ J6
   ♥ 83
   ♦ 542
   ♣ KJ10982

f) ♠ J853
   ♥ 10976
   ♦ J5432
   ♣ —

g) ♠ 104
   ♥ KQJ63
   ♦ Q532
   ♣ 64

h) ♠ 965
   ♥ K102
   ♦ 85432
   ♣ 62

Example 97) hands are responding to the opening bid of two clubs.

Example 97a) would be treated as a positive response by those who count points. After all, there are 6 HCP present. However, the club holding may be completely wasted facing shortness in opener's hand. This hand does not meet the requirements for a positive response of two diamonds, and should make the negative response of two hearts. If partner's rebid is two notrump, showing a balanced hand it is reasonable to continue to three notrump. All of the secondary honors are facing some length in opener's hand.

Example 97b) can make a positive response to show a good spade suit. In response to two clubs, two spades promises a suit at least five cards long including two of the top three honors.

Example 97c) assumes that one of the two queens will be a working card. With that assumption responder makes the positive response of two diamonds.

Example 97d) makes the positive response of three diamonds. This shows a six card suit with two of the top three honors. If the suit were only five cards, the loss of bidding space would not justify a jump to three diamonds.

Example 97e) has a good club suit, but the suit does not include two of the top three honors. Those who use the old method of two diamonds waiting and cheapest three as a second negative will never be able to show this good suit. When that is the agreement, it needs to be understood that responder can make an immediate positive in clubs holding any reasonable suit, rather than need to wait for two of the top three honors. If two diamonds is a positive response, there is no problem showing this good club suit at responder's rebid.

Example 97f) needs to play in a suit—any suit but clubs. If partner rebids in notrump after either a two diamond or negative two heart response, this hand can use Stayman to get to a suit contract. However, if responder can bid two hearts as a negative response and opener rebids in any of the top three suits, responder can then splinter in clubs to show a useful hand without much in values.

Example 97g) has a positive response in hearts. If two diamonds is an omnibus response, responder bids two hearts to show this good suit. If two diamonds is positive and two hearts is negative, responder artificially shows a good heart suit by responding two notrump.

Example 97h) looks very bleak, but is a positive response to the opening bid of two clubs. The king is an adequate value.

High Level Opening Bid Exercises

Plan your opening bid in any position and subsequent auction with each of these hands.

1. ♠ 7
   ♥ QJ10763
   ♦ A942
   ♣ 54

2. ♠ 83
   ♥ 65
   ♦ AKQJ975
   ♣ 92

3. ♠ AKQ9753
   ♥ 6
   ♦ 872
   ♣ 102

4. ♠ AKQJ932
   ♥ 62
   ♦ —
   ♣ AK54

5. ♠ 104
   ♥ AQJ107643
   ♦ A62
   ♣ —

6. ♠ AQJ10
   ♥ A53
   ♦ AKJ2
   ♣ AK

7. ♠ 632
   ♥ 95
   ♦ —
   ♣ KJ1097654

8. ♠ 54
   ♥ AQJ1082
   ♦ 76
   ♣ A103

9. ♠ KJ10754
   ♥ 63
   ♦ A82
   ♣ 95

10. ♠ K93
    ♥ 65
    ♦ A
    ♣ AKQJ952

11. ♠ 62
    ♥ AKQJ63
    ♦ 852
    ♣ 93

12. ♠ KQJ108754
    ♥ —
    ♦ AQ3
    ♣ 94

With these hands you are responding to a weak two bid in hearts. What action do you take?

13. ♠ A62
     ♥ Q1074
     ♦ 6
     ♣ K10975

14. ♠ Q4
     ♥ —
     ♦ KQJ9753
     ♣ K853

15. ♠ AQ3
     ♥ 84
     ♦ A1072
     ♣ KJ107

16. ♠ KQ1092
     ♥ Q3
     ♦ AK62
     ♣ 82

With these hands you are responding to an opening bid of three notrump. Assuming that this opening bid is **Gambling**, how do you continue?

17. ♠ AK52
     ♥ AK83
     ♦ —
     ♣ A9654

18. ♠ Q954
     ♥ A876
     ♦ 85
     ♣ 932

19. ♠ AK953
     ♥ KQJ2
     ♦ 6
     ♣ 876

20. ♠ A843
     ♥ KQ2
     ♦ 95
     ♣ A1076

With these hands you are responding to the opening bid of four clubs, playing the **Namyats** convention. What action do you plan?

21. ♠ 10975
     ♥ 82
     ♦ AK6
     ♣ J654

22. ♠ 876
     ♥ K93
     ♦ A3
     ♣ AKQ65

23. ♠ A
    ♥ 8652
    ♦ KQJ102
    ♣ AK6

24. ♠ K82
    ♥ 97
    ♦ AJ53
    ♣ Q1064

With these hands you are responding to an opening bid of two clubs. Plan your auction.

25. ♠ 854
    ♥ AQJ95
    ♦ Q6
    ♣ 432

26. ♠ K83
    ♥ 854
    ♦ 9876
    ♣ 1032

27. ♠ J873
    ♥ 6
    ♦ QJ84
    ♣ J1095

28. ♠ KQJ4
    ♥ 8753
    ♦ A6
    ♣ 1052

Answers _____

1. Two hearts. If partner asks, show a good hand with a bad suit.

2. Three notrump, assuming that the agreement is **Gambling**. If that is not your agreement, one diamond is better than three diamonds.

3. Three spades if vulnerable vs. not. You have seven winners. At any other vulnerability bid four spades.

4. Two clubs. No, you do not need to open two clubs for fear that an opening bid of one spade would be passed out. However, you have a completely solid suit and nine winners. You can express that fact after opening two clubs by jumping to three spades.

5. Four clubs, assuming that you play **Namyats**. You have the correct suit quality and the right number of tricks.

6. Two clubs. What else? If you are playing that two diamonds is positive, you will be able to rebid two notrump, and partner then might use **Stayman** or make a **transfer** bid. If you are not up to date and two diamonds is not positive, you will need to jump to three notrump to show your values, and a superior major suit contract will be impossible to reach.

7. Four clubs is the classic opening bid with this hand. If you have agreed to play **Namyats**, you will open three notrump instead.

8. Open one heart in first, second, or third seat. Open two hearts in fourth.

9. Open two spades in any seat except fourth. You will seldom hold this hand after three passes.

10. Three notrump if playing **Acol**. Perhaps you will hold this hand in fourth seat, which is the only seat in which we recommend this agreement. Otherwise open one club. Under no circumstances should you believe that this hand should be opened with two clubs. If you open one club and partner responds one heart, rebid three notrump.

11. Open two hearts. If partner uses **Ogust**, bid three notrump to show a solid suit.

12. Open one spade. This hand is far too good for any preemptive opening bid. It has the wrong suit quality for **Namyats**. If partner makes a minimum response, you will jump rebid four spades to show a self-sufficient suit.

13. Four hearts. A bid of a gamble, but in keeping with **The Law of Total Tricks**. If you do not make four hearts, your result will be a good save against a making contract by the other side.

14. Three diamonds. Aren't you glad that we have agreed that a new minor suit is not forcing?

15. Two notrump. If partner has a good suit, game will be easy. If partner has a bad suit, you can still speculate.

16. Two spades. Do not woodenly bid two notrump when you can get vital information that may be of greater help. If partner fits spades, game is a good bet. If there is no spade fit, it may be best to stop at three hearts.

17. Six diamonds. Partner's solid suit will work well as trumps. But you cannot expect to make three notrump without an entry to those seven tricks.

18. Four clubs. Run to the best place without values. Partner will pass or correct.

19. Four diamonds. Partner will pass or correct to five clubs. We expect to make five clubs, but only four diamonds.

20. Pass. With stoppers in every side suit, partner's trick source will produce what we need.

21. Four diamonds. No need for this hand to declare. Let partner do it.

22. Four diamonds and then four spades, an **Asking Bid**. If partner holds a second round control in spades we can make a slam in hearts.

23. Four spades. **Roman Key Card** (see Chapter Twelve), checking for controls. Partner may hold a suit headed by the ace and king, in which case a small slam is clear. But partner could hold those cards and the diamond ace, in which case we can bid and make seven hearts.

24. Four hearts. With tenaces everywhere this hand should declare.

25. Two notrump. This shows a very good heart suit and reasonable values.

26. Two diamonds. Precious little, but the king is a control card and may be all that partner needs for game or slam.

27. Two hearts. A negative response. But if partner shows any suit except hearts, our next call will be a **splinter** to show four card support and shortness in hearts.

28. Two diamonds. An ordinary positive response. Partner's rebid will direct the auction.

CHAPTER TEN
Intruding When They Have Opened the Bidding

Synopsis: Thus far discussion in Chapter Ten has covered overcalls in notrump and in suits, balancing, takeout doubles, and the **Michaels Cue Bid**.

Chapter Ten continues with presentation of a difficult to bid hand type which the expert community has largely ignored, and discussion of the controversy that surrounds it. Among the several solutions offered is the use of conventional jump overcalls. The problems of balancing when the opponents have stopped at one notrump are discussed. Responsive doubles, Snapdragon doubles and honor redoubles are presented. More types of cue bids are examined. The chapter concludes with conventions to be used as defenses against the opening bid of one notrump, and against a strong, forcing club.

Definitions

When competitive auctions are discussed, references to the opener and the responder are present in virtually all discussions and are familiar to the reader. Not so familiar are the terms that describe members of the opposing side that interrupts the auction.

The opponent who enters the auction, generically known as the "intruder," may have entered the auction in one of three ways.

1. The intrusion may be a double. When made early in the auction, most often this double will be intended for takeout.

2. The intrusion may be an overcall. This overcall may be in a suit or in notrump at the immediate level or as a jump.
3. The intrusion may be a cue bid.

The partner of the "intruder" is always called the "advancer." This is true no matter which form of intrusion has occurred.

Reference to these terms will be frequent in this and the following chapter.

The Hand That Nobody Can Bid _____

Well, that is not quite the case. We refer to the hand that has a four card (or weak five card) major and a longer and/or stronger minor. There are ways to bid this type of hand, but it is difficult to convince recognized authorities that it even presents a problem. Every January, May, and September Mary and I are privileged to be panel members in the Bridge World's Master Solvers Club. The moderators when we are panelists are David Berkowitz and Larry Cohen. They have used problems of this nature to see what guesses a panel of experts will make because there is no recognized methodology for describing the hand type.

Suggestion that methodology (rather than guesswork) is correct has been rebuffed. The only answers permitted are those which are part of the consensus system called Bridge World Standard. Suggested conventions which describe this hand but are not part of Bridge World Standard are not permitted. Any answer outside the permitted system is changed to "abstain."

Again, the problem is showing a hand with a longer/stronger minor and a weaker/shorter major after the opponents have opened the bidding. The guessers sometimes overcall in the four card major, sometimes overcall in the longer/stronger minor, sometimes double for takeout despite a missing major suit, and sometimes overcall one notrump with a dubious stopper in opener's suit.

The first hand of this nature appeared as Problem A in the November 1993 Master Solver's Club. At IMPs partner as dealer has passed and right hand opponent has opened one diamond. What action do you take with: ♠K6 ♥AJ105 ♦Q6 ♣KQ986? Twenty eight expert panelists replied. One heart received 16 votes, and two clubs received seven. The other five were scattered among pass, double, and one notrump. Unfortunately, that was not one of our months on the panel, but it prompted us to seek and share bidding methods to describe those elusive hands.

The methods developed to define this hand type appeared to be easily workable. *Competitive Bidding with Two Suited Hands*, which was published in 1997, presented those answers, taking into account which two suits were held in various auctions. Certainly other solutions must be available, but thus far not only have alternate solutions not been presented—those suggested have been ignored. Sadly, this will not change until a majority of experts comes to the conclusion that a problem exists. Bridge World Standard, which is the accepted guide for expert bidding, cannot change until a majority of experts polled agrees that there is a problem and that a solution should be found.

In the January 1997 issue of *The Bridge World*, Berkowitz and Cohen presented Problem A at matchpoints with both vulnerable. After two passes RHO opened with one diamond and your hand is: ♠A1086 ♥K6 ♦Q6 ♣AQ732. Thirteen panelists voted for pass, seven for two clubs, two each for one notrump, one spade, and double, and our vote was changed to "abstain." We were given a nice paragraph in which to lament the lack of interest in finding a true solution for this hand type, and given a chance to plug *Competitive Bidding With Two Suited Hands*, for which we thank David and Larry.

In the September 1997 issue, Problem D was at IMPs with your side vulnerable. RHO has opened one diamond which could be as short as two, and you hold: ♠J6 ♥A985 ♦Q3 ♣AK765. Note that this time the heart suit was less hefty by design. This time there were 16 votes for pass, ten for two clubs, and only one for one heart. Our vote was changed to "abstain." Enough commentary, let us get back to the work of descriptive bids.

There are three possible suit combinations that may need description.

1. When the two suits held are the two highest, make a takeout double and

use "equal level correction" if partner should happen to bid the lowest suit (for which you have no support).

2. When the two suits held are the highest and lowest ranking, use the Top and Bottom Cue Bid (the minor suit will usually be longer and/or stronger).

3. When the two suits held are the two lowest ranking, one will be the unbid minor and the other will be hearts. To show these suits use a conventional jump overcall.

Further discussion of takeout doubles and cue bids happens later in this chapter.

Jump overcalls after the opponents have opened the bidding in a minor suit are used to show a shorter or weaker heart suit and a longer or stronger holding in the other minor suit. The original 1997 presentation used a jump overcall in the unbid minor to show this hand. When the opening bid was one club, it was a jump to two diamonds. When the opening bid was one diamond, it was a jump to three clubs.

Assigning a conventional meaning to the two diamond jump presented no problem. A preemptive jump to three diamonds was still available. Assigning a conventional meaning to the jump overcall of three clubs was less acceptable as it left no preemptive jump in clubs short of the four level, and when the contract was in hearts the three level was frequently too high. An old friend came to the rescue.

Bill Parks, a one time bridge pro on the Western circuit, suggested that instead of jumping conventionally to three clubs, a jump to two hearts be used for this purpose. This worked well because:

1. It gave back a preemptive jump in clubs.
2. It allowed play in hearts at the two level when necessary instead of at the three level.

No problem with giving up the preemptive jump in hearts at the two level because the natural preemptive jump in hearts to the three level was still available. So with the Master Solver hands of November 1993 and September 1997 complete description was made possible by a jump overcall of two hearts.

Example 98)

a) ♠ 8
    ♥ KQ98
    ♦ AQJ92
    ♣ 953

b) ♠ 75
    ♥ AJ104
    ♦ AKQ92
    ♣ 54

Holding either of the hands in Example 98) how do you compete when the opening bid is one club? If you overcall one diamond, you may lose the heart suit entirely. If you overcall one heart, you may play an inadequate fit when diamonds is the right place. If you can make the jump overcall of two diamonds conventionally to show diamonds and hearts with longer/stronger diamonds, your problem is solved.

Example 99)

a) ♠ Q
    ♥ 98652
    ♦ A9
    ♣ AKJ107

b) ♠ 4
    ♥ A1094
    ♦ Q10
    ♣ AJ10632

The two hands of Example 99) are hands 9 and 21 from Chapter One (and Chapter Six) of *Competitive Bidding With Two Suited Hands*. When the opening bid on your right is one diamond, how do you compete? Either one heart or two clubs could be right or wrong. If you can jump to two hearts to show clubs and hearts with longer/stronger clubs, have you not described the hand you hold?

Balancing When the Opponents Stop at One Notrump ___

Volume I mentioned various means for balancing. A double by the balancer is usually for takeout.

When the opponents have bid one or two suits and stop at one notrump, double is not for takeout. It is a penalty double. It says that the hand that doubled in the balance position has passed because it holds the suit bid by the opponent in front of the balancer. When the values of the two sides are about equal but dummy's suit is trapped in front of a defender who also holds that suit, the favorable value placement for the defense will usually cause the defenders to prevail. Double by the balancer asks partner to pass and lead dummy's suit.

In order to make a takeout call in the balancing position when the opponents stop at one notrump, the partnership must have a specific agreement. The common expert agreement is to use an artificial bid of two clubs as a takeout call. The artificial takeout promises support for all unbid suits. If clubs happens to be one of the unbid suits, intruder has support for clubs as well.

Example 100)

a) ♠ 1083
    ♥ A95
    ♦ AK862
    ♣ J2

b) ♠ K83
    ♥ Q1063
    ♦ A82
    ♣ J43

c) ♠ K83
    ♥ AQ1063
    ♦ A8
    ♣ J42

d) ♠ KJ3
    ♥ 95
    ♦ A862
    ♣ Q1082

With all Example 100) hands your LHO and partner have passed and RHO opens one heart. You pass and LHO bids one notrump. Two passes follow and it is your turn in the balance position. What action do you take?

Example 100a) should bid two diamonds. Your hand and suit were not good enough to overcall at your first turn, but are quite adequate for a balance now.

Example 100b) should pass. You have no reason to take any action. On a good day your side will beat this contract because the values in the deck are divided about equally and declarer has few heart tricks.

Example 100c) should double. You have reason to believe that with a heart lead you will beat this contract easily.

Example 100d) wants to make a takeout call. Since double is for penalty, your partnership should have the agreement that two clubs in this auction is takeout for the unbid suits.

More About Takeout Doubles

Volume I discussed three hand types that might be expected when a takeout double is used.

Type 1. The doubler has roughly the values of an opening bid (or more) and support for all of the unbid suits. Advancer is asked to select one of those suits to be the trump suit for the intruding side.

Type 2. The doubler has a hand that would like to overcall with a very good suit and superb values. Fearing that an overcall would cause a game to be missed, intruder describes this hand by starting with a takeout double. Advancer believes this to be Type 1 and bids accordingly. When doubler then bids either a different suit or notrump, partner knows this double is not truly for takeout, but prefaces the message of a hand too good to make an overcall.

Type 3. Remember, some inexperienced bidders believe that a takeout double shows thirteen points, regardless of distribution. It is not truly a double for takeout. It is just a double that shows values. Most bidders of this ilk fail to mark their convention cards properly and fail to alert. They have the right to bid this way if they wish, but their non-standard approach must be alerted.

Type 4. There is yet a fourth type of takeout double. When the intruder holds support for the two highest ranking of the three unbid suits, a takeout double is possible if the partnership has agreed to use "equal level correction." What this means is that if advancer bids the lowest ranking of the unbid suits, the only one for which the doubler does not have support, doubler can then bid the next higher ranking unbid suit. In this auction, doubler does not promise a Type 2 hand but instead denies support for the lowest suit (which advancer has bid) and offers a choice between the two highest ranking of the unbid suits.

Of course, if doubler corrects to the higher ranking of the remaining suits, it is not "equal level correction" since it would force a choice at too high a level. That correction would show a Type 2 hand (too good to overcall). When doubler holds a Type 2 hand and has the "equal level correction" suit, it must be shown by a jump rather than by a simple correction.

When the opening bid has been in a minor suit, the Type 4 double shows the majors (the two highest ranking unbid suits) and denies support for the unbid minor. In this auction the doubler will usually have somewhat equal holdings in the two major suits. If advancer bids the other minor, the "equal level correction" will be made in the heart suit.

When the opening bid has been in a major suit, the Type 4 double shows the other major and diamonds, and denies support for clubs. In this auction the doubler will usually have four cards in the unbid major, but may have longer and/or stronger diamonds. The major will not have been good enough to over-call, but the diamond suit may be quite good. If advancer bids clubs, the "equal level correction" will be in diamonds. This is our second means of bidding hands with a shorter/weaker major and a longer/stronger minor.

Example 101)

a) ♠ KQ104
    ♥ AJ763
    ♦ K2
    ♣ 94

b) ♠ AKQ1085
    ♥ K85
    ♦ AQ3
    ♣ 3

c) ♠ AJ85
    ♥ 64
    ♦ AQ9854
    ♣ 7

d) ♠ 64
    ♥ AJ85
    ♦ AQ9854
    ♣ 7

e) ♠ AJ1083
    ♥ KQ974
    ♦ 6
    ♣ 104

f) ♠ AQ3
    ♥ AKQ1085
    ♦ K85
    ♣ 3

With Example 101a) how do you compete when an opponent opens in a minor suit? If your agreement includes Type 4 doubles with "equal level correction," you have no problem. Double for takeout, and if partner bids the other minor, bid hearts as cheaply as possible for "equal level correction."

With Example 101b) when the opponents open in any of the three lower ranking suits, your hand is too good to overcall one spade. Make a takeout double (Type 2) and bid spades at your next turn. No matter which suit was opened and which suit the advancer has bid, your rebid in spades will show an excellent hand and a fine suit that was too good for an overcall.

With Example 101c) if the opening bid is one heart, how do you compete? If you overcall in diamonds, you may miss a spade fit. If Type 4 doubles are part of your partnership agreement, show this hand by doubling. If partner bids spades or diamonds, you are pleased, but if partner bids clubs, you can make the "equal level correction" to diamonds.

With Example 101d) if the opening bid is one spade, you have the same problem. Double, and correct clubs to diamonds.

With Example 101e) after a minor suit opening bid, most will use a Michaels Cue Bid. However, those who adopt the recommended approach to competitive bidding which includes Top and Bottom Cue Bids will not have that convention available. Make a Type 4 double and if partner bids the unbid minor, correct to hearts.

With Example 101f) you are too good to overcall in hearts after a minor suit opening bid. Make a Type 4 double. If partner bids the other minor, you cannot bid just two hearts as that would be "equal level correction." To show that you have a true Type 2 double, you must jump to three hearts.

Responsive Doubles _____

When our side intrudes with either a double or an overcall and responder raises the opening bid, the most descriptive continuation may be a **responsive double**. Note that this convention applies only when opener and responder have bid the same suit, partner has intruded, and advancer has a message to send. The message differs depending on the nature of the intrusion.

When the intrusion by partner is a takeout double and responder raises, a **responsive double** carries a message that relates to the unbid suits. The meaning of the double varies based on the suits opener and responder have bid.

When opener has bid a minor suit, partner has made a takeout double, and responder has raised opener, the **responsive double** asks opener to pick a major suit. You will usually hold four cards in each of the major suits and at least the values of a minimum response.

When the opening bid has been one heart, partner has doubled for takeout, and responder has raised hearts, it is easy for advancer to bid spades. In this auction if you make a **responsive double**, it asks the intruder to pick a minor suit.

When the opening bid has been one spade, partner has doubled for takeout, and responder has raised spades, bidding hearts is not so easy. If you bid three hearts, you promise game invitational values of 9+ to 12– HCP. You may have four hearts and fewer values, and be unable to bid hearts at the three level even though the takeout double has suggested that hearts should be the trump suit.

If you stretch to bid three hearts, when partner holds better than minimum values (14+ HCP), there will be a raise to game which you do not want to hear. Instead, make a **responsive double** which asks partner to select a minor. Once partner selects a minor, you then bid three hearts. This is a "slow-down" auction designed to show that your values were not sufficient for a direct call of three hearts.

Example 102)

a)   ♠ QJ65
     ♥ K1083
     ♦ 942
     ♣ 86

b)   ♠ KJ85
     ♥ 62
     ♦ Q1043
     ♣ J75

c)   ♠ 75
     ♥ 862
     ♦ KJ105
     ♣ AQ73

d)   ♠ 85
     ♥ KQ83
     ♦ J1064
     ♣ J72

e)   ♠ 85
     ♥ KQ83
     ♦ AJ104
     ♣ J72

f)   ♠ KJ85
     ♥ 62
     ♦ AQ103
     ♣ J85

Example 102a) would make a responsive double **after an opening minor suit bid by LHO, a takeout double by partner, and a raise of the opening minor by RHO. This would ask partner to pick a major suit.**

After an opening bid of one heart, a takeout double by partner, and a raise to two hearts, Example 102b) has an easy bid of two spades.

After an opening bid in either major suit, a takeout double by partner, and a raise of the opening bid to the two level, Example 102c) would make a responsive double. This would ask partner to choose a minor.

After an opening bid of one spade, a takeout double by partner, and a raise to two spades, Example 102d) would like to bid hearts but does not have the values to bid at the three level. This hand makes a responsive double which asks partner to pick a minor suit. After the doubler bids a minor suit as requested, this hand corrects to three hearts. This shows the desire to compete to the three level in hearts, but denies that advancer holds game invitational values.

After an opening bid of one spade, a takeout double by partner, and a raise to two spades, Example 102e) bids three hearts. This promises the values of a game invitation.

After the opening bid of one heart, a takeout double by partner, and a raise to two hearts, Example 102f) jumps to three spades to invite game.

When the intrusion has been an overcall, the **responsive double** conveys an entirely different meaning. It shows the two unbid suits. Again, opener and responder must have both bid the same suit. Advancer's holding in the two unbid suits is expected to be five-five. The overcaller is encouraged to bid one of the two unbid suits on a three card holding. On occasion advancer may hold five cards in one of the unbid suits and have a good four card holding in the other. If the overcaller happens to bid the suit in which the doubler has only four cards, the four-three fit needs to be good enough to play reasonably well.

Example 103)

a) ♠ Q10843
    ♥ 6
    ♦ KJ982
    ♣ 84

b) ♠ AQ104
    ♥ 63
    ♦ KJ982
    ♣ 84

After an opening bid of one club, an overcall of one heart by partner, and a raise to two clubs, Example 103a) has a classic hand for a responsive double. This double shows the two unbid suits and encourages partner to bid one of them if holding three cards in the suit.

In the same auction Example 103b) should also make a responsive double despite being short a spade. The four card suit is good enough to encourage partner to bid spades with only three of them.

Most users of the **responsive double** apply it through the level of three spades. After an opening bid, an intrusion, and a jump raise to the three level, advancer's double is **responsive**. Also, after an opening weak two bid, a takeout double, and a raise of the weak two bid, double by advancer is played by most as **responsive**.

Understand that the **responsive double** applies only when opener and responder have found a fit. If the opening bid was in a minor suit and the responder bids one notrump, responder is deemed to have shown a fit for the minor. However, in all other auctions after the intrusion of a takeout double, when responder's call does not show a fit, double is not **responsive**; it is penalty oriented.

Example 104)

a) ♠ K4
    ♥ KJ964
    ♦ 975
    ♣ Q87

b) ♠ Q4
    ♥ KJ7
    ♦ 9754
    ♣ J876

After an opening bid of one club, a takeout double by partner, and a response of one heart, Example 104a) should double. This double is not responsive **because responder has not shown a fit for opener. The double shows four or more cards in the suit that responder has bid and is for penalty. Because the takeout double only guarantees two quick tricks, the penalty double should include a surprise for the responder.**

In the same auction Example 104b) should bid one notrump to show scattered minimum response values and imply a stopper in each suit bid by the opposition.

The Snapdragon Double

When the intrusion has been an overcall and responder bids a third suit, double by the advancer takes on a different systemic meaning. Double in this auction is known as **Snapdragon** (some call it the fourth suit double). It shows two things. It says that the doubler holds five (or more) cards in the unbid suit, and also has support for the suit of the overcall. The support for partner will minimally be a doubleton high honor or three small cards.

The auction must be such that the advancer asks the intruder to bid at the two level, but no higher. Advancer must hold adequate values to make a two level contract feasible.

Negative inferences are available when advancer either raises the overcall or bids freely in the fourth suit. The raise of the overcall usually denies as many as five cards in the fourth suit, and a free bid in the fourth suit denies a fit for the overcall.

Example 105)

a)
- ♠ 843
- ♥ KQJ987
- ♦ 62
- ♣ A7

b)
- ♠ 843
- ♥ KQJ7
- ♦ 962
- ♣ Q74

c)
- ♠ Q85
- ♥ A109763
- ♦ 763
- ♣ 4

d)
- ♠ K43
- ♥ Q10975
- ♦ K6
- ♣ 754

The auction has been one club by LHO, one diamond by partner, and one spade by RHO.

With Example 105a) bid two hearts. As you show your good suit you also deny a fit for diamonds.

With Example 105b) bid two diamonds. Your hearts are very good but you do not hold enough length to show them.

With Example 105c) make a Snapdragon double to show five or more hearts and a fit for diamonds.

With Example 105d) your doubleton diamond king in addition to five hearts makes this hand also appropriate for a Snapdragon double.

Honor Redoubles

When partner has overcalled and there has been a **negative double** by responder, **redouble** becomes available. It makes sense to assign a specific meaning to an available bid. We use **redouble** to promise the ace or king of partner's suit, at least doubleton. If we later defend, this information will allow partner to underlead the ace of his suit, which may be the best start for the defense. Ordinarily leading or underleading unsupported aces against suit contracts is to be avoided. Knowledge that partner holds one of the top two honor cards becomes very useful.

It follows that advancer's raise of the overcall tends to deny the ace or the king of the overcalled suit. The negative inference is as important as positive information. The instance in which advancer holds a top honor card and does not redouble is when a preemptive jump raise is used. It will often be more important to preempt than to show the top honor.

Example 106)

a) ♠ 642
   ♥ J84
   ♦ A3
   ♣ J8765

b) ♠ 6
   ♥ K6532
   ♦ J93
   ♣ 8765

c) ♠ 642
   ♥ K84
   ♦ A3
   ♣ J8765

d) ♠ 642
   ♥ K4
   ♦ A93
   ♣ J8765

After an opening bid of one diamond, partner has overcalled one heart and there has been a negative double.

Example 106a) has an easy raise to two hearts. Partner will know not to expect a high heart honor.

Example 106b) should make a preemptive jump raise to four hearts. This neither promises nor denies a high honor in hearts.

Example 106c) should redouble **to show the ace or king of hearts. Given an opportunity to make a minimum raise later, that raise will show a fit for hearts as well and some extra values.**

Example 106d) should redouble **to show ace or king of hearts. Plan no further action in this auction.**

Cue Bids _____

Volume I presented the **Michaels Cue Bid**. It was introduced in 1966 and rapidly gained favor with most competitive bidders. Today it is considered the standard cue bid when the opponents have opened the bidding.

There are several additional types of cue bid listed in the *Encyclopedia of Bridge*. The one we believe to be the most important is the **Top and Bottom Cue Bid**.

As its name suggests, this cue bid shows the highest and lowest ranking of the unbid suits. When the opening bid is in spades, these suits are hearts and clubs. When the opening bid is in clubs, these suits are spades and diamonds. When the opening bid is in either hearts or diamonds, these suits are spades and clubs.

The expected hand when this cue bid is used has a longer/stronger minor suit, with the higher ranking major being shorter/weaker. The typical pattern is four-six, although four-five is frequent when the minor suit is of good quality, or five-five when the major is poor. This is the third element of our complex to show hands of this nature.

Conventional jump overcalls that show the two lowest ranking suits, and the **Type 4 takeout double** to show the two highest ranking suits were covered earlier in this chapter. Inclusion of the **Top and Bottom Cue Bid** gives us a way to bid all of the possible combinations of suits when the opponents have opened the bidding and we hold a two suited hand in which the minor is longer/stronger.

The values shown by the use of this cue bid vary based upon the position in the auction. If partner has not yet called, the cue bidder promises roughly the values of an opening hand. Most particularly, the cue bidder promises two defensive tricks. Facing a passed partner, the cue bidder no longer needs to meet this criterion. Any reasonable hand with the right pattern is acceptable.

Advancer knows that the minor is a safe haven. Intruder will hold six cards or a very good five, and when advancer needs a place to escape it is reasonable to seek the minor even when holding a doubleton. When advancer holds three cards in the major and two in the minor, with most ordinary hands it is right to bid the minor. The known fit is at least five-two, and often six-two.

If advancer bids the major with only three, it must be for good reason. Advancer will not bid the lower suit with a singleton or a void. In those cases a bid of the major with only three cards will be the best available escape. Do what seems to be prudent. When advancer bids the major, it will usually be because a fit has been found. Advancer probably has four (or more) cards in the major suit.

There will be occasional hands in which the intruder has two suits and excellent values. In these cases intruder uses the cue bid to identify the suits. When advancer bids the minor suit and intruder then volunteers the major, that shows at least five-five with an excellent hand. If one suit is longer, it will be the minor. Advancer should then know what to do.

Example 107)

a) ♠ AJ94
♥ 82
♦ 6
♣ KQJ632

b) ♠ 82
♥ AJ94
♦ 6
♣ KQJ632

c) ♠ AJ94
♥ 82
♦ KQJ632
♣ 6

d) ♠ QJ104
♥ 82
♦ 6
♣ KJ10854

e) ♠ 97632
♥ A2
♦ 6
♣ AKJ103

f) ♠ AKJ103
♥ 8
♦ 6
♣ AKQ852

If the opening bid is either one diamond or one heart, Example 107a) makes a Top and Bottom Cue Bid **to show clubs and spades with longer/stronger clubs.**

If the opening bid is one spade, Example 107b) makes a Top and Bottom Cue Bid **to show clubs and hearts with longer/stronger clubs. If the opening bid is one diamond, this hand makes the conventional jump overcall of two hearts.**

If the opening bid is one club, Example 107c) makes a Top and Bottom Cue Bid **to show spades and diamonds with longer/stronger diamonds. If the opening bid is one heart, this hand makes a Type 4 takeout double.**

Example 107d) has the pattern for a Top and Bottom Cue Bid **but will do so only if partner is a passed hand. If partner has not passed, this hand needs to have two defensive tricks.**

Example 107e) is best described by use of the Top and Bottom Cue Bid **after a red suit opening bid because of the poor quality of the five card spade suit.**

Example 107f) makes a Top and Bottom Cue Bid **after a red suit opening. If partner seeks the sanctuary of the expected longer/ stronger club suit, this intruder bids spades voluntarily to show a superb hand with at least five-five distribution. If responder raises opener's suit, shutting partner out of the auction, this hand is good enough to bid three spades.**

Example 108)

a) ♠ 983
    ♥ J832
    ♦ K654
    ♣ Q5

b) ♠ Q83
    ♥ J9832
    ♦ K654
    ♣ 5

c) ♠ J1053
    ♥ J32
    ♦ K654
    ♣ 105

d) ♠ QJ43
    ♥ A952
    ♦ A62
    ♣ 105

The auction has been an opening bid of one diamond by LHO, a Top and Bottom Cue Bid **of two diamonds by partner, and pass by RHO.**

Example 108a) bids three clubs. There is at least a five-two fit in clubs and likely only a four-three in spades.

Example 108b) bids two spades. Better to play a four-three than a possible five-one.

Example 108c) bids two spades. The four-four spade fit could not have been found if partner had overcalled in clubs.

Example 108d) should jump in spades. If you are a passed hand, invite game by jumping to three spades since partner may have pattern without much in values. If you are not a passed hand, partner must have full opening bid values. Jump to four spades.

Intruding After an Opening Bid of One Notrump

When the opponents have opened one notrump, there are many ways to compete. Natural bidding came first, but many conventions have been created to make competing easier and more descriptive. In *Competitive Bidding With Two Suited Hands*, nineteen different conventions created for this purpose are discussed. Our purpose here is to present the few that we find most acceptable and practical.

The conventions for this use can be separated into two groups. One group uses double for penalty. The other group assigns an artificial meaning to double. They use it to show a single suited hand. We feel that it is important to be able to double for penalty with an appropriate hand. The conventions we recommend all retain the penalty double.

Landy

The very first artificial method for intruding against an opening bid of one notrump was the **Landy** convention. It is quite simple. Two clubs is an artificial takeout for the major suits. As with all conventions with this purpose, clubs cannot be played at the two level. However, if the intruder is a passed hand, double shows the major suits so that clubs can be bid naturally.

Cappelletti/Hamilton/Helms _____

This convention is claimed by all three experts who have been named. It is commonly called Cappelletti in the eastern United States, and Hamilton in the west. Few players who use the convention know the claim of Jerry Helms. We do not care who the originator might have been, but do recommend this convention to casual partnerships as it is widely known and easy to adopt without discussion. Of course, it retains the important penalty double. Here are the parameters:

1. Double is for penalty.
2. Two clubs shows some single-suited hand. Advancer is asked to bid two diamonds to allow intruder to show the single suit.
3. Two diamonds shows both majors.
4. Two hearts shows hearts and a minor suit. If advancer cannot stand to play in hearts, two notrump asks intruder to bid the minor suit.
5. Two spades shows spades and a minor suit. If advancer cannot stand to play in spades, two notrump asks intruder to bid the minor suit.
6. Two notrump shows both minor suits.

The major weakness in this convention is that when you hold a nice major suit, you cannot bid it. You are required to bid two clubs with your single-suited hand when it could be far more effective to take up bidding space by introducing the major suit.

An important adjunct is the use of double by a passed hand. The passed hand that doubles cannot have the values to penalize the opening notrump bid. Double suggests that advancer bid clubs. Intruder will then pass with clubs or bid two diamonds to show both red suits.

Hello _____

That is not a greeting. It is the name of the convention that we find most to our liking. Its origin is a refinement of the convention just presented. Jerry Helms set out to correct the weakness of not being able to bid a single major suit immediately. Working with one of his regular partners, Bill

Lohman, Helms created the convention which bears the first part of each of their last names, **Hello**. This is how it works:

1. Double is for penalties.
2. Two clubs shows either diamonds or a major–minor two suiter. Advancer is asked to bid two diamonds. Intruder passes or raises with diamonds, or corrects to the major. When advancer has no support for the major, a continuation to two notrump asks intruder to bid the minor.
3. Two diamonds shows hearts. The transfer effect puts the opening notrump bidder on lead.
4. Two hearts shows both majors.
5. Two spades shows spades (wonders never cease!!).
6. Two notrump shows clubs.
7. Three clubs shows both minors.
8. Three diamonds shows both majors with a very good hand.
9. Double by a passed hand shows either clubs or both red suits.

Example 109)

a)
♠ 76
♥ 843
♦ KQ10985
♣ A6

b)
♠ K4
♥ AQJ1083
♦ J97
♣ 86

c)
♠ J10875
♥ J107632
♦ 4
♣ 9

d)
♠ AJ10764
♥ 3
♦ KJ102
♣ 84

e)
♠ 7
♥ 93
♦ Q1087
♣ KQJ1063

f)
♠ 7
♥ 93
♦ AQ982
♣ KQJ109

g)
♠ KQJ954
♥ A62
♦ K7
♣ A3

h)
♠ AQJ83
♥ KQJ952
♦ —
♣ Q6

All Example 109) hands are bidding after an opposing opening bid of one notrump.

Playing either Hamilton **or** Hello, **Example 109a) bids two clubs, asking partner to bid two diamonds. You intend to pass.**

Playing Hamilton, **Example 109b) bids two clubs to show a single suited hand. When partner bids two diamonds as requested, bid two hearts. Playing** Hello, **bid two diamonds to show hearts.**

Playing Landy, **Example 109c) should bid two clubs to show major suits. If you are a passed hand, double to show major suits. Playing** Hamilton, **bid two diamonds to show both majors. Playing** Hello, **bid two hearts to show both majors.**

Playing Hamilton, **Example 109d) should bid two clubs to show a single suiter. When partner bids two diamonds as requested, bid two spades. Playing** Hello, **bid two spades. Do not consider this hand to be a two suiter with spades and diamonds. If the suit lengths were reversed, it would make more sense to show two suits, but not when the major suit is a good six and the minor suit only four cards.**

Example 109e) is not an easy hand to show. Playing Landy, **you cannot bid and show clubs at the two level unless you are a passed hand. That is also true using other conventions. As a passed hand playing either** Hamilton **or** Hello, **you can double to show clubs. As an unpassed hand playing** Hamilton, **you must either bid two clubs, then three clubs, or make an immediate call of three clubs. In these instances, two clubs followed by three clubs should show a better hand than an immediate three clubs. Playing** Hello, **bid two notrump to show clubs.**

Example 109f) bids two notrump to show both minors unless playing Hello, **in which case three clubs shows both minors.**

Example 109g) should double one notrump for penalty. You have an excellent trick source and should be able to take at least seven tricks even if partner is broke.

Example 109h) wants to show both majors and make a strong try for game. Playing Landy, **bid two clubs and raise the major**

that partner bids. Playing Hamilton, **bid two diamonds to show majors and raise the major that partner bids. Playing** Hello, **bid three diamonds to show a hand with both majors that can almost produce game without any help.**

Defending Against the Artificial Forcing Opening of One Club

You will find yourself playing against opponents who use one club as an artificial, forcing opening bid. The minimum strength will vary. It will usually be sixteen high card points or more. You have an advantage against this system when you hold a distributional hand. Your advantage is the ability to interfere so that it becomes difficult for the strong opening bidder to be able to define the good hand that opened the bidding.

It is best to compete after an artificial one club opening bid whenever your hand allows. The more bidding space you can take away, the harder it is for the one club bidder to describe the big hand. It behooves you to have methods to disrupt after the opening one club bid is made.

Understand that the opening bidder's good hand may be based on distribution and/or a very strong suit. There is no reason to believe that just because an opponent has shown a strong hand our side cannot play and make a contract, even at the game level.

We believe that the best simple defense is this:

1. Overcall whenever you have a good suit.
2. Double to ask partner to bid a major.
3. Bid one notrump to ask partner to bid a minor.

This defense is known as **Mathe**. It was devised by the deceased California expert who also created the **Mathe Asking Bid** (see Chapter Eight). What is required is judgment. You should intrude whenever you have any reasonable excuse.

A more sophisticated defense is known as **CRASH**. This is an acronym for color, rank, shape. It allows for the description of various two suited hands.

After the opening bid of one club, an intrusion in the immediate seat should have a transfer effect. If our side declares, we want the opening one club bidder to be on lead, leading from the honor cards known to be in the strong hand. We take into account that major suited hands are important, but allow two suited hands to be shown, keeping in mind that the opening bidder should be on lead against any contract that our side declares.

1. Double—shows two suits of the same color—either both black suits or both red suits.
2. One diamond is a transfer to hearts.
3. One heart is a transfer to spades
4. One spade shows two suits of the same rank—either both majors or both minors.
5. One notrump shows two suits of the same shape—either both pointed suits or both rounded suits.
6. Two clubs shows a three suited hand.
7. All suit bids at any level beyond these conventional calls are transfer bids, showing the suit that ranks directly beyond the suit actually bid.
8. Since two spades transfers to clubs, two notrump is set aside to show both minors with game interest.
9. With a very good major two suiter, bid one spade to show two suits of the same rank and then bid again.

Bearing in mind that we want the opening club bidder to be on opening lead, when the auction begins with one club and there is no immediate intrusion, responder will most often artificially bid one diamond to show some hand with limited values. In this auction our natural intrusions are designed so that if the we declare the opening one club bidder will be the opening leader.

So, after one club—pass—one diamond:

1. Double shows two suits of the same color.
2. One heart is natural.
3. One spade is natural.
4. One notrump shows two suits of the same rank.
5. Two clubs shows two suits of the same shape.
6. Two diamonds shows a three suiter.

7. All higher ranking suit bids are natural.

8. Two notrump still shows a minor two suited hand with interest in game.

9. Good major two suiters start with two clubs.

Overcalling with your own suit should be done so as to take up as much space as appropriate. Good single suited hands may be shown by jumps. When advancer holds moderate values and a fit for overcaller's suit, a raise may enable a fitting game despite the strong opposing opening bid.

It is important that the undefined strong hand held by the opposition be given problems. Showing two suits without specifying which two can be an advantage to the intruding side. Knowing that a fit exists, advancer assumes that the intruder holds an average hand and bids immediately to the highest level deemed to be safe. This places great pressure on the opening one club bidder.

When partner has shown two suits of the same color and advancer holds length in one red suit and one black suit, advancer bids immediately to the highest level that seems safe in one of those suits, knowing that partner will pass or correct to the suit of the other color. Whichever happens, advancer feels comfortable with the level that has been reached.

The same type of auction occurs when partner shows two suits of the same rank and you hold one major and one minor, or when you hold one pointed and one rounded and partner shows two of the same shape. Bid to the highest reasonable level with the expectancy that partner will either pass or correct.

Consuming bidding space when a fit is assured is easy. However, when advancer's suits are both of the same color, rank, or shape, it is likely that partner holds the other set and that there is no true fit. Assuming this to be the case, make the cheapest possible call in the nearer or longer of the two suits that are not really held. Partner will usually hold that pair of suits and will pass.

When advancer bids a suit that the intruder does not hold, correction is automatic. Having announced two suits, the intruder has the obligation to get the bidding side to one of those suits. Pass is not permitted even when partner has forced the auction to some high level. Partner's reason for getting the auction so high is based on a fit for a shown suit, no matter what they may be. Never assume that partner's jump is in a long and strong suit—it is always done with a known fit for one of the suits shown by the intrusion.

Suppose that advancer is 2-4-5-2. LHO opens with a forcing club and partner shows two suits. If the intrusion is one spade showing two suits of the same rank (both majors or both minors), advancer knows that either diamonds or hearts will match. Bid in diamonds to the highest level at which a diamond or heart contract would be reasonable. Partner will pass holding minors, but will correct to hearts at that level holding majors.

Or suppose that intruder bids one notrump to show two suits of the same shape (both pointed or both rounded). Again, jump in diamonds to the highest level at which a diamond or heart contract would be reasonable. Partner will pass holding pointed suits or will correct to hearts holding rounded suits.

If partner doubles to show two suits of the same color, there is no guarantee of a fit.

Since you hold red suits, partner is likely to hold black suits. Assume this to be the case and bid only one spade, the cheapest available call in a black suit. When intruder's suits are black, this is as far as the auction will go. But when intruder holds red suits, a correction will be made to diamonds—the cheapest call available in one of the suits actually held. When that correction occurs, you know there are fits and can compete further.

The secret is for advancer to bid to the most expressive level when a fit is guaranteed, but to bid cheaply in the nearest or longest non-suit when there may be no fit. With a guaranteed fit, advancer bids to the level that should produce a plus score when partner holds an average hand. When partner holds a better than average hand, bidding on to a game becomes possible.

Example 109) again (see page 155)

The hands that would compete against an opening bid of one notrump would also compete against the opening bid of a

forcing club. **Reviewing the hands of Example 109) these are the competitive calls that would be used against the opening bid of one club, forcing and artificial with those hands.**

With Example 109a) playing Mathe, **overcall one diamond. Playing modified CRASH, with transfers in the immediate seat, you would need to bid three clubs. Do so only at favorable vulnerability.**

With Example 109b) playing Mathe, **overcall one heart. Playing CRASH, make the transfer overcall of one diamond. If there has been a one diamond response to one club, make a natural overcall of one heart.**

With Example 109c) playing Mathe, **double to show both majors. Playing CRASH, bid one spade to show two suits of the same rank.**

With Example 109d) playing Mathe, **overcall one spade. Playing CRASH, make the transfer overcall of one heart. If there has been a one diamond response to one club, make a natural overcall of one spade.**

With Example 109e) playing Mathe, **overcall two clubs. Playing CRASH, make the transfer overcall of two spades if the vulnerability is favorable; otherwise pass. If there has been a one diamond response to one club, make the natural overcall of two clubs.**

With Example 109f) playing Mathe, **bid one notrump to show minors. Playing CRASH, bid one spade to show two suits of the same rank.**

With Example 109g) playing Mathe, **overcall one spade. Playing CRASH, make the transfer overcall of one heart. If there has been a one diamond response to one club, make a natural overcall of one spade.**

With Example 109h) playing Mathe, **double to show majors. Playing CRASH, bid one spade to show two suits of the same rank.**

Example 110)

a) ♠ Q853
    ♥ J62
    ♦ 84
    ♣ Q1076

b) ♠ 84
    ♥ Q10973
    ♦ 6
    ♣ KJ432

c) ♠ Q853
    ♥ J952
    ♦ 6
    ♣ Q1076

d) ♠ Q8543
    ♥ Q109
    ♦ Q62
    ♣ 106

Your left hand opponent has opened with a forcing club. Your partner has made a CRASH call.

With Example 110a) if partner doubles to show two suits of the same color, bid one heart. Partner will pass or correct to spades. If partner bids one spade to show two suits of the same rank, bid two clubs. Partner will pass or correct to hearts, which you will correct to spades. If partner bids one notrump to show two suits of the same shape, bid two clubs. If partner corrects to diamonds to show the pointed suits, you will correct further to two spades.

With Example 110b) if partner doubles to show two suits of the same color, bid three clubs. You expect to make a three level contract either in clubs or hearts. If partner corrects to diamonds to show red suits, you will correct further to hearts. If partner bids one spade to show two suits of the same rank, again you should bid three clubs. Partner will pass with minors or correct to three hearts with majors, and you will pass expecting the contract to make. If partner bids one notrump to show two suits of the same shape, bid two spades. If partner has rounded suits and corrects to three clubs, you will be at the three level where you want to play. At match points you will correct to three hearts.

With Example 110c) you are well placed no matter what pair of suits partner shows. If partner doubles to show two suits of the same color, bid one heart. If partner corrects to spades to show black suits, pass. If partner bids one spade to show two suits of the same rank, bid two clubs. Partner will pass with minors or correct to hearts with majors. If partner bids one notrump to show two suits of the same shape, bid two hearts. Partner will pass or correct to spades.

With Example 110d) if partner doubles to show two suits of the same color, bid two hearts. Partner will pass with red suits or correct to spades with black suits. If partner bids one spade to show two suits of the same rank, bid two diamonds. Partner will pass or correct to two hearts, in which case you will correct further to two spades. If partner bids one notrump to show two suits of the same shape, bid two hearts. Partner will pass with rounded suits or correct to spades with pointed suits.

Intruder's Exercises _____

Determine what you would do after any natural opening bid at the one
level including a standard opening one notrump, and also against the artificial opening bid of one club. Plan your auction including rebids, both as a
passed and unpassed hand.

1. ♠ 92
   ♥ AQJ6
   ♦ 5
   ♣ KJ10943

2. ♠ 92
   ♥ AQJ6
   ♦ KJ10943
   ♣ 5

3. ♠ KQ103
   ♥ 64
   ♦ AKJ62
   ♣ 87

4. ♠ KQ1082
   ♥ AJ653
   ♦ J9
   ♣ 4

5. ♠ KQJ95
   ♥ —
   ♦ 62
   ♣ AQJ1064

6. ♠ AJ5
   ♥ AKQ1093
   ♦ K6
   ♣ 84

7. ♠ 64
   ♥ —
   ♦ AQJ62
   ♣ KQ10985

8. ♠ AK92
   ♥ 8
   ♦ 62
   ♣ QJ10754

9. ♠ 8
   ♥ 62
   ♦ KJ1082
   ♣ QJ975

10. ♠ 87542
    ♥ A6
    ♦ KQJ105
    ♣ 3

11. ♠ K2
    ♥ AKJ10
    ♦ Q10753
    ♣ 92

12. ♠ KQ76
    ♥ 7
    ♦ QJ10754
    ♣ 85

13. ♠ 6
    ♥ 72
    ♦ AKJ1073
    ♣ AQ104

14. ♠ AQJ3
    ♥ Q10975
    ♦ 62
    ♣ K3

15. ♠ AKQ1093
    ♥ K6
    ♦ AJ5
    ♣ 84

16. ♠ AJ103
    ♥ 4
    ♦ K10987
    ♣ AQ3

Your left hand opponent has opened one club, partner has passed, and right hand opponent has bid one spade. You have passed and opener has rebid one notrump, followed by two passes. What action do you take?

17. ♠ AQ1054
    ♥ 63
    ♦ KQ10
    ♣ K62

18. ♠ J10
    ♥ QJ102
    ♦ AK103
    ♣ 932

19. ♠ 762
    ♥ Q10854
    ♦ K2
    ♣ AJ3

20. ♠ KQ93
    ♥ A42
    ♦ 632
    ♣ A105

The auction has been one spade on your left, double by partner, and a raise to two spades on your right. What action do you take?

21. ♠ 63
    ♥ 954
    ♦ KJ95
    ♣ A1087

22. ♠ 63
    ♥ KJ95
    ♦ 954
    ♣ A1087

23. ♠ 63
    ♥ AQ105
    ♦ 954
    ♣ A1087

24. ♠ 6
    ♥ 854
    ♦ 632
    ♣ KJ10942

Your left hand opponent has opened two hearts, your partner has doubled, and right hand opponent has raised to three hearts. What action do you take?

25. ♠ K1084
    ♥ 65
    ♦ K862
    ♣ A32

26. ♠ QJ84
    ♥ 65
    ♦ K862
    ♣ Q74

Your left hand opponent has opened one club, partner has overcalled one spade, and right hand opponent has made a **negative double**. What action do you take?

27. ♠ J94
    ♥ 86
    ♦ A10542
    ♣ K65

28. ♠ A93
    ♥ 86
    ♦ J10542
    ♣ K65

Answers

1. If the opening bid is one club, overcall one heart. You have a chunky suit and length in the suit bid at your right. If the opening bid is one diamond, jump to two hearts to show hearts and clubs with longer/stronger clubs. If the opening bid is one heart, overcall two clubs. If the opening bid is one spade, make a **Top and Bottom Cue Bid**. If the opening bid is one notrump, playing **Hamilton**, bid two hearts to show hearts and a minor. Playing **Hello**, bid two clubs and after partner bids two diamonds as requested, bid two hearts to show hearts and a minor. If the opening bid is a forcing club, playing **Mathe**, you have no systemic device—a two club overcall seems best. Playing **CRASH**, you can bid one notrump to show two suits of the same shape.

2. If the opening bid is one club, make a conventional jump overcall of two diamonds to show diamonds and hearts with longer/stronger diamonds. If the opening bid is one diamond, overcall one heart. If the opening bid is one heart, overcall two diamonds. If the opening bid is one spade, make a type four takeout double—if partner bids clubs, make an "equal level correction" to diamonds. If the opening bid is one notrump and you are playing **Hamilton**, bid two hearts. If you are playing **Hello**, bid two clubs and correct two diamonds to two hearts. If the opening bid is a forcing club, playing **Mathe**, overcall one diamond. Playing **CRASH**, double to show two suits of the same color.

3. If the opening bid is one club, make a **Top and Bottom Cue Bid**. If the opening bid is one diamond, overcall one spade. If the opening bid is one heart, make a type four takeout double—if partner bids clubs, make an "equal level correction" to diamonds. If the opening bid is one spade, overcall two diamonds. If the opening bid is one notrump, playing **Hamilton**, overcall two spades to show spades and a minor. Playing **Hello**, bid two clubs and correct two diamonds to two spades. If the opening bid is a forcing club, playing **Mathe**, you take your best guess, but do bid. Playing **CRASH**, bid one notrump to show two suits of the same shape.

4. If the opening bid is either one club or one diamond, you cannot use **Michaels** since you have agreed to play **Top and Bottom Cue Bids**. However, you can make a type four takeout double and if partner bids the unbid minor make an "equal level correction" to hearts. If the opening bid is one heart, overcall one spade. If the opening bid is one spade, pass. Your heart suit is not good enough for a two level overcall. If the opening bid is one notrump, playing **Hamilton**, bid two diamonds to show both majors. Playing **Hello**, bid two hearts to show both majors. If the opening bid is a forcing club, playing **Mathe**, double to show the majors. Playing **CRASH**, bid one spade to show two suits of the same rank.

5. If the opening bid is one club, overcall one spade. If the opening bid is either one

diamond or one heart, make a **Top and Bottom Cue Bid**. If advancer bids clubs as expected, volunteer two spades to show your wonderful hand. If the opening bid is one spade, overcall two clubs. If the opening bid is one notrump, playing **Hamilton**, overcall two spades to show spades and a minor. Playing **Hello**, bid two notrump to show clubs, then continue to three spades. If the opening bid is a forcing club, playing **Mathe**, start by bidding two clubs and plan to bid spades at your next turn. Playing **CRASH**, start with double to show two suits of the same color.

6. If the opening bid is one club, one diamond, or one spade, double planning to bid hearts next. If you double one minor and advancer bids the other, you will need to jump to three hearts since a bid of two hearts would be "equal level correction." If the opening bid is one notrump, you are happy that you can make a penalty double. If they open a forcing club, overcall one heart playing **Mathe** or bid one diamond to show hearts playing **CRASH**.

7. If the opening bid is one club, overcall one diamond and plan to bid clubs later. If the opening is one diamond, overcall two clubs. If the opening bid is in a major suit, you have a choice. You can overcall diamonds and bid clubs later, risking a **false preference** to diamonds, or you can overcall two clubs and plan to bid notrump at your next turn to show that you also hold diamonds. If the opening bid is one notrump, bid two notrump to show both minors unless playing **Hello**—bid three clubs to show both minors then. If the opening bid is a forcing club, playing **Mathe**, bid one notrump to show both minors. Playing **CRASH**, bid one spade to show two suits of the same rank.

8. If the opening bid is one club, overcall one spade. If the opening bid is either one diamond or one heart, make a **Top and Bottom Cue Bid**. If the opening bid is one spade, overcall two clubs. If the opening bid is one notrump, playing **Hamilton**, overcall two spades showing spades and a minor. Playing **Hello**, bid two clubs and correct two diamonds to two spades to show spades and a minor. If the opening bid is a forcing club, playing **Mathe**, a two club overcall is probably best. Playing **CRASH**, double to show two suits of the same color.

9. If the opening bid is one club, overcall one diamond as a lead director. If the opening bid is one diamond, pass. If the opening bid is one of a major suit, bid two notrump unless the vulnerability is unfavorable. If the opening bid is one notrump, playing **Hamilton**, bid two notrump or playing **Hello**, bid three clubs if the situation calls for a risky action. If the opening bid is a forcing club, playing **Mathe**, bid one notrump. Playing **CRASH**, bid one spade to show two suits of the same rank.

10. If the opening bid is one club, make a **Top and Bottom Cue Bid**. If the opening bid is one diamond an overcall in spades is risky and does not help partner with a lead. However, when partner fits spades finding that fit will produce a good situation. If

the opening bid is one heart, make a type four takeout double. If the opening bid is one spade, overcall two diamonds. If the opening bid is one notrump, playing **Hamilton**, bid two spades to show spades and a minor. Playing **Hello**, bid two clubs and correct two diamonds to two spades. If the opening bid is a forcing club, playing **Mathe**, overcall one diamond. Playing **CRASH**, bid one notrump to show two suits of the same shape

11. If the opening bid is one club, jump to two diamonds to show diamonds and hearts. If the opening bid is one diamond, overcall one heart. If the opening bid is one heart, pass. If the opening bid is one spade, make a type four takeout double. If the opening bid is one notrump, playing **Hamilton**, bid two hearts. Playing **Hello**, bid two clubs and correct two diamonds to two hearts. If the opening bid is a forcing club, playing **Mathe**, make your best guess, but do not pass. Playing **CRASH**, double to show two suits of the same color.

12. If the opening bid is one club, make a **Top and Bottom Cue Bid** if partner has passed, but otherwise pass. If the opening bid is one diamond, a spade overcall is possible but risky. If the opening bid is one heart or one spade, pass. If the opening bid is one notrump, it is reasonable to show diamonds unless the vulnerability is bad, but your hand is not good enough to show both suits. If the opening bid is a forcing club, do something to get in their way. Playing **Mathe**, you could overcall one diamond but that does not take away much space. Playing **CRASH**, you can bid one notrump to show two suits of the same shape, but only if the vulnerability is right.

13. If the opening bid is one club, overcall one diamond. If the opening bid is one diamond, pass, but bid diamonds at your next turn. If the opening bid is one of a major suit, overcall two diamonds. Plan to bid notrump at your next turn to show both minors with a discrepancy between them. If the opening bid is one notrump, bid two clubs to show diamonds. If the opening bid is a forcing club, playing **Mathe**, overcall in diamonds. Playing **CRASH**, bid three clubs to transfer to diamonds.

14. If the opening bid is one club or one diamond, make a type four takeout double. If the opening bid is one heart, overcall one spade. If the opening bid is one spade, pass. If the opening bid is one notrump, it is reasonable to show both majors. Playing **Hamilton**, bid two diamonds; playing **Hello**, bid two hearts. If the opening bid is a forcing club, playing **Mathe**, double. Playing **CRASH**, bid one spade to show two suits of the same rank.

15. If the opening bid is one club, one diamond, or one heart, start with double. You intend to bid spades at your next turn. If the opening bid is in a minor suit and advancer bids the other minor, two spades will be enough. Spades is not the "equal level correction" suit, so this type two double will be understood. If the opening bid

is one notrump, double for penalty. If the opening bid is a forcing club, bid or show spades.

16. If the opening bid is one club, make a **Top and Bottom Cue Bid**. If the opening bid is one diamond, overcall one spade. If the opening bid is one heart, make a type one takeout double. If the opening bid is one spade, pass. If the opening bid is one notrump, it is reasonable to show diamonds and spades. If the opening bid is a forcing club, playing **Mathe**, you have no good call. Playing **CRASH**, it is reasonable to show diamonds and spades.

17. Double. You did not bid spades because they beat you to them. You believe that a spade lead would beat one notrump, and that is what your double asks for.

18. Two clubs. A takeout for the unbid suits. You were almost good enough to double at your first turn, but it is clear now to ask partner to bid a red suit.

19. Two hearts. Your suit was not good enough for an overcall, but now you know that your side has values and you do not want to sell out.

20. Double if you need a swing. You do have well placed spades, but they may have enough tricks

21. Double. Ask partner to bid a minor suit.

22. Double. After partner bids a minor suit, you will correct to hearts. Partner will know that you do not have game invitational values.

23. Three hearts. You have enough values to bid hearts directly this time.

24. Two notrump. This asks partner to bid three clubs. An early look at Chapter Eleven.

25. Three spades at matchpoints, four spades at IMPs. You like your hand for this auction.

26. Double. Assuming that your agreement is that this double is **responsive**. If that is not your agreement, you will need to bid three spades but not like it a lot.

27. Two spades. Raise partner whenever you can.

28. Redouble. It is more important to tell partner that you have a high honor than to raise at once.

CHAPTER ELEVEN
When They Intrude

Synopsis: Thus far in Chapter Eleven you have learned how to defend against overcalls by bidding at the one level, raising partner simply, pre-emptively, or by making a cue bid, making free bids, and using **action doubles** and the **negative double**, how to defend against an overcall in notrump and against the **unusual notrump**, how to defend against takeout doubles and when to redouble, and how to defend against **Michaels**.

As Chapter Eleven continues you will learn how to compete by using **The Law of Total Tricks**, all about Lebensohl, doubles to combat intrusion, and how competition affects **Hardy Raises**.

Sometimes the opponents have entered into our auction. Sometimes we have entered theirs. What we most need to know is simply how far can we safely compete? There is a guide. It is known as **The Law of Total Tricks**. In 1992 Larry Cohen brought this concept to the attention of American bidders with his great book, *To Bid or Not to Bid*. This swept through the world of bridge and helped many to understand when it is right to compete, and when not.

In 1978 a wonderful collection of cameos by expert contributors was published under the title *Expert Bridge*. Marty Bergen was one of those contributors. His article was titled "The Law of Total Tricks—The Key to Competitive Bidding." With permission from both Marty and the Publisher of that book, here is that ground-breaking presentation which did not get nearly the attention that it should have been given then. Thank you, Marty Bergen.

THE LAW OF TOTAL TRICKS—
THE KEY TO COMPETITIVE BIDDING
By Marty Bergen

One of the first things that a rubber bridge player notices during his initial duplicate session is the extremely competitive nature of the auctions. Everyone bids aggressively, trying to make life difficult for their opponents. And, indeed, the most difficult bidding problems are the ones that arise in competitive auctions. We have all been confronted many times with the classic decision after:

NORTH	EAST	SOUTH	WEST
1♠	2♥	2♠	3♥
Pass	Pass	?	

Is it right to bid? Pass? Double? Most players rely on their judgment in these situations; this may work well for the expert but usually results in a guessing game for those of more modest talents.

Is there a scientific way for the average player to improve his "guessing" on these competitive hands? In the late 1960's a Frenchman named Jean-Rene Vernes proposed a rule to accomplish this end. He called it **The Law of Total Tricks**. Vernes wrote an article about it which appeared in the June, 1969 issue of *The Bridge World*.

This is Vernes' law: "THE NUMBER OF TOTAL TRICKS IN A HAND IS APPROXIMATELY EQUAL TO THE TOTAL NUMBER OF TRUMPS HELD BY BOTH SIDES, EACH IN THEIR RESPECTIVE SUIT."

Once this total number of tricks is determined, it is possible to use this number to take effective competitive action, i.e., whether to pass or what level to bid to. The result is that the determining factor in competitive bidding now becomes the total trump length of the opposing sides. And this outweighs the other factors to be taken into account such as distribution, high cards, and trump strength.

For the law to work it is necessary for certain criteria to be met. What follows is an explanation of WHY and HOW **The Law of Total Tricks** operates. Here is a hand from actual play, where the strength was fairly equally divided and the bidding was keenly contested:

Dealer South
Neither vulnerable

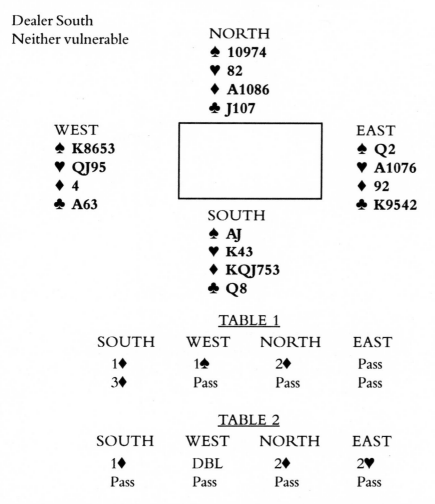

NORTH
♠ 10974
♥ 82
♦ A1086
♣ J107

WEST
♠ K8653
♥ QJ95
♦ 4
♣ A63

EAST
♠ Q2
♥ A1076
♦ 92
♣ K9542

SOUTH
♠ AJ
♥ K43
♦ KQJ753
♣ Q8

TABLE 1

SOUTH	WEST	NORTH	EAST
1♦	1♠	2♦	Pass
3♦	Pass	Pass	Pass

TABLE 2

SOUTH	WEST	NORTH	EAST
1♦	DBL	2♦	2♥
Pass	Pass	Pass	Pass

North-South made nine tricks in comfort in diamonds at the first table, and their teammates easily made three hearts at table two. The aggressive bidding paid off to the tune of six IMPs.

Let us consider how **The Law of Total Tricks,** as stated, applies. What is the total number of tricks that can be made by both sides combined, each playing in its best trump suit? In this deal it is 18....nine for North-South in diamonds and nine for East-West in hearts. For this hand Vernes' law holds true: The number of total tricks in the hand is equal to the total number of trumps held by both sides. North-South have ten diamonds, East-West have eight hearts for a total of 18.

Here is another illustration, taken from the 1956 World Championship:

Dealer East
Both vulnerable

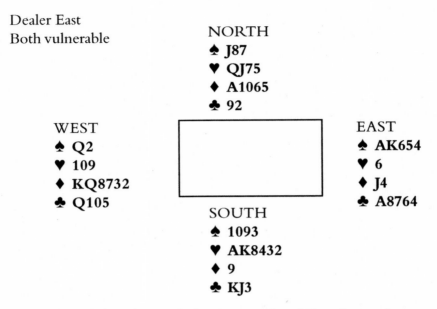

NORTH
♠ J87
♥ QJ75
♦ A1065
♣ 92

WEST
♠ Q2
♥ 109
♦ KQ8732
♣ Q105

EAST
♠ AK654
♥ 6
♦ J4
♣ A8764

SOUTH
♠ 1093
♥ AK8432
♦ 9
♣ KJ3

In one room, North–South for France played four hearts down one, losing three spades and a club. In the other room their East–West pair was allowed to play in four diamonds and were also down one, losing two trumps, a club and a heart. Once again you can see that the number of total tricks is 18 (nine tricks for North–South in hearts and nine tricks for East–West in diamonds), the same as the total number of trumps (East–West have eight diamonds, North–South have ten hearts).

Although **The Law of Total Tricks** may seem surprising at first, an analysis of the two hands will show why it works. In the first example given, North–South could not know which opponent had the ace of hearts. Had it been with West, South would have made one trick fewer. However, East would then be able to take one trick more playing in hearts. Therefore, although the number of tricks made by one declarer may vary according to the location of a key card, the total number of tricks on each hand is not dependent on finesses.

In the second hand, West was unlucky to find diamonds splitting four–one against him. If South held one of North's diamonds, and North one of South's clubs, East–West would probably have made another trick playing in diamonds. But then South in his four heart contract would have had to lose a diamond trick and would have made one trick less. Once again the number of total tricks is constant.

How accurate is the law? Vernes did a study based on ten years of World Championships which showed that the law was exactly right in one-third of the deals, and within one trick on 80% of all of them. In the years since I read about **The Law of Total Tricks**, I have used it for my competitive decisions, and have also found it to be extremely accurate. Most hands either conform exactly to the law or are off by only one trick. The number of hands where the law is off by two or more tricks is very small.

Although this law is very accurate, yet very simple, there are some factors which can cause a slight adjustment in the law. This is analogous to the factors of hand evaluation which cause good players to adjust their point-count totals.

The most important factor is the existence of a double fit. If both sides have eight or more cards in each of two suits, the number of total tricks on a hand will usually be one greater than the number of trumps. The second factor, although a less crucial one, is the possession or absence of trump honors. If all the trump honors are owned by one side, the number of total tricks will be higher than the number of trumps. Therefore, beware of bidding too high with queens or jacks in the opponents' trump suit.

Factors which cause you to bid one more are extra trump length, existence of a double fit, or possession of trump honors, in that order. On the other hand, you should tend to stop bidding when you have a minimum number of trumps, or no strong side suit, or if your trump suit is missing honors. (Notice the relative unimportance of high cards.)

Now back to our original auction of:

NORTH	EAST	SOUTH	WEST
1♠	2♥	2♠	3♥
Pass	Pass	?	

The time to bid three spades is when you and your opponents have a total of 18 trumps in your respective suits, since it is then likely that each side can make a three level contract. On the other hand, with 16 trumps, it is wrong to bid three spades; even if you can make your bid they are going down two, and the most likely case is that each side is down one. Since you will show a small profit in the long run when the total is 17, this becomes the minimum number needed to outbid the opponents at the three level. A bid at this level is not crucial, however, since normally one (but not both) contract will make.

Unfortunately it is not always easy to figure out how many trumps the opponents have, but there are some assumptions and inferences that can be made. A takeout double of one major usually shows four of the other major. A weak jump overcall or weak two bid shows a six card suit. An opening bid in a major shows a minimum of four or five cards, depending on system. A three level preemptive opening bid shows seven while an overcall shows a minimum of five cards in the bid suit. You certainly should be able to tell how many trumps your side has, even if you are unable to be absolutely certain about the opponents. Fortunately, this is usually sufficient information to enable **The Law of Total Tricks** to be applied with almost complete accuracy.

Now let us consider our original sequence,

NORTH	EAST	SOUTH	WEST
1♠	2♥	2♠	3♥
Pass	Pass	?	

one more time. North is presumed to have five spades for his opening bid, since even four card majorites are very unlikely to open one spade on four when they do not have heart length. If South has four spades, he can be pretty certain that his partnership must have nine. Since East-West must have a minimum of eight hearts, there are at least 17 tricks on the hand, so a bid of three spades is likely to show a profit, and at worst will break even.

The situation changes drastically, though, when South has only three trumps. Now the partnership is presumed to have only eight trumps. If East-West have only eight as well, a bid of three spades will probably change a plus score into a minus.

After you examine several of the competitive bidding problems at various levels, you would find that there is a simple, practical rule that can be applied to each individual case. In fact, this rule is so important that I believe that everyone who calls himself a bridge player must know and understand it: "YOU ARE SAFE IN CONTRACTING FOR AS MANY TRICKS AS YOUR SIDE HOLDS TRUMPS." Therefore, with eight trumps you can bid with virtually no danger to the two-level, with nine trumps to the three-level, with ten to the four-level, etc. In each case you are likely to make your bid or enjoy a cheap sacrifice against the opponents' contract.

This rule is extremely accurate for competitive bidding up to the small slam level, with only one exception: It usually pays to compete to the three level in a lower ranking suit when holding only eight trumps. This is obviously good bridge and also comes under the heading of balancing. If the opponents are about to make two spades, it is wise to bid three diamonds, even though you don't expect to make nine tricks, with the hope of pushing the opponents one level too high.

Application of the trump rule thus becomes the determining factor in competitive decisions. OF COURSE, THE HIGH CARD POINTS MUST BE FAIRLY EVENLY DISTRIBUTED, USUALLY NO GREATER THAN 17-23. Vulnerability is, as always, a consideration—you must be careful before venturing to the four or five level when vulnerable.

Since the key to applying this practical rule is knowledge of how many trumps your side possesses, it is easiest to use **The Law of Total Tricks** after partner makes a preemptive bid. However, you must not use that as a rationalization for not employing **The Law of Total Tricks** on every competitive hand, merely because you are not sure about the number of trumps held by partner. In addition, I can tell you from experience that you will be able to work out the number of trumps held both by partner and the opponents on many more hands than you think possible.

You will be able to make many discoveries and observations by becoming a student of **The Law of Total Tricks**. Here's one of them: You should practically never sacrifice with only eight trumps. Without sufficient trumps, there just won't be enough tricks in the hand. The only exception, of course, is when there is a big double fit or your suit is lower than theirs and you are pushing them to the three level.

Although you may not be aware of it, one of the most popular modern treatments, the preemptive jump raise of an overcall, is based on **The Law of Total Tricks**. After:

NORTH	EAST	SOUTH	WEST
1♥	1♠	2♣	?

most good players would bid three spades on ♠KJ106 ♥75 ♦J9764 ♣52 even if vulnerable, showing four trumps and a weak hand. Partner will then be well placed to judge whether to sacrifice. Since **The Law of Total Tricks** tells you that your side should compete to the three level with nine trumps (remember, partner has at least five for his overcall), and it clearly puts more pressure on the opponents if you bid the inevitable three spades immediately, I strongly recommend this treatment to all tournament players: you aren't giving up anything since you can cue bid if you hold a better hand.

To summarize:

Total Trumps	Appropriate Action
16	Compete to the two level. Compete to the three level **only** when your suit is lower than your opponents.
17	Compete to the three level (if your opponents bid a higher ranking suit at the three level, pass).
18	Compete to the three level. Usually compete to the four level when your suit is lower than your opponents'.

FACTORS TO CONSIDER WHEN MAKING A CLOSE DECISION

Plus Factors—   1. High cards in your trump suit
2. A double fit

Minus Factors—   1. Queens and jacks in opponents' suit
2. Unfavorable vulnerability

All of the following hands are taken from actual play; some occurred in World Championships. Notice in how many situations **The Law of Total Tricks** aids in competitive decisions. YOU ARE SOUTH IN ALL CASES.

1. Neither side vulnerable, IMPs: ♠J107532 ♥A ♦10643 ♣A5

SOUTH	WEST	NORTH	EAST
—	—	—	1♦
1♠	DBL	2♠	4♥

At first it seems right to save, which is what was done at the table. However, partner can only be counted on for three trumps; he is unlikely to have four since he didn't make a weak jump raise. In addition to the fact that your side is unlikely to have ten trumps, consider how many trumps the opponents have. The four heart bidder probably has only four, five would be most unlikely. The negative doubler is also likely to have four. Therefore the most likely number of total tricks is 17, nine for you, eight for them. This means that if they can make four hearts, you will go down three. Even if there is an 18th trump around, you might go down two versus their game, certainly no bargain. And you might find that both four hearts and four spades would go down. Therefore, PASS.

2. Both vulnerable, IMPs: ♠K64 ♥8 ♦AJ753 ♣AJ72

SOUTH	WEST	NORTH	EAST
1♦	1♥	1♠★	4♥

★ shows five spades

Again four spades was bid at the table, and again it was wrong. Since your side can only be guaranteed to hold eight spades in this competitive auction, you shouldn't bid four spades. Partner has two or three hearts, so there are "only" 17 or 18 tricks in the hand. At best you would be taking a 500 point loss. At worst (which actually happened on this hand) you go down 500 when the opponents were about to be set. Remember, partner is still there. Partner's actual hand was: ♠J10875 ♥K74 ♦Q8 ♣Q83.

3. Neither vulnerable, Match Points: ♠8765 ♥K43 ♦Q7643 ♣8

SOUTH	WEST	NORTH	EAST
—	—	1♦	DBL
2♦	3♣	3♦	4♣
?			

You might have bid a preemptive three diamonds on the round before, announcing five trumps and very little defense. Partner's bid of three diamonds should show five trumps since he can only count on you for four trumps after your two diamond bid, and he chose to compete on the three level after the opponents were already there. Therefore you are entitled to compete to the four level since your side should have ten trumps.

4. Neither vulnerable, IMPs: ♠K732 ♥QJ ♦Q109 ♣A864

SOUTH	WEST	NORTH	EAST
—	—	2♥	3♣
?			

Partner has six hearts and is more likely to have two clubs than any other number (since he has six hearts, he has a total of seven cards in the other three suits, an average of 2 1/3 for each). Therefore we probably have fifteen trumps. Even if we add one to this total because each side is likely to have all the minor honors in its respective trump suit, we only get a total of sixteen. Therefore a pass is indicated.

5. Both vulnerable, IMPs: ♠KQ ♥A8764 ♦A53 ♣Q74

SOUTH	WEST	NORTH	EAST
—	—	1♦	1♠
2♥	Pass	3♦	Pass
3NT	DBL	4♥	4♠
?			

What started off as a nice tame auction has suddenly taken several unexpected turns. Partner has gone out of his way to emphasize the length and strength of his diamonds, since he obviously has the three hearts needed to raise that suit on the previous round. We can therefore place him with six-three or seven-three in the red suits. It now becomes apparent that this is a big double-fit hand, where we have nine or ten diamonds and they must have nine or ten spades despite West's failure to raise that suit earlier. The doubler must have been playing a waiting game with a heart stack. If we add one to the number of trumps for the double fit, we get a grand total of about twenty. It now becomes clear that double is out of the question, since even if we defeat four spades, we should make eleven tricks in diamonds: since partner can't have too much strength in hearts and spades, he must have a club honor to justify his opening bid. The diamonds are likely to run, based on partner's three diamond bid and your holding. Therefore you should bid four notrump. Partner's actual hand was: ♠86 ♥K53 ♦KQ109862 ♣A. In four spades the opposition would take nine or ten tricks.

6. Neither vulnerable, IMPs: ♠10752 ♥A87 ♦K843 ♣J6

SOUTH	WEST	NORTH	EAST
—	1♠	2NT	4♠
?			

Partner's two notrump call showed both minor suits. Descriptive calls like Michaels or the unusual notrump are very helpful to those using **The Law of Total Tricks** since there is now precise information available about suit length as well as possible double fits. Since partner is presumed to have five-five in the minors, we can calculate the total trumps as 17 or 18 (nine for us, eight or nine for them). Once again it is right to pass, since a save would probably go for −500 or −800 if they can make ten tricks. (And if they can't you are due for a plus score.)

7. Vul vs not, IMPs: ♠86 ♥Q874 ♦K1073 ♣942

SOUTH	WEST	NORTH	EAST
—	—	1♥	1♠
2♥	2♠	Pass	Pass
?			

This should be easy. Whether you play four or five card majors, you want to push the opponents up to the three level. You shouldn't worry about the vulnerability or the weakness of your hand; it should go against your "bridge sense" to sell out here. Even if partner has four hearts, there must be 16 trumps, so they are cold for two spades; you mustn't allow them to play there.

8. Not vul vs vul, Match Points: ♠Q873 ♥5 ♦Q1084 ♣10432

SOUTH	WEST	NORTH	EAST
—	1♥	1♠	2♣
?			

It seems likely that the opponents will bid four hearts and your side will sacrifice, but there is no reason to mastermind. Simply bid three spades, telling partner about your hand, and leave the decision to him. He is, after all, the one who knows the heart situation. When partner doubles, you can pass with confidence, having shown no defense. In the actual hand partner held: ♠AJ1064 ♥AQ106 ♦5 ♣K85 and collected 500 points.

9. Neither vulnerable, IMPs: ♠K654 ♥532 ♦K7 ♣K764

SOUTH	WEST	NORTH	EAST
Pass	Pass	1♦	Pass
1♠	Pass	2♣	Pass
Pass	3♣	Pass	Pass
?			

You assume that partner has four spades, and therefore you should not bid higher with only eight spades. You also know that partner has a full opening bid; otherwise he would have passed your one spade. Most players would pass at IMPs, although they might double at match points. However, if partner can sit for the double, which he should do unless holding a singleton club, you should have a nice plus score. If there are indeed 15 trumps (your side holding eight spades and your opponents seven clubs), it would be quite amazing if they made their contract. That would indicate that your side could only take six tricks in spades, which you don't believe. At the table a double produced a 500 point penalty with partner merely holding: ♠QJ83 ♥AJ10 ♦10863 ♣A10.

10. Both sides vulnerable, IMPs: ♠8763 ♥Q104 ♦A43 ♣Q83

SOUTH	WEST	NORTH	EAST
—	—	1♠	2♥
2♠	3♥	Pass	Pass
?			

You should pass, despite the four trumps. You have nothing to ruff, nor is there any chance of a double fit. Your side is likely to be missing honors in the trumps suit, and you know that the opponents are missing some of theirs. It wouldn't be surprising to discover that both three hearts and three spades are down one. (This hand is an exception, for the reasons stated, to the general rule.)

11. Neither vulnerable, Match Points: ♠98 ♥J10764 ♦Q74 ♣A54

SOUTH	WEST	NORTH	EAST
—	1♦	1♥	1♠
?			

Normally you would bid to the four-level with ten trumps (partner has five for his overcall). However, with no singleton or void, and with a minor honor in the diamond suit, three hearts is enough. You don't need much to bid to the two or three level, but opponents don't need much to double at the four or five level.

12. Both vulnerable, IMPs: ♠A654 ♥8 ♦KJ1075 ♣984

SOUTH	WEST	NORTH	EAST
—	1♥	4♣	4♥
?			

Partner should have seven or eight clubs; the opponents probably have ten hearts. With 20 trumps in the hand the five club save must be a good one.

The bridge expert has long appreciated the value of extra trumps. He bids four hearts over one heart with: ♠953 ♥Q8752 ♦KJ62 ♣8, and three hearts (a limit raise) over one heart with: ♠85 ♥KQ72 ♦K10964 ♣92, not at all concerned if either of these contracts should fail, since he can console himself with the knowledge that the opponents could have made something. Now you too can exhibit expert judgment in competitive auctions by applying **The Law of Total Tricks**.

Although **The Law of Total Tricks** did not catch the eye of the tournament world until 1992, it has been around far longer. We thank Marty Bergen for allowing this reprint of his presentation which was made fourteen years earlier.

Lebensohl

The convention known as **Lebensohl** is one of the most powerful in modern bidding. It uses a bid of two notrump artificially as a relay to three clubs. This relay allows for the different description of many hand types. It appears in many different auctions. We have already seen this relay in action in several auctions.

We have learned to use the two notrump response to an opening bid of one notrump as a relay to three clubs. In this context responder is able to escape holding a weak hand with long clubs, or the auction may continue to allow responder to show a three suited hand with interest in slam.

We have learned that responder can use the two notrump relay after opener has **reversed** to slow down the auction and describe several hand types. The two notrump relay in this instance is a request rather than a command. When responder's rebid after the **reverse** is two notrump, opener is asked to bid three clubs, but not required. When opener holds values enough for game facing a minimum response, opener will not comply, for responder might pass three clubs and a game might be missed. Also, when a diamond opening bidder holds a wonderful diamond suit and nothing in clubs, opener will bid three diamonds instead of three clubs. It would be wrong to bid three clubs and play there when a diamond contract is far more desirable.

What follows are various other uses of the two notrump relay. Some of them might have been in the previous chapter since they are generated by the side that intrudes into the auction. They are all presented here rather than scattered.

Lebensohl After Interference Over an Opening One Notrump Bid _____

The primary situation for use of this relay is as a defense against intrusion after our side has opened one notrump. Sometimes the intrusion does not disturb our normal auction, but when it does a systemic procedure is necessary.

When the intrusion is double, the normal notrump response structure is not impeded. Two clubs can still be used as **Stayman**, and transfers and other calls are intact. When the intrusion is two clubs, if that call is artificial, double becomes **Stayman** and the system again remains intact. **Lebensohl** applies whenever the interference is a natural call of two clubs, or any other two level call whether natural or artificial.

The two notrump relay is used for one of three purposes:

1. To distinguish among forcing, non-forcing and invitational auctions.
2. To affirm or deny stoppers in the opponents' suit(s) when bidding game in notrump.
3. To affirm or deny stoppers in the opponents' suit(s) when using **Stayman**.

Assume that partner has opened one notrump and there has been a natural overcall of two clubs, or any other suit at the two level whether natural or artificial. If the interference is two spades, no action by responder at the two level is possible. When the interference is something less than two spades, responder may introduce a suit at the two level. When responder does bid a suit at the two level, it is natural and non-forcing.

If responder bids a suit at the three level, it will sometimes be a jump but will often not be a jump. If the suit bid at the three level is a major suit, the call is natural and forcing, promising a five card suit.

Responder's suit will not be longer than five, for with six or more and good values, responder would have used a **Texas Transfer**. Opener is asked to raise responder's major to game holding three or more card support, or to bid three notrump holding a doubleton in responder's major.

If the three level call is in a minor suit, it will usually not be a jump. The meaning varies based upon partnership agreement. Some partnerships play that it is natural and forcing; others play that it is natural and invitational to game.

The only reason for such a call to be forcing is that responder feels the possibility of slam in the minor exists. Although such hands will occur, the frequency with which responder will wish to seek a slam in a minor suit is not at all great.

Much more frequently responder will hold a reasonably good suit and wish to invite game in notrump. In fact, that is the function of the bid of three of a minor suit in response to one notrump when there has been no interference. The minor shown is six or seven cards long and headed by the ace-queen or the king-queen (ace-king is too good).

When opener holds no unstopped suit and a fit for the minor, three notrump becomes a good contract. When opener has a poor fit for the minor suit or a wide open suit, the invitation is declined and the minor suit part score contract is played.

Our preference is clearly for the use of the bid of a minor suit at the three level to be invitational rather than forcing, simply because of frequency. We suggest that your partnership make its own determination.

In order to compete and make a non–forcing call at the three level, responder uses the two notrump relay. When responder relays, then bids a suit at the three level, it is natural and non–forcing.

In some auctions a new suit can be introduced in any of three ways:

1. At the two level.
2. At the three level with or without a jump.
3. At the three level after the relay.

When all three auctions are possible, the jump to the three level is natural and forcing. In those auctions when the relay is used and the suit is then introduced at the three level, the auction is invitational.

Example 111)

	a)	♠ KJ853	b)	♠ KJ853
		♥ J4		♥ 74
		♦ AJ6		♦ KJ6
		♣ 1083		♣ 1083

	c)	♠ KJ853	d)	♠ 7
		♥ 74		♥ KJ853
		♦ J65		♦ K654
		♣ 1083		♣ 1083

	e)	♠ J62	f)	♠ 6
		♥ K4		♥ 932
		♦ 5		♦ AQ9853
		♣ AKJ9853		♣ 1083

Example 111) hands are responders to the opening bid of one notrump after an interfering bid at the two level.

Example 111a) jumps to three spades. This is forcing, showing a five card suit. Partner is asked to raise holding three or four spades, or bid three notrump with a spade doubleton.

Example 111b) bids two notrump to relay to three clubs, then bids three spades. This auction is invitational. Opener may bid four spades or three notrump with a maximum or may pass three spades.

Example 111c) bids two spades. This is natural and non-forcing. Opener is asked to pass.

If the interference is a call of two spades, Example 111d) has the choice of bidding three hearts which is forcing, or bidding two notrump to relay to three clubs, then three hearts which is not forcing. No invitational auction is available. If the interference is in a lower ranking suit, Example 111d) can bid two notrump to relay to three clubs, then bid three hearts. This auction is invitational to game. Opener can bid four hearts, three notrump, or pass.

Example 111e) would like to invite a slam in clubs. When the partnership agreement is that three clubs is forcing, this hand can make that call. If the partnership agreement is that three clubs is game invitational, this hand must find some other slam invitation.

Example 111f) wants to invite game in notrump and show a source of tricks in diamonds. When the partnership agreement is that after interference a bid of three in a minor suit is invitational, rather than forcing, responder can still bid three diamonds to show this hand. If the agreement is that three diamonds is forcing, this hand must find some other call.

The second use of the two notrump relay is in auctions in which responder holds the values to bid game in notrump. As game is bid, responder can show or deny stoppers in the suit(s) shown by the interference.

A direct jump to three notrump denies such stoppers. Opener knows not to pass and play three notrump unless holding stoppers. Without stoppers, opener will seek a makeable contract, and will start bidding four card suits up the line at the four level.

Sometimes the interference will be natural, and the stopper needed will be in that suit. Sometimes the interference will be artificial, showing a known suit in which a stopper is needed. Sometimes the interference will show two known suits, but in other instances the interference will show two suits, only one of which is known.

The use of **Lebensohl** revolves around known suits. When two suits are known, responder's jump to three notrump denies stoppers in both known suits. When responder uses the relay, then bids three notrump, a stopper or stoppers in all known suits are promised. Holding a stopper in one of the known suits, responder cue bids that suit. The cue promises a stopper in the suit bid and denies a stopper in the other known suit.

Example 112)

a) ♠ K5
   ♥ QJ3
   ♦ A1074
   ♣ J986

b) ♠ 85
   ♥ QJ3
   ♦ A1074
   ♣ K1098

Example 112) hands are responders after an opening bid of one notrump and an interfering bid by RHO.

Regardless of the suit shown by the interference, Example 112a) holds a stopper. Responder uses the two notrump relay, then bids three notrump to show a stopper in the suit of the intruder.

If the interfering call shows spades, Example 112b) jumps to three notrump to show the values for game but deny a stopper in spades. If the interference shows spades and an unknown second suit, responder's action is the same. If the interference shows both major suits, responder makes a cue bid of two hearts. This promises the values for game and a stopper in hearts, but denies a spade stopper.

The third use of the relay occurs in **Stayman** auctions.

After interference, a cue bid becomes **Stayman**. If the interference is natural, responder bids that suit as **Stayman**. If the interference is artificial showing a known suit, a cue bid of the known suit is **Stayman**. When responder makes this cue bid directly as **Stayman**, a stopper in the suit bid or shown is denied. To show a stopper, responder uses the two notrump relay, then makes the cue bid.

When the interference is a natural call of two clubs, a cue bid of three clubs is **Stayman** without a club stopper. To use **Stayman** and show a club stopper, responder bids two notrump to relay to three clubs. When opener bids three clubs as required, responder continues by bidding three diamonds as **Stayman** with a club stopper.

This cannot be construed as a signoff or an invitation in diamonds. After the natural call of two clubs, responder was able to bid two diamonds naturally to sign off or three diamonds to invite.

Example 113)

	a)		b)	
♠	A84		62	
♥	QJ93		QJ93	
♦	62		A84	
♣	K1062		K1062	

c) ♠ K1062
   ♥ QJ93
   ♦ A84
   ♣ 62

d) ♠ K1062
   ♥ QJ93
   ♦ 62
   ♣ A84

Example 113a) responds to the opening bid of one notrump after an overcall of two spades. This responder bids two notrump to relay to three clubs, then bids three spades as Stayman **showing four hearts and promising a stopper in spades. If the overcall is an artificial bid of two diamonds which promises spades and another suit, responder generates the same auction.**

Example 113b) responds to the opening bid of one notrump after an overcall of two spades. This responder bids three spades which is Stayman **without a spade stopper. If the overcall is an artificial bid of two diamonds which promises spades and another suit, responder bids two spades which again is Stayman without a spade stopper.**

Example 113c) responds to the opening bid of one notrump after an artificial overcall of two clubs. Responder doubles which is Stayman. **If the overcall of two clubs is natural, responder bids three clubs which is Stayman without a club stopper.**

Example 113d) responds to the opening bid of one notrump after the natural overcall of two clubs. Responder bids two notrump to relay to three clubs, then bids three diamonds which is Stayman **promising a club stopper.**

The McCabe Adjunct

When our side makes a weak two bid and there is a takeout double, it is essential to raise the weak two bid whenever possible. The preemptive raise will sometimes keep the advancer from entering the auction. The responder's most effective auction is one in which, holding a fit, he can also help opener make a profitable opening lead if the advancer becomes declarer. The complex known as the **McCabe Adjunct** is designed to facilitate good opening leads.

After the takeout double if responder raises the suit partner has opened, it shows the ace or king of the weak two bidder's suit. Knowledge of this high honor makes the lead of the weak two bid suit very easy. A response in a lower ranking suit at the three level is also lead directing. Opener is asked not to pass, but to return to the suit of the weak two bid. Responder has a holding in the suit bid at the three level that makes a lead of that suit a good idea if opener has a lead problem, and also holds a fit for the weak two bid.

Without a fit for the suit of the weak two bid and the need to escape to a different suit, responder bids two notrump as a relay to three clubs. After opener bids three clubs as requested, responder passes or corrects to the suit that responder wishes to play as the trump suit.

With a fit for the weak two bid but no good lead to indicate, responder again uses the two notrump relay. After opener bids three clubs, responder returns to opener's suit at the three level. Responder denies a good lead to suggest and a high honor in the suit of the weak two bid.

Example 114)

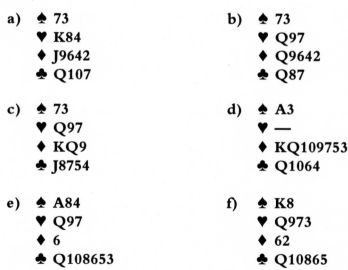

a) ♠ 73
    ♥ K84
    ♦ J9642
    ♣ Q107

b) ♠ 73
    ♥ Q97
    ♦ Q9642
    ♣ Q87

c) ♠ 73
    ♥ Q97
    ♦ KQ9
    ♣ J8754

d) ♠ A3
    ♥ —
    ♦ KQ109753
    ♣ Q1064

e) ♠ A84
    ♥ Q97
    ♦ 6
    ♣ Q108653

f) ♠ K8
    ♥ Q973
    ♦ 62
    ♣ Q10865

All Example 114) hands are responders after the opening bid of two hearts and a takeout double.

Example 114a) raises to three hearts. This extends the auction pre-emptively but also promises that an opening heart lead, even away

from the ace, will be just fine. Responder promises one of the top two honors in hearts.

Example 114b) also wishes to preempt, but cannot bid three hearts without a top honor. This responder bids two notrump to relay to three clubs, then bids three hearts.

Example 114c) bids three diamonds to indicate a good lead if the advancer declares. Opener knows that this shows a heart fit.

Example 114d) needs to escape to diamonds. Because three diamonds is not natural but lead directing, responder bids two notrump to relay to three clubs. When opener bids three clubs responder corrects to diamonds—to play.

Example 114e) occurred in a Regional Knockout. After the double, responder bid three diamonds to ask for a lead in that suit. Playing a four spade contract with a diamond lead, declarer won the first trick cheaply, but responder took the first trump, put partner in with a heart, and got a diamond ruff which turned out to be the setting trick.

Example 114f) should consider all that has been discussed, then should bid four hearts. The Law of Total Tricks makes this a safe action since there should be ten hearts between the two bidders.

Lebensohl After the Double of a Weak Two Bid

When partner has doubled an opening weak two bid, the advancer has little room in which to show or deny values. If advancer bids a higher ranking suit at the two level, it is because the values held are not sufficient for an invitational jump. However, in many auctions, advancer may need to bid a lower ranking suit at the three level. When the doubler has a good hand, further action may be dangerous unless the advancer's values are known. The use of **Lebensohl** solves this problem.

When advancer bids a new suit at the three level in response to the takeout double, the values of about seven to eleven high card points are guaranteed. With more in values the advancer will be able to cue bid, but with less the advancer does not immediately bid at the three level. Instead, advancer bids two notrump, asking the doubler to bid three clubs. When the doubler bids three clubs as requested, the advancer then passes with clubs or corrects to another suit, and values of less than seven high card points have been shown.

The doubler will not always bid three clubs after the two notrump request. Holding a self-sufficient suit, doubler will bid it rather than bid clubs and take the chance that partner will pass.

Example 115)

a) ♠ K983
   ♥ 54
   ♦ J76
   ♣ 10542

b) ♠ KJ83
   ♥ 54
   ♦ A76
   ♣ J1042

c) ♠ J76
   ♥ 54
   ♦ K9853
   ♣ 1052

d) ♠ K93
   ♥ 54
   ♦ KQ983
   ♣ 1052

e) ♠ KJ8
   ♥ A4
   ♦ 10962
   ♣ A875

f) ♠ KJ62
   ♥ 5
   ♦ AQJ964
   ♣ A3

g) ♠ KJ62
   ♥ 54
   ♦ AJ96
   ♣ A103

h) ♠ AK8
   ♥ K4
   ♦ AJ964
   ♣ A103

Example 115a) bids after an opening bid of two hearts by LHO and a takeout double by partner. With meager values, this hand bids two spades.

Example 115b) bids after an opening bid of two hearts by LHO and a takeout double by partner. This hand jumps to three spades to show invitational values.

Example 115c) bids after an opening bid of two hearts by LHO and a takeout double by partner. Not having the values to bid at the three level, this hand bids two notrump to ask partner to bid three clubs. If partner bids as requested, this hand will sign off at three diamonds.

Example 115d) bids after an opening bid of two hearts by LHO and a takeout double by partner. This hand bids three diamonds which promises values in the range of 7 to 11 HCP.

Example 115e) bids after an opening bid of two hearts by LHO and a takeout double by partner. This hand makes a cue bid of three hearts to show excellent values.

Example 115f) has made a takeout double of a two heart opening bid. When partner bids two notrump to request a rebid of three clubs, this hand bids three diamonds. If this hand bids three clubs as requested, partner might pass and an inferior trump suit might result.

Example 115g) has made a takeout double of a two heart opening bid. When partner bids two notrump to request a rebid of three clubs, this hand obliges and makes that call.

Example 115h) has made a takeout double of a two heart opening bid. If partner bids three clubs or three diamonds promising values, this hand bids three notrump. Knowledge of partner's values makes this game a good prospect. If partner's call had not shown values, this hand would not be able to bid on.

The Good-Bad Two Notrump

There are many competitive auctions in which a bid freely made at the three level will leave partner guessing as to values. To solve this problem another form of **Lebensohl** is available. When this usage is agreed, a bid made at the three level shows sound values, while the desire to compete is expressed by the use of the two notrump relay.

There are many possible nuances involved in the use of this agreement. Rather than spend space here repeating information from the authoritative source, we refer the reader to *Better Bidding With Bergen*, volume two, pages 112 to 124. Bergen explains the origin of this method, presents a list of exceptions in which it does not apply, and gives several examples of when and how to apply it, continuations when partner has used it, and continuations when partner has bid at the three level rather than use it.

The Support Double and Redouble

When there has been an opening bid and response, if the opponent next to bid makes an overcall or doubles, opener has an obligation. Finding fits is important in any auction. After the overcall, opener needs to show a fit for responder's suit whenever one exists.

Opener—and only opener—can use a **Support Double** or **Redouble**.

It may be very important for responder to know the nature of opener's fit. When **Support Doubles** and **Redoubles** are available, opener will be able to differentiate between a fit of three cards and a fit of four cards for responder's suit. The four card fit is shown by a direct raise. Opener shows a three card fit by making an artificial double or redouble after the intrusion.

The obligation to show or deny a fit takes precedence over other actions that are available to opener. Opener will wait for a later turn to show another four card suit or rebid the six card or longer suit of the opening bid.

The use of the **Support Double** or **Redouble** applies only in auctions in which it is possible for opener to raise responder's suit to the two level. If a raise to the two level is not possible, a double by opener does not show support—it is a penalty double.

Example 116)

a)   ♠ K84
        ♥ 84
        ♦ AKJ1062
        ♣ J8

b)   ♠ A1076
        ♥ K84
        ♦ 5
        ♣ AJ1052

c) ♠ K4
♥ 62
♦ AJ953
♣ AQ108

d) ♠ K84
♥ 93
♦ K1062
♣ AK53

With Example 116a) you have opened one diamond. If partner responds one spade and RHO doubles, this hand makes a Support Redouble. If RHO bids two clubs, this hand makes a Support Double. It is more important to show three card support for spades than to rebid your good diamond suit. If partner's response has been one heart and RHO doubles or bids two clubs, rebid diamonds.

With Example 116b) you have opened one club. If partner responds one spade and RHO bids two diamonds, raise to two spades to show four card support. If partner responds one heart and RHO bids two diamonds, make a Support Double to show three card heart support. Showing the heart fit takes precedence over showing the four card spade suit.

With Example 116c) you have opened one diamond and partner has responded in a major suit. If RHO overcalls two clubs, you would like to double for penalty, but you cannot. A double by you would be a Support Double showing three card support for partner's major suit. You pass, hoping that partner will reopen with an action double (see Volume I, page 222) so that you can penalize the overcall.

With Example 116d) you have opened one club and LHO has overcalled one heart. Partner has bid one spade (showing a five card suit—a negative double would show four spades after the overcall) and RHO has raised to two hearts. Even though you know that partner holds five spades, you must make a Support Double rather than a direct raise in spades. It is important for partner to know that your support is exactly three cards.

The Maximal Overcall Double _____

In a competitive auction a rebid at the three level of the suit agreed by our side is not a try for game, but is simply competitive. Game tries by opener must be made in suits other than the agreed trump suit.

If we bid and raise spades and the opponents overcall and raise clubs, opener is able to make a game try in either diamonds or hearts after the three club call. As a game try, opener will choose the red suit in which help is needed.

If we bid and raise spades and the opponents overcall and raise diamonds, opener's game try options are severely limited. Opener can bid only three hearts as a try for game, whether that call is descriptive or not. Responder must understand that this is an omnibus try which says nothing about hearts, but simply asks responder to bid game with a good raise but sign off at the three level with a bad raise.

When we bid and raise spades and the opponents overcall and raise hearts, no suit in which to make a game try is available. No suit ranks higher than hearts and lower than spades. The opponents have bid maximally to take up the available bidding space. In this auction, the agreement to use **Maximal Overcall Doubles** is necessary if a game try is to be made. Opener doubles the raise to three hearts, not for penalty, but as an artificial try for game.

It is important to understand that the opponents must have found a fit. Both of them must have bid or shown the suit that takes game try space away from our side. If there is no immediate overcall of the one spade opening bid and responder raises opener's spades after a pass, if the other opponent then overcalls three hearts, no such fit has been displayed. Opener in that auction has no available game try, since double is for penalty.

The **Maximal Overcall Double** is also available in auctions in which our side has bid and raised hearts and both opponents have bid diamonds. After the diamond raise, opener can make a game try by using the **Maximal Overcall Double.**

Example 117)

a) ♠ AKQ85
  ♥ J82
  ♦ AQ4
  ♣ 86

b) ♠ A5
  ♥ KQJ963
  ♦ 105
  ♣ AJ2

With Example 117a) you have opened one spade, LHO has overcalled in a suit at the two level, partner has raised to two spades, and RHO has raised the overcall to the three level. If the overcall has been in clubs, make a natural game try by bidding three diamonds. If the overcall has been in diamonds, make a game try by bidding three hearts. This is not really expressive but is the only game try available. If the overcall has been in hearts, make a Maximal Overcall Double as your only game try.

With Example 117b) you have opened one heart, LHO has over-called in a suit, partner has raised to two hearts, and RHO has raised the overcall. If the overcall has been one spade, make your natural game try of three clubs. If the overcall has been two clubs, make a game try by bidding three diamonds. This is not expressive but is your only available game try. If the over-call has been two diamonds, make a Maximal Overcall Double as your only game try.

The Responsive Double Facing a Negative Double _____

In virtually all circumstances a **Responsive Double** can only be made by the advancer after there has been an opening bid, an intruding overcall or takeout double, and a raise of the opening bid. One other circumstance exists in which a **Responsive Double** can be made.

When there has been a minor suit opening bid, a spade overcall, a **Negative Double**, and a raise in spades, opener will sometimes hold four hearts. Since the **Negative Double** has promised four or more hearts in responder's hand, opener will wish to announce a fit for responder's heart suit. The problem presented is one of values.

If opener bids three hearts in this auction, sound values are promised—opener does not hold a minimum opening bid. Responder needs this information in order to know when to pass and when to raise to game. If opener freely bids three hearts showing a hand that would accept a game invitation, when responder's values are invitational, game will be bid.

When opener does not have maximum values, there must be a means of showing the heart fit. Opener uses the **Responsive Double** to show four hearts and minimum opening bid values, allowing responder to either compete to three hearts or bid on to game when adequate values are known to be held by the bidding side.

Example 118)

a) ♠ 84   b) ♠ 8
   ♥ KJ63   ♥ KJ63
   ♦ Q85   ♦ A105
   ♣ AQ102   ♣ AQ1062

With both Example 118) hands you have opened one club, there has been an overcall of one spade, partner has made a Negative **Double, and RHO has raised to two spades.**

Example 118a) would like to bid hearts but does not hold the required extra values. This hand makes a Responsive Double **to show four hearts but deny the values to bid them at the three level.**

Example 118b) has extra values and bids three hearts. Partner will pass with minimum values (5+ to 9– HCP), but will bid game with invitational values (9+ to 12– HCP) or more.

The Exclusion Double

In two specific auctions there is a special kind of takeout double known as the **Exclusion Double**. The first of these is by a major suit opener after a **forcing notrump** response and an overcall. When the suit of the overcall is opener's shortest suit, opener can use the **Exclusion Double**. Opener assumes that responder will often hold a five card (or longer) suit. The function of the **Exclusion Double** is to show support for unbid suits and urge responder to bid.

When opener has bid one heart and after the **forcing notrump** response the overcall is in a minor suit, double shows at least three cards in spades and in the unbid minor, sometimes four in either.

When the opening bid has been one spade, after a **forcing notrump** response the **Exclusion Double** will usually show exactly three hearts. If opener holds four hearts, it will be more important to bid them than to make the **Exclusion Double**.

The other specific auction is after an opening bid of one notrump by LHO, an interference bid of two clubs which shows a single suited hand (Hamilton) by partner, and a bid by responder. Responder's bid of two diamonds or two hearts may be natural but may be intended as a transfer bid. You must determine which meaning applies in the auction.

When your shortest suit is shown, you will have support for the suit of the two club bidder no matter which it might be. When you hold adequate values, make an **Exclusion Double** to show support for partner's suit whatever it is, and urge a bid in that suit.

Example 119)

a)
♠ KQJ4
♥ KQ876
♦ —
♣ AJ103

b)
♠ AK108
♥ KQ876
♦ 5
♣ KQ2

c)
♠ AQ1075
♥ KJ4
♦ 6
♣ QJ62

d)
♠ AQ1075
♥ QJ62
♦ 6
♣ KJ4

e)
♠ Q95
♥ 62
♦ K1082
♣ QJ54

f)
♠ 62
♥ QJ54
♦ Q95
♣ K1085

Example 119a) and Example 119b) have opened one heart. After a forcing notrump **response there has been an overcall of two diamonds. Both of these hands should make an** Exclusion Double **to indicate shortness in diamonds and support for each of the unbid suits. Since partner's** forcing notrump **has denied four spades, very good spades are required.**

Example 119c) has opened one spade. After a forcing notrump **response there has been an overcall of two diamonds. This hand should make an** Exclusion Double **to indicate shortness in diamonds and support for each of the unbid suits.**

Example 119d) has opened one spade. After a forcing notrump **response there has been an overcall of two diamonds. This hand should continue by bidding two hearts rather than make an** Exclusion Double. **The importance of major suits should be noted.**

Example 119e) bids after an opening bid of one notrump by LHO, **a call of two clubs which artificially shows a single suit by partner, and a bid by RHO. If RHO has bid two hearts naturally, or has bid two diamonds as a transfer to hearts, this hand should make an** Exclusion Double **to show shortness in hearts and urge partner to bid the suit that has been announced.**

Example 119f) bids after an opening bid of one notrump by LHO, a **call of two clubs which artificially shows a single suit by partner, and a bid by RHO. If RHO has bid two spades naturally, or has bid two hearts as a transfer to spades, this hand should make an** Exclusion Double **to show shortness in spades and urge partner to bid the suit that has been announced.**

Flip-Flop

After a minor suit opening bid and a takeout double, **Inverted Raises** no longer apply. Jump raises are weak as they would have been without the double. The single raise is no longer strong and forcing. It denies a four card or longer major suit and shows support for opener's minor suit (at least four cards) and minimum response values of 5+ to 9– HCP.

After a takeout double most players use a conventional agreement known as **Jordan**. A jump to two notrump promises a limit raise for opener's suit. When the opening bid has been in a major suit, this approach works well since opener will declare and the takeout doubler will be on opening lead, leading away from the values held.

When the opening bid has been in a minor suit, the contract will often be in notrump rather than in opener's minor. If responder jumps to two notrump to show a limit raise in opener's minor suit and opener either passes or raises notrump, the contract plays from the wrong side. The takeout doubler's partner will be on opening lead, leading from a long suit, with the doubler playing third to the first trick.

A better idea would be to have the takeout doubler on opening lead, not knowing what partner's long suit might be, and leading away from the values known to be held. To achieve this end, the convention known as **Flip-Flop** has been adopted by thinking partnerships. After the takeout double, responder inverts the two normal calls that show a fit for opener's minor suit. The preemptive raise is shown by a jump to two notrump rather than by a jump raise. The limit raise is shown by a jump raise rather than by a jump to two notrump.

When opener has more than minimum values and believes that a game in notrump will make, opener then bids three notrump and the contract is right-sided. The takeout doubler is on opening lead, not knowing which suit is long in partner's hand, and leading away from the values known to be held.

Therefore, when **Flip-Flop** is agreed:

1. After a minor suit opening bid and a takeout double, a jump to two notrump shows a preemptive raise for opener's minor suit (alert).
2. After a minor suit opening bid and a takeout double, a jump raise of the minor suit shows a limit raise (9+ to 12– HCP) (alert).

Hardy Raises After Interference _____

When partner has opened in a major suit and RHO has either made a take-out double or an overcall, the call often will not interfere with responder's ability to make a **Hardy Raise**.

When the interference is double, a response of one notrump is no longer forcing. Responder loses the ability to show the bad limit raise (three trumps and no side shortness) by first using the **forcing notrump**, then jumping in opener's major suit. This problem is solved by the use of **Jordan** (the jump to two notrump after the double). Of course, the jump to two notrump after the double will no longer be the **Jacoby Two Notrump**, but that should not matter often. When the takeout doubler holds expected values, it will be extremely rare for responder to hold the values (15+ HCP) required for the use of the **Jacoby Two Notrump** within the framework of **Hardy Raises**.

When the interference after a major suit opening bid is an overcall at the two level, it will often interfere with responder's ability to use the **Hardy Raise** complex.

If the opening bid has been one heart, an overcall of one spade leaves responder's conventional jumps intact. After an opening in either major suit, an overcall of two clubs takes away a jump response of three clubs. If the overcall is two diamonds, there cannot be a jump response to three diamonds.

When the overcall takes away the jump to three clubs, responder uses a simple cue bid to show any good balanced raise. However, game forcing raises that show shortness require definition that cannot be shown by a simple cue bid. In such situations, the **Over** and **Under Jump Shift** and **Inverted Trump Swiss** are set aside in favor of direct **Splinter** bids to the four level. Knowledge of the **Splinter** is too important to ignore.

Similarly, if the opening bid has been one spade, an overcall of two clubs or two diamonds takes away ability to show the good limit raise by jumping to three clubs. Responder falls back on a simple cue bid to show both the bad limit raise and the good limit raise, but still has available the **Under**

Jump Shift of three hearts. If the overcall is two hearts, responder again must set aside **Inverted Trump Swiss** and show the good raises which include shortness by use of a direct **Splinter** to the four level. When responder holds the hand that would have used an **Over Jump Shift** but is denied that tool, the unexpected extra values held may require later additional action by responder.

When responder holds the hand that would have used **Inverted Trump Swiss** but is denied that tool, a simple cue bid again must be used. Responder will have extra values to show later in the auction.

Summary: **Hardy Raises** in Competition

1. After an opposing takeout double of a major suit opening bid
    a. All suit jumps that show conventional raises still apply.
    b. Since a response of one notrump is no longer forcing, both the bad limit raise and the good raise that would have been shown by the **Jacoby Two Notrump** jump to two notrump.
2. After a suit overcall
    a. If the overcall is one spade over one heart, all suit jumps still apply.
    b. If the overcall is two clubs, all good raises that do not include **Splinters** make a cue bid.
    c. If the overcall takes away responder's **Under Jump Shift,** hands that would have made concealed **Splinters** make direct **Splinters** instead.

Exercises to Combat Intrusion _____

You are responding to an opening bid of one notrump after an overcall of two clubs. What call do you make and why?

1. ♠ 8632
    ♥ KQJ4
    ♦ 93
    ♣ A76

2. ♠ A863
    ♥ 93
    ♦ KQJ4
    ♣ 1076

With these hands you are responding to the opening bid of one notrump after a bid of two diamonds which shows both major suits. What call do you make and why?

3. ♠ K65
    ♥ A9
    ♦ Q10974
    ♣ J103

4. ♠ K103
    ♥ 96
    ♦ KQ965
    ♣ QJ4

With these hands you are responding to the opening bid of one notrump after a natural overcall of two hearts. What call do you make and why?

5. ♠ AJ1095
    ♥ 43
    ♦ KQ2
    ♣ 1098

6. ♠ K43
    ♥ 862
    ♦ AQJ4
    ♣ J75

7. ♠ 84
    ♥ 9
    ♦ 1062
    ♣ KQ108543

8. ♠ QJ1074
    ♥ 43
    ♦ A62
    ♣ 1098

9. ♠ KQ84
    ♥ A6
    ♦ J8654
    ♣ 83

10. ♠ J10743
    ♥ 6
    ♦ Q1074
    ♣ Q52

11. ♠ 862
    ♥ K43
    ♦ AQJ4
    ♣ J75

12. ♠ KQ84
    ♥ 83
    ♦ J8654
    ♣ A6

With these hands you are responding to an opening bid of two spades (weak) after a takeout double. What call do you make and why?

13. ♠ J954
    ♥ 62
    ♦ Q10843
    ♣ J3

14. ♠ 1087
    ♥ 62
    ♦ AQ103
    ♣ J964

15. ♠ —
    ♥ 62
    ♦ AQ97653
    ♣ J1092

16. ♠ A84
    ♥ 62
    ♦ Q10843
    ♣ J73

With these hands you are bidding after a weak two spade bid on your left, a takeout double by partner, and a pass by responder. What call do you make and why?

17. ♠ 83
    ♥ A54
    ♦ 962
    ♣ KQ1062

18. ♠ 83
    ♥ A53
    ♦ J10962
    ♣ 765

19. ♠ 83
    ♥ AJ6
    ♦ AJ104
    ♣ Q853

20. ♠ 83
    ♥ Q1094
    ♦ 642
    ♣ QJ86

With these hands you have opened one heart, partner has responded one spade, and LHO has intruded by bidding two clubs or by doubling. What call do you make and why?

21. ♠ A104
     ♥ AQJ92
     ♦ 5
     ♣ K1043

22. ♠ A1043
     ♥ AQJ92
     ♦ 5
     ♣ K103

With these hands you have opened one spade, partner has responded with a **Forcing Notrump**, and there has been an overcall of two clubs. What call do you make and why?

23. ♠ A10963
     ♥ AQ4
     ♦ KJ86
     ♣ 4

24. ♠ A10963
     ♥ KJ86
     ♦ AQ4
     ♣ 4

With these hands your partner has opened one diamond and there has been a takeout double by RHO. What call do you make and why?

25. ♠ K83
     ♥ 5
     ♦ J76542
     ♣ 983

26. ♠ K83
     ♥ 54
     ♦ AQ942
     ♣ J65

With these hands your partner has opened one heart and there has been an overcall of two diamonds. You have agreed to play **Hardy Raises**. What call do you make and why?

27. ♠ A54
     ♥ KJ3
     ♦ 62
     ♣ Q10954

28. ♠ A5
     ♥ AQJ3
     ♦ K95
     ♣ 10873

29. ♠ 5
     ♥ AQJ3
     ♦ K95
     ♣ 108743

30. ♠ 5
     ♥ AQJ3
     ♦ K95
     ♣ A10873

31. ♠ A543
    ♥ KJ10
    ♦ 9
    ♣ Q8742

32. ♠ AQ5
    ♥ KJ104
    ♦ 83
    ♣ AQ62

Answers

1. If two clubs is artificial, double. This is **Stayman**. If two clubs is natural, bid two notrump to relay to three clubs. When partner bids three clubs, bid three diamonds. This is **Stayman** promising a stopper in clubs.

2. If two clubs is artificial, double. This is **Stayman**. If two clubs is natural, bid three clubs. This is **Stayman** which denies a club stopper.

3. Bid two notrump to relay to three clubs, then bid three notrump. This promises stoppers in both major suits.

4. Bid two spades. This shows the values to at least invite game, promises a spade stopper, and denies a heart stopper.

5. Bid three spades. This is forcing, showing exactly five spades. Partner will bid three notrump with a doubleton spade or will raise holding three or more spades.

6. Bid three notrump. This shows values to be in game but denies a stopper in hearts.

7. Bid three clubs. This shows a good club suit and game invitational values. Partner will pass unless holding a high club honor and no unstopped suits. With those attributes partner will bid three notrump.

8. Bid two notrump to relay to three clubs, then bid three spades. This shows a five card spade suit and game invitational values.

9. Bid two notrump to relay to three clubs, then bid three hearts. This is **Stayman** showing four spades and also promising a stopper in hearts.

10. Bid two spades. This is natural and non-forcing.

11. Bid two notrump to relay to three clubs, then three notrump to show a heart stopper.

12. Bid three hearts. This is **Stayman** showing four spades but denying a heart stopper.

13. Bid two notrump to relay to three clubs, then bid three spades. This extends the auction preemptively showing a spade fit, but denies any good holding in which you would like to suggest an opening lead.

14. Bid three diamonds. This shows a spade fit and asks for a diamond lead on defense.

15. Bid two notrump to relay to three clubs, then bid three diamonds. This is an escape auction. You cannot make a direct call of three diamonds as that would not be natural—it would show a spade fit.

16. Bid three spades. This extends the auction preemptively and promises a high honor in spades.

17. Bid three clubs. This is natural and promises values in the range of 7 to 11 HCP.

18. Bid two notrump to relay to three clubs, then bid three diamonds. This gets you to the place in which you wish to play and shows values of less than seven HCP.

19. Bid three spades. This shows opening bid values and asks partner to describe further.

20. Bid two notrump to relay to three clubs, then bid three hearts. You cannot bid three hearts directly as that would promise greater values.

21. Double. No, this is not for penalties. It promises three card support for partner's spade suit.

22. Bid two spades. This promises four card support.

23. Double. This shows that you are short in clubs and have support for the unbid suits.

24. Bid two hearts. This does not deny diamond support, but it is important to bid majors when possible.

25. If your agreement is **Flip-Flop**, bid two notrump to show a preemptive diamond raise.

26. Playing **Flip-Flop**, bid three diamonds to show a limit raise.

27. You have a bad limit raise for hearts. Your plan was to bid a **Forcing Notrump**, then jump to three hearts. The overcall has made that impossible. Bid three diamonds to show some good heart raise.

28. Without the overcall you would have used **Inverted Trump Swiss** and jumped to four clubs to show a balanced hand with 12+ to 15- HCP and good four card trump support. After the overcall you cannot make that call since four clubs would be a **Splinter** in support of hearts. Bid three diamonds to show some good heart raise.

29. Without the overcall you would have made an **Under Jump Shift** to show a game forcing limit raise with some shortness. Since you can no longer jump in diamonds, make the direct **Splinter** call of three spades.

30. Without the overcall you would have made an **Over Jump Shift** to show four card support, 12+ to 15- HCP, and shortness in some side suit. After the overcall your only descriptive call is to **Splinter** to three spades. You have more in values than partner expects, but for the moment this is the best you can do.

31. Without the overcall you would have jumped to three clubs to show a good limit raise containing either four trumps or three trumps with a ruffing value. Since you can no longer jump in clubs you should cue bid three diamonds to show a good heart raise.

32. Without the overcall you would have used the **Jacoby Two Notrump** to show a very good four card heart raise and ask opener for further description. Since two notrump will no longer be a jump, you should cue bid to show some good heart raise.

CHAPTER TWELVE
Slam Bidding

Synopsis: Chapter Twelve has covered slam tries below the level of game, the **Blackwood** and **Gerber** conventions, how to cue bid to slams, the meanings of jumps to five of a major suit, and the Grand Slam Force.

As Chapter Twelve continues you will learn about showing controls in response to the opening bid of two clubs and the Serious Three Notrump Slam Try in a cameo by Eddie Wold. We investigate the finding of controls by looking into **Roman Gerber, Roman Key Card Blackwood** (including the showing of specific kings rather than kings by number), **Kickback**, the use of four of an agreed minor suit as control asking, showing voids in response to **RKC**, using **RKC** when there has been interference, and **Exclusion RKC**. We then look into slam tries after **Stayman** has found a fit, **Walsh Relays**, a refinement to the Grand Slam Force, and **Walsh Asking Bids**.

Control Responses to the Opening Bid of Two Clubs _____

An approach with some following is the use of responses to an opening bid of two clubs to show the controls held by responder. An ace is considered to be two controls, and a king is one control. Responder uses steps to show how many controls are held.

1. A response of two diamonds shows zero or one control.
2. A response of two hearts shows two controls. Responder has either one ace or two kings.
3. A response of two spades shows three controls. Responder's specific holding is one ace and one king.

4. A response of two notrump also shows three controls. Responder's specific holding is three kings. The theory is that when notrump is played, the hand with kings should declare to protect those kings from attack on the opening lead.

5. A response of three clubs shows four controls.

Each step beyond three clubs shows an additional control.

It is clear that this approach relates to slam bidding, but it has serious drawbacks. If slam is to be a good prospect, the first requisite is that the bidding side find the fits that will take the tricks needed at the slam level. When responder shows controls, the finding of fits is put on hold in favor of the second necessity for making slams. It is easier to find fits first, then seek controls, than it is to determine controls first, then begin a search for fits. It is wrong to put the cart before the horse.

The opening two club bidder will often have the values for game in hand, but usually will need one working card from responder in order to successfully fulfill a game contract. It is for that reason that the most popular modern approach to responding to two clubs is to have responder affirm or deny a working card. Opener then has plenty of room in which to pursue the search for fits. If responder bids two diamonds to show zero or one control, opener does not know whether or not responder holds any useful value.

Although this approach has some expert following, it is not recommended here.

In some auctions the search for slam below the level of game can make use of an expert approach which is presented here by guest expert World Champion Eddie Wold.

THE SERIOUS THREE NOTRUMP SLAM TRY
By Eddie Wold

A popular approach used by many experts that play Two Over One is a method called the Serious 3NT Slam Try. The basic assumption used in this convention is that once your side finds a confirmed eight card (or longer) fit in a major, there is relatively little need to play in 3NT. Therefore, 3NT

is used conventionally to send the message that you are in the slam zone
even if your partner has minimum values for the previous bidding. The
corollary to this 3NT bid is that if you cue bid immediately without using
3NT first, you have only mild slam interest and are economically showing
your good control structure in case partner has more serious aspirations
toward slam. The best way to explain this method is with some examples.

Example 120)

OPENER	RESPONDER
♠ AKJ854	♠ Q63
♥ AQ2	♥ 86
♦ K4	♦ AQJ952
♣ 65	♣ A8

THE BIDDING

1♠	2♦
2♠	3♠
3NT★	4♣
4NT	5♠
6♦	7♠

Opener uses the 3NT convention to show partner serious slam interest.
After responder cue bids clubs, opener uses **Roman Key Card Blackwood**
to find out about controls. When responder shows that the partnership holds
all of the **Key Cards**, opener shows interest in a grand slam by cue bidding
the diamond king. Responder can count 13 tricks and bids the grand slam.

Example 121)

OPENER	RESPONDER
♠ J65	♠ Q84
♥ KQJ872	♥ A53
♦ A8	♦ QJ752
♣ AQ	♣ K9

THE BIDDING

1♥	2♦
2♥	3♥
3NT★	4♥!!
Pass	

In this Example the 3NT is used to show serious slam aspirations but de-nies a spade control. Here the partnership can stop safely in four hearts while even five hearts is in jeopardy.

Example 122)

OPENER	RESPONDER
♠ J9865	♠ 4
♥ AQJ3	♥ K1095
♦ A3	♦ KQJ765
♣ 63	♣ A4

THE BIDDING

1♠	2♦
2♥	3♥
4♦★	4NT
5♣	6♥

There are two things to notice about this example. First, serious 3NT is in effect even though responder has raised opener's second suit. Second, opener is able to make a light slam try based on good trumps and fitting honor in responder's suit. Note: if responder's hand were: ♠K4 ♥K1095 ♦KJ765 ♣AQ4, despite more high cards there would be no slam try because this hand would not be the magic fitter needed opposite a LIGHT slam try.

Example 123)

OPENER	RESPONDER
♠ KJ65	♠ AQ82
♥ A	♥ 64
♦ AQJ874	♦ K2
♣ 87	♣ A9653

THE BIDDING

1♦	2♣
2♠	3♣
3NT★	4♣
4NT	5♠
5NT	6♦
7♣	

In this example opener needs to know about a club control and can show a serious slam try without using up valuable bidding room. Partner's club cue bid prompts the use of **Roman Key Card Blackwood** and specific king asking 5NT to bid the light-HCP grand slam.

If the partnership agrees, serious 3NT can also be used in non two over one auctions where there is a confirmed eight or nine card major suit fit. Two sequences where this works well are when one of a major is answered by an immediate limit or forcing raise. Now there is no need for 3NT to be natural, so some artificial meaning can be assigned to it, and serious 3NT is a good choice.

Example 124)

OPENER	RESPONDER
♠ AQJ84	♠ K963
♥ A	♥ KQ5
♦ 654	♦ QJ7
♣ KQ82	♣ AJ3

THE BIDDING

1♠	2NT (Jacoby raise)
3♥ (short)	3♠
3NT★	4♣
4♥	4♠
Pass	

Here the 3NT bid initiates cue bidding and yet the partnership can stop at four spades by discovering the lack of a diamond control. Notice from these last two examples that the number of high card points is less important than the value of controls and fits.

I do not play the serious 3NT convention after interference for two reasons:

1. In a contested auction partner might be forced to raise with less than the normal number of trumps because there is no other convenient action.
2. 3NT might be the best contract when your side finds out that a side suit is not splitting well. For example:

Example 125)

OPENER	RESPONDER
♠ QJ3	♠ K65
♥ KQ10963	♥ J74
♦ 6	♦ KQJ54
♣ AJ4	♣ K8

THE BIDDING

1♥	(1♠)	2♦
2♥		3♥
3NT		Pass

Here the one spade overcall warned the partnership that a spade ruff is likely, and therefore opener offers 3NT as a possible final contract. Responder with an aceless hand and an additional spade stopper is happy to go along.

Our thanks to Eddie Wold for this presentation.

Roman Gerber

In **Blackwood** and **Gerber** auctions a modern response structure has emerged. **Roman** responses make use of calls to show one of two widely separated things. In most auctions there will be evidence that makes clear which meaning is intended. The occasions on which it will not be possible to tell which answer is meant will be very few, and in those instances safeguards are provided.

In **Gerber** auctions responses to four clubs are:

1. Four diamonds, the first step, shows zero or three aces.
2. Four hearts, the second step, shows one or four aces.
3. Four spades, the third step, shows two aces, but denies interest in slam.

4. Four notrump, the fourth step, shows two aces and interest in slam. This interest is not because of maximum HCP, but because of one or more trick sources.

If the **Gerber** bidder continues with five clubs, kings are shown using the same schedule. When responder has shown two aces and either affirmed (4NT) or denied (4 spades) slam interest, that interest can be described further if responder also has two kings to show.

Example 126)

a) ♠ A3
    ♥ A94
    ♦ KQ1062
    ♣ K103

b) ♠ K105
    ♥ KQ43
    ♦ K2
    ♣ KQ62

c) ♠ A652
    ♥ QJ3
    ♦ A962
    ♣ A4

d) ♠ AJ
    ♥ A1032
    ♦ K864
    ♣ K65

All Example 126) hands have opened one notrump. Partner has bid four clubs which is Roman Gerber.

Example 126a) bids four notrump to show two aces and interest in playing a slam. If partner continues by bidding five clubs to ask for kings, your source of tricks should cause you to show continued slam interest and bid five notrump.

Example 126b) bids four diamonds which shows either zero or three aces. Partner should be able to determine which.

Example 126c) also bids four diamonds to show zero or three aces. Again, partner should be able to determine which.

Example 126d) bids four spades to show two aces without interest in slam. If partner bids five clubs to ask for kings, bid five spades to show two kings and reaffirm your lack of slam interest.

Roman Key Card Blackwood _____

The second part of the modern structure takes into account the fact that when a trump suit has been agreed, the king and queen of the agreed trump suit are important cards that responder should be able to show or deny. The king of the trump suit is designated with the four aces as a **Key Card**. When controls are shown in response to **Roman Key Card Blackwood**, the response is based on the five **Key Cards**.

In response to a **Blackwood** bid of four notrump:

1. Five clubs, the first step, shows zero or three **Key Cards**.
2. Five diamonds, the second step, shows one or four **Key Cards**.
3. Five hearts, the third step, shows two **Key Cards**, but denies the queen of the trump suit.
4. Five spades, the fourth step, shows two **Key Cards** and promises the queen of the trump suit.

When the **Blackwood** user discovers that there are insufficient key cards for slam to be reasonable, there will be a signoff in the agreed suit at the five level. If the **Blackwood** user is not sure how many **Key Cards** responder holds, again there will be a signoff in the agreed suit at the five level.

If responder has shown zero or three **Key Cards** and holds zero, the signoff will be honored. This is also true if responder has shown one or four **Key Cards** and holds one.

But when responder holds the greater number, the signoff will not be honored. Responder will continue to slam, believing that the **Blackwood** bidder signed off expecting the lesser number.

Since responder is expected to continue after a signoff when holding the greater number of **Key Cards**, the **Blackwood** bidder must hold at least one **Key Card** in order to use the convention. If slam is to be bid, at least four **Key Cards** are needed. If the **Blackwood** bidder holds none and the responder continues to slam with three, the slam will usually fail.

When the **Blackwood** response has been one of the first two steps, nothing has been said about the trump queen. Should the **Blackwood** bidder need to know about the trump queen, the cheapest call that is not a return to the agreed trump suit is used. Assuming spades to be the agreed suit, after a five club response, five diamonds asks for the trump queen; after a five diamond response, five hearts asks for the trump queen.

Responder denies the trump queen by returning to the agreed suit at the five level. Holding the trump queen but no outside king, responder bids five notrump. Holding the trump queen and one or more outside kings, responder bids in the suit of the nearest king.

With spades as trumps, when five diamonds has asked, five spades denies the trump queen; five notrump shows the queen and denies outside kings; five hearts shows the trump queen and the heart king; six clubs shows the trump queen and the club king but denies the heart king; six diamonds shows the trump queen and the diamond king but denies the heart and club kings.

With spades as trumps, when five hearts has asked, five spades denies the trump queen; five notrump shows the queen and denies outside kings; six clubs shows the trump queen and the club king; six diamonds shows the trump queen and the diamond king but denies the club king; six hearts shows the trump queen and the heart king but denies the club and diamond kings.

When responder shows the nearest king, the **Blackwood** user can ask for other kings which have not been denied. After a five club response to four notrump, when five diamonds has asked and responder has bid five hearts to show the nearest king and the trump queen, the **Blackwood** bidder can bid six clubs to ask for the club king, or six diamonds to ask for the diamond king. Holding that king, responder bids six notrump. Without that king, responder bids six spades (the agreed trump suit). If the club king has been asked for and responder does not hold it but does have the diamond king, a bid of six diamonds sends this message.

After a five diamond response to four notrump, when five hearts has asked and responder has shown the trump queen and the nearest king by bidding six clubs, the **Blackwood** bidder can ask for the diamond or heart king by bidding that suit. Again, six notrump shows the king asked for and six spades denies. If the ask is for the diamond king, six hearts also denies that king but shows the heart king.

When a specific king has been sought, if responder holds that king and the queen as well, responder raises the ask to the seven level. When responder does not hold the specific king but has a singleton in the suit and unannounced extra trump length, responder jumps to a grand slam in the agreed suit.

After **Key Cards** have been shown at the five level, if the **Blackwood** bidder wants to try for a grand slam, the next call will be five notrump. The five notrump call says:

1. We have all of the **Key Cards**.
2. If you hold a trick source that you have not yet shown, bid seven of our agreed suit.
3. If you are unable to bid the grand slam, show specific kings by bidding the lowest ranking king you hold.

If responder bids six clubs to deny the ability to bid a grand slam and show the club king, the **Blackwood** bidder can then ask for the diamond or heart king by bidding that suit. Responder again shows the king sought by bidding six notrump or denies by bidding six spades. If the diamond king is asked for, responder can deny that king and show the heart king by bidding six hearts.

If responder bids six diamonds to show the diamond king but deny the club king, the **Blackwood** bidder can ask for the heart king by bidding that suit. Responder affirms the heart king by bidding six notrump or denies it by bidding six spades.

Example 127)

a) ♠ AQ54
   ♥ 6
   ♦ A73
   ♣ AKQ65

b) ♠ AQ8543
   ♥ K4
   ♦ 7
   ♣ KQ54

Example 127a) opens one club and after a one spade response makes a jump reverse **by bidding three hearts. Partner then bids four notrump,** Roman Key Card Blackwood. **Bid five clubs to show either zero or three** Key Cards.

If partner then signs off by bidding five spades, raise to six since you hold three Key Cards **rather than zero.**

If partner bids five notrump asking for a grand slam if you hold an undisclosed trick source, bid seven spades because of your solid club suit.

If partner bids five diamonds to ask for the spade queen, bid six clubs to show that card and the club king. If partner over six clubs bids either six diamonds or six hearts to ask for a king, bid six spades to deny that king.

Example 127b) bids one spade and partner jumps to two notrump—a Jacoby **raise promising four card trump support and asking for a further description of the opening hand. Bid three diamonds to show shortness. If partner marks time by bidding three spades, bid four clubs to show values in that suit. If partner then bids four notrump,** Roman Key Card Blackwood, **bid five diamonds to show one or four** Key Cards.

If partner signs off by bidding five spades, pass since you hold one rather than four Key Cards.

If partner bids five notrump which guarantees all of the Key Cards **and asks you to bid a grand slam with an undisclosed trick source, bid seven spades. You know that there are no losers in any suit.**

If partner bids five hearts to ask for the spade queen, bid six clubs to show that card and the club king. If partner then bids six hearts to ask for that king, bid six notrump to show that you hold it. If partner bids six diamonds to ask for that king, bid six hearts to deny the diamond king and show the heart king.

Kickback _____

All of this works well when spades is the agreed trump suit. There is ample bidding space for all necessary information to be exchanged and for the **Blackwood** bidder to sign off at the five level. When another trump suit is agreed, there may not be enough space in which to investigate and still sign off at the five level.

Assume that hearts has been agreed. The **Blackwood** bidder holds one **Key Card** and bids four notrump. Responder bids five spades to show two **Key Cards** and the queen of hearts. Whoops!! We belong in five hearts but cannot get there. We simply need more bidding space in which to operate. There must be four steps for responder to use without bypassing the agreed trump suit at the five level. How can we manage that?

The answer is another Marty Bergen suggestion. Start **Blackwood** one or more calls lower than four notrump, depending on the trump suit that has been agreed. Bergen calls this treatment **Kickback**. If **Kickback** has been agreed, the suit ranking directly above the agreed trump suit is used at the four level to ask for **Key Cards**.

When the agreed suit is hearts, if four spades becomes **Blackwood** responder has four steps and still will not exceed five hearts. When the agreed suit is diamonds, if four hearts becomes **Blackwood** responder has four steps and still will not exceed five diamonds. When the agreed suit is clubs, if four diamonds becomes **Blackwood** responder has four steps and still will not exceed five clubs.

Using Four of the Agreed Minor as RKC _____

Most expert partnerships have carried this idea one step further. When no major suit fit is found and a minor suit fit exists, if the bidding side has the values to reach game, the first game sought will be three notrump.

When one suit is unstopped, with a shortness control in that suit and good values in all other suits, the bidding side will try to reach slam in the agreed minor. Once three notrump is bypassed, the bidding side will reach either five or six in the minor. The auction will rarely stop at the four level when a fit exists and game values are held.

For this reason, in such auctions a bid of four in the agreed minor suit is forcing. Many expert pairs have the agreement that four of the agreed minor suit is a **Roman Key Card** ask. For this agreement to be firm, one of two things must be true:

1. Agreement on the minor suit has been established before the auction reaches the four level.
2. Agreement on the minor suit is established by a jump to the four level in that suit which becomes **RKC**.

In each of the following auctions, four diamonds is **RKC:**

1. 1♦ – pass – 1♠ – pass, 2♣ – pass – 3♦ – pass, 4♦
2. 1♦ – pass – 1♠ – pass, 2♦ – pass – 4♦
3. 1♠ – pass – 2♦ – pass, 3♦ – pass – 4♦

In 1 and 3 agreement was established before the four level was reached. In 2 the jump to four diamonds established suit agreement as it asked.

When agreement is made at the four level without a jump, it establishes the minor and is not **RKC**. In such auctions the bidder next to speak can ask for **Key Cards** by using **Kickback**.

In the auction: 1♦ – pass – 1♠ – pass, 3♦ – pass – 4♦ – pass, a continuation to four hearts would be **RKC**. However, in the auction: 1♦ – pass – 1♥ – pass, 3♦ – pass – 4♦ – pass, a continuation of four hearts is an offer to play in partner's suit. Opener holds a heart fit which could not be shown earlier. Because four hearts is a delayed natural call, **Kickback** must be to the next higher suit. In this auction a bid of four spades would be **Kickback**.

To summarize the calls that are used as **Roman Key Card**, when spades is the agreed suit, four notrump asks. When hearts is the agreed suit, four spades asks. When a minor suit is agreed, four of the minor suit asks whenever suit agreement has been established before the four level is reached, or when agreement is established by a jump to four of the minor suit. When agreement is established at the four level, **Kickback** is used.

Showing Voids in Response to RKC

Question—can a void be shown when partner uses **RKC**? Answer—yes, but it should be shown only when it is a "working" void. A void in a suit that partner has bid naturally is not an asset. When partner's high cards face shortness they lose value. Such a void is not a "working" void and should not be shown. If the void is an unbid suit, it is a "working" void and may reasonably be shown.

Voids are shown by use of steps beyond the first four. The fifth step shows two **Key Cards** and a working void, the sixth step shows one **Key Card** and a working void, and the seventh step shows three **Key Cards** and a working void. This order is based on practicality. Two **Key Cards** is the most likely holding, one **Key Card** will usually be enough for a small slam, and showing three **Key Cards** may facilitate reaching a grand slam.

Example 128)

a) ♠ AJ65
    ♥ —
    ♦ Q93
    ♣ AQJ1042

b) ♠ AJ65
    ♥ Q93
    ♦ —
    ♣ AQJ1042

With both Example 128) hands you have responded to an opening bid of one heart by bidding two clubs. Partner rebids two spades and you raise to three spades. Partner then bids four notrump, Roman Key Card Blackwood.

With Example 128a) bid five hearts to show two Key Cards **without the queen of spades. Do not show a void in partner's first bid suit.**

With Example 128b) bid five notrump to show two Key Cards **and a working void. Partner will know that you would not show a heart void because that void would not be "working." Since you have bid clubs and spades, partner will know that your void is in diamonds.**

Combating Interference in RKC Auctions _____

If the opponents interfere after a **Roman Key Card** ask, double is for penalty, pass shows zero or three **Key Cards**, and steps beyond the interfering
call are used in order to show other holdings. However, if the interference is
in a denomination beyond the suit agreed by the bidding side at the five
level, **DEPO** is used—double shows an even number of **Key Cards** and
pass shows an odd number.

Exclusion RKC _____

When the hand that wishes to seek **Key Cards** held by partner includes a
void, the bidder may use **Exclusion RKC**. The **Exclusion** call is a high
level jump in the suit of the void.

When spades is the agreed suit, that jump is to the five level in any of the other
three suits. When hearts is the agreed suit, jumps to five of a minor are **Exclusion** as well. Since four spades is normal **RKC** with hearts agreed, four notrump
becomes **Exclusion** in the spade suit. When diamonds is the agreed suit a
jump to four in a major suit or five clubs is **Exclusion**. When clubs is the agreed
suit a jump to any higher ranking suit at the four level is **Exclusion**.

When **Exclusion** has been used, responder to that call is asked to show
Key Cards but to exclude the ace of the void suit.

Slam Tries After Stayman Finds a Fit _____

When responder to the opening bid of one notrump uses **Stayman**, after
opener's rebid a jump to four notrump does not ask for controls—it is a
quantitative slam try denying that a fit has been found. When a fit is found,
responder has three ways in which to seek a slam:

1. Responder may ask for **Key Cards** by using **Roman Key Card Gerber**.
   A jump to four clubs becomes **Gerber**, agreeing on the major suit shown
   in response to **Stayman**, and asks for **Key Cards**.
2. When responder does not wish to take control, a jump to four diamonds

announces a fit for the major suit opener has shown, interest in a slam, and denies that responder holds a **Splinter**. Opener can sign off at game or pursue slam further.

3. When responder does not wish to take control, a call in the other major at the three level is artificial, showing a fit for the major suit that opener has bid, interest in a slam, and that responder has shortness (a singleton or void) in some suit. Opener can sign off at game in the agreed major, or may make the cheapest call to ask about responder's shortness.

    a. When the agreed suit is hearts and responder has bid three spades, opener bids three notrump to ask the location of the shortness. Responder bids four clubs or four diamonds to show shortness in the suit bid, or four hearts to show spade shortness.

    b. When the agreed suit is spades and responder bids three hearts, opener bids three spades to ask for the location of the shortness. Responder shows a singleton by bidding that suit at the four level, or bids three notrump to show that the shortness held is a void. Opener then bids four clubs to ask the location of the void and responder bids the red suit of a void or bids four spades (the agreed suit) to show a club void.

Example 129)

a)   ♠ QJ73
       ♥ 5
       ♦ KQJ63
       ♣ AK4

b)   ♠ A2
       ♥ A954
       ♦ K1093
       ♣ AJ10

c)   ♠ AQ53
       ♥ KJ109
       ♦ —
       ♣ A9874

d)   ♠ AQ53
       ♥ 6
       ♦ AK1074
       ♣ Q92

All Example 129) hands respond to an opening bid of one notrump by using Stayman.

With Example 129a) when partner bids two spades, all you need to know is about partner's Key Cards. **Jump to four clubs,** Roman Key Card Gerber. **If partner shows two** Key Cards **by bidding four spades, pass. If partner shows three** Key Cards **by bidding four diamonds (cannot hold zero with 15HCP), bid**

six spades. If partner shows four Key Cards by bidding four hearts (cannot hold one with 15HCP), bid seven spades.

With Example 129b) when partner bids two hearts, jump to four diamonds to show a four card heart fit, interest in a slam, and no splinter. If there is slam interest, let partner ask for Key Cards since you hold so many. With hearts agreed, four spades would be RKC and four notrump would be to play.

With Example 129c) if partner bids two hearts, jump to three spades to show a four card heart fit, slam interest, and shortness somewhere. If partner bids three notrump to ask the location of your shortness, bid four diamonds.

If partner bids two spades, bid three hearts to show a four card spade fit, slam interest, and shortness somewhere. If partner bids three spades to ask about your shortness, bid three notrump to show that it is a void. When partner then bids four clubs, show that your void is in diamonds.

With Example 129d) if partner bids two hearts, bid three diamonds as a natural slam try. If partner then bids three spades, that will show a four card spade suit as well as four hearts and you can pursue a spade slam by cue bidding your diamond ace.

If partner bids two spades, bid three hearts to show a four card spade fit, slam interest, and some shortness. If partner bids three spades to ask about your shortness, bid four hearts to show a singleton there.

Walsh Relays _____

In Volume I you were given minor suit slam suggestion auctions following the use of **Stayman**. A more sophisticated approach to minor suit slam bidding is available. It is the **Walsh Relay**.

The beginning of the relay will appear to be a **transfer** to hearts. Responder to the opening bid of one notrump bids two diamonds which is announced as a **transfer**. After opener bids two hearts, responder continues by bidding two spades. This cancels the **transfer** and requires opener to bid two notrump so that responder may describe a specific slam try. Opener must alert the two spade bid.

Responder's continuation shows the nature of the slam try:

1. Three clubs shows a slam try with a broken six card or longer club suit.
2. Three diamonds shows a slam try with a broken six card or longer diamond suit.
3. Three hearts shows a slam try with a one loser six card or longer club suit.
4. Three spades shows a slam try with a one loser six card or longer diamond suit.
5. Three notrump shows a slam try with some completely solid suit of at least six cards, and exactly seven winners. Opener will know which suit responder holds. It will be the one in which opener has no honor cards.

Once responder has shown the specific nature of the slam try, opener can reject by bidding (or passing) three notrump, or can make move towards reaching slam. Opener's continuation in the agreed suit at the four level becomes **Roman Key Card**. Opener's continuation in any other suit is a cue bid, agreeing to the slam try and showing a control.

When responder bids two diamonds to initiate the relay, opener expects that responder has shown a heart suit. To make a super acceptance for hearts only one call carries that message. Opener must bid two spades.

When responder holds hearts, a continuation of two notrump becomes a repeat transfer, requiring opener to bid hearts. When responder continues by making any call at the three level after opener's super acceptance of two spades, responder is bidding as though the relay had been completed.

Example 130)

a) ♠ A2
♥ 5
♦ AQ3
♣ KJ98754

b) ♠ AK3
♥ 6
♦ J83
♣ AQJ1074

c) ♠ K3
    ♥ 2
    ♦ KQJ10754
    ♣ A109

d) ♠ 102
    ♥ AKQJ953
    ♦ 6
    ♣ J109

e) ♠ KQ2
    ♥ 3
    ♦ AJ10754
    ♣ K103

f) ♠ AKQJ103
    ♥ 4
    ♦ A65
    ♣ 1082

g) ♠ A2
    ♥ AJ53
    ♦ KQ102
    ♣ K87

h) ♠ 96
    ♥ K10964
    ♦ A3
    ♣ 10965

Example 130a) responds to an opening bid of one notrump by bidding two diamonds which opener announces as a transfer. Opener bids two hearts and responder bids two spades which opener alerts as a cancellation of the transfer. Opener bids two notrump as required and responder bids three clubs to show a broken club suit slam try.

Example 130b) also uses the relay, then bids three hearts to show a one loser club suit.

Example 130c) uses the relay, then bids three spades to show a one loser diamond suit.

Example 130d) uses the relay, then bids three notrump to show a completely solid suit and exactly seven winners.

Example 130e) uses the relay, then bids three diamonds to show a broken diamond suit slam try.

Example 130f) uses the relay, then bids three notrump to show a solid suit with exactly seven winners.

Example 130g) opens one notrump. When responder bids two diamonds, opener announces "transfer," then bids two spades to show a super accept for hearts. Example 130h) bids two notrump to repeat the transfer to hearts. In many auctions Example 130h) would not know whether or not to bid game, but the super acceptance makes a four heart call easy. Hands similar to Example 130a) through 130f) would also bid as though the relay had been completed.

A Refinement for the Grand Slam Force _____

An unusual jump to five notrump is the **Grand Slam Force**, asking partner to bid a grand slam in the agreed suit if holding two of the top three honors. When eight or nine trumps are held in the partnership, all three top trump honors are needed to make the grand slam a near certainty. When the bidding side holds ten trumps, the ace and king are still necessary, but the queen is usually not needed. Our refinement allows bidding the grand slam when the queen is missing if the bidding side holds ten trumps.

In response to the jump to five notrump, when you hold only one high trump, bid six clubs to announce that you hold either the ace or the king, but not the queen. When partner knows that our side holds ten trumps, the grand slam can be bid. When partner knows that at least nine trumps are held, a continuation of six diamonds asks if you hold one trump more than you have already shown. If you might have raised earlier with three card support and you actually hold four, bid the grand slam. If your earlier raise promised four cards and you actually hold five, bid the grand slam. When you do not hold the extra trump partner has sought, just bid a small slam in the agreed suit.

Example 131)

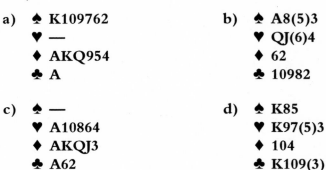

a) ♠ K109762
♥ —
♦ AKQ954
♣ A

b) ♠ A8(5)3
♥ QJ(6)4
♦ 62
♣ 10982

c) ♠ —
♥ A10864
♦ AKQJ3
♣ A62

d) ♠ K85
♥ K97(5)3
♦ 104
♣ K109(3)

Example 131a) opens one spade and Example 131b) raises to two spades. Opener then jumps to five notrump, the Grand Slam Force.

Example 131b) bids six clubs to deny two of the top three honors, but promise the ace or king. Opener then bids six diamonds to ask if responder holds extra length in spades. Responder's original raise promised at least three spades, but if responder holds four, the grand slam can be bid without the queen since the bidding side will hold ten trumps. When Example 131b) holds only three spades (and four hearts), there is no extra length and responder bids six spades. When Example 131b) holds four spades (and only three hearts), the fourth spade is extra length and responder bids the grand slam.

Example 131c) opens one heart and responder makes a limit raise which promises four card support for hearts. Opener then jumps to five notrump, the Grand Slam Force.

Example 131d) bids six clubs to deny holding two of the top three honors but promise the ace or king. Opener bids six diamonds to ask for extra length. With four card support there are only nine trumps, but if responder holds five card support there are ten trumps and the grand slam should be bid.

Walsh Asking Bids

There will be hands in which the bidding of a slam depends on finding partner with control in a specific suit. In many such instances it will be possible to inquire about the specific control needed. When the partnership has agreed to use this tool, these bids are **Asking Bids**:

1. A jump shift response after a weak two bid or an opening three bid is an **Asking Bid**.
2. A new suit response to the opening bid of four in a major suit is an **Asking Bid**.

3. After an opening **Namyats** bid of four clubs or four diamonds and a relay to the anchor suit, responder's continuation in a new suit is an **Asking Bid**.
4. After the opening bid of two clubs and the waiting response of two diamonds, a jump to three of a major by opener announces a completely solid suit and asks responder to show controls. Responder must bid a suit in which an ace is held. With more than one ace, the nearest one is shown. When responder holds no aces but does have other controls, that is shown by a bid of three notrump. Holding no controls, responder raises opener's suit to game. Opener's further bids in any suit are **Asking Bids**.

Responses to **Asking Bids** are these:

1. The cheapest call in notrump promises the king of the **Asking Bid** suit at least doubleton. When the eventual contract is in notrump this protects what may be the only stopper in that suit. Other than the cheapest call in notrump:
2. The first step shows no control. This means no ace, king, void or singleton.
3. The second step shows second round control. This means a singleton with at least two trumps, or the king and the queen.
4. The third step shows first round control. This means the ace or a void with at least one trump.
5. The fourth step shows absolute control. This means the ace and king or a void with at least two trumps.

Although finding first and second round controls is the primary reason for using **Asking Bids**, there will be times when a third round control is needed. If an **Asking Bid** is used when first and second round controls have been denied, third round control is sought. Responder to the **Asking Bid** uses steps as follows:

1. The first step denies a third round control.
2. The second step shows third round control in the form of a doubleton.
3. The third step shows third round control in the form of the queen.

Example 132)

	a)	OPENER	RESPONDER
		♠ 5	♠ 86
		♥ KJ10975	♥ AQ8
		♦ Q73	♦ A4
		♣ 984	♣ AKQ762

b)

OPENER	RESPONDER
♠ Q75	♠ —
♥ 8	♥ Q54
♦ 82	♦ AKQ753
♣ KQ109876	♣ A542

c)

OPENER	RESPONDER
♠ AQJ10953	♠ K62
♥ 7	♥ 85
♦ K63	♦ A2
♣ 93	♣ AKQ852

d)

OPENER	RESPONDER
♠ K5	♠ —
♥ AQJ108532	♥ K94
♦ 92	♦ AKQ863
♣ 7	♣ 9842

e)

OPENER	RESPONDER
♠ A5	♠ 9
♥ AKQJ943	♥ 65
♦ AQ8	♦ K654
♣ A	♣ 987542

f)

OPENER	RESPONDER
♠ AKQJ874	♠ 96
♥ A	♥ 8754
♦ AK952	♦ Q63
♣ —	♣ 9852

With Example 132a) opener bids two hearts and responder jumps to three spades which is an Asking Bid. Opener bids four diamonds, the second step (excluding notrump), to show second round control. Responder can now bid six hearts.

With Example 132b) opener bids three clubs and responder jumps to four hearts which is an Asking Bid. Opener bids five clubs, the second step (excluding notrump), to show second round control. Responder then bids six clubs. Holding a heart suit, responder would first bid three hearts which is forcing, then four hearts to play.

With Example 132c) opener bids four spades and responder bids five hearts, an Asking Bid. With no control opener would bid five spades which would be a safe place to play. Opener, however, bids six clubs, the second step (excluding notrump), to show second round control, and responder bids six spades.

With Example 132d) opener bids four clubs, a Namyats call showing a heart suit with eight or eight and one half tricks. Responder first bids four diamonds to relay to four hearts, then bids five clubs which is an Asking Bid. Opener bids five hearts, the second step, to show second round control, and responder bids six hearts.

With Example 132e) opener bids two clubs and after a positive response of two diamonds jumps to three hearts to set the trump suit. Responder bids three notrump to show some controls which are not aces, and opener makes an Asking Bid by bidding four diamonds. Responder bids four notrump to show the guarded diamond king. Opener then bids five spades, another Asking Bid. Responder bids six diamonds, the second step (excluding notrump), to show second round control, and opener then bids seven hearts.

With Example 132f) opener bids two clubs and after a negative response of two hearts jumps to three spades to set the trump suit. Responder raises to four spades to deny any first or second round control. Opener then bids five diamonds, an Asking Bid, to seek third round control. Responder bids five notrump, the third step, to show the diamond queen, and opener bids seven spades.

Slam Bidding Exercises _____

With these hands you are responding to an opening bid of two clubs. What call do you make and why?

1. ♠ 8643
   ♥ 92
   ♦ J863
   ♣ Q102

2. ♠ 8643
   ♥ 92
   ♦ K863
   ♣ Q102

With these hands you have opened one spade and rebid two spades after a two club response. Partner raises to three spades. What call do you make and why?

3. ♠ AJ10753
   ♥ AK4
   ♦ 63
   ♣ K5

4. ♠ AJ10753
   ♥ AK4
   ♦ 63
   ♣ 85

With these hands you have opened one notrump and partner has bid four clubs, **Roman Gerber**. Plan the auction that follows.

5. ♠ A8
   ♥ KQ104
   ♦ K65
   ♣ A1093

6. ♠ 62
   ♥ A104
   ♦ KQJ73
   ♣ KQJ

With these hands you have responded one spade to the opening bid of one diamond and partner has jump raised to three spades. You have cue bid four clubs and partner has bid four notrump, **Roman Key Card Blackwood**. How do you respond?

7. ♠ KQ984
   ♥ K85
   ♦ —
   ♣ AJ765

8. ♠ KQ984
   ♥ —
   ♦ K85
   ♣ AJ765

With these hands you have responded one spade to partner's opening bid of one club and partner has jump raised to three spades. After you cue bid four hearts, partner bids four notrump, **Roman Key Card Blackwood**. You respond five diamonds to show one **Key Card** and partner bids five notrump. What call do you make and why?

9.	♠ Q10984	10.	♠ Q10984
	♥ AQ2		♥ A
	♦ KJ2		♦ KQJ42
	♣ K5		♣ K5

With these hands you have raised a one heart opening bid to two hearts and partner has bid five notrump, the **Grand Slam Force**. You have bid six clubs to show that you do not hold two of the top three honors, but do hold ace or king. Partner has bid six diamonds. What call do you make and why?

11.	♠ J1087	12.	♠ J1087
	♥ K1052		♥ K102
	♦ K53		♦ K853
	♣ 86		♣ 86

With these hands you have opened two spades and partner has jumped to four diamonds, an **Asking Bid**. What call do you make and why?

13.	♠ AJ9854	14.	♠ AJ9854
	♥ 962		♥ 962
	♦ 4		♦ K4
	♣ Q107		♣ Q107

With these hands you have opened two clubs and partner has made a positive response of two diamonds. You have jumped to three spades to set the trump suit and partner has bid three notrump to show some controls other than aces. Plan the following auction.

15.	♠ AKQJ1065	16.	♠ AKQJ1065
	♥ —		♥ 85
	♦ A		♦ A
	♣ AK643		♣ AKQ

Answers

1. If you are showing controls, in response to two clubs you will bid two diamonds to show zero or one control. If you are using standard modern responses, you will bid two hearts, a negative response to deny as much as an ace, a king, or two queens.

2. If you are showing controls, in response to two clubs you will bid two diamonds to show zero or one control. If you are using standard modern responses, you will bid two diamonds to show a working card.

3. Bid three notrump to make a serious slam try. If partner bids four clubs you will bid four hearts and leave further exploration to partner.

4. Make a cue bid of four hearts. Partner will understand that you have the heart ace but hold minimum values—not enough to bid three notrump.

5. Bid four notrump to show two aces with interest in slam. If partner bids five clubs to ask for kings, bid five spades to show that your interest is only moderate.

6. Bid four hearts to show one ace. If partner then bids five clubs to ask for kings, bid five notrump to show two kings with definite interest in slam.

7. Bid five spades to show two **Key Cards** and the spade queen. Do not show a void in partner's first bid suit.

8. Bid five notrump to show two **Key Cards** and a working void.

9. Bid six clubs to show the club king and deny the ability to bid a grand slam.

10. Bid seven spades. You know that there are five diamond tricks available.

11. Bid seven hearts. You showed only three hearts with your raise and you hold four.

12. Bid six hearts. Sorry partner, no extra length.

13. Bid four spades, the second step, to show second round control of diamonds.

14. Bid four notrump to show the protected diamond king.

15. Bid four clubs, an **Asking Bid**. If partner denies first or second round control, repeat the **Asking Bid** to seek third round control.

16. Bid four hearts, an **Asking Bid**. Partner does not hold the heart ace but might have a void or second round control.

FINAL EXERCISES

The final exercises are organized as follows:

With each of the following hands you are the opening bidder. Plan your opening bid and your rebid.

1. ♠ A53
    ♥ 6
    ♦ AKJ10
    ♣ J9765

2. ♠ Q107543
    ♥ AQJ4
    ♦ 5
    ♣ A3

3. ♠ 5
    ♥ K4
    ♦ AQ2
    ♣ AKQ7542

4. ♠ 83
    ♥ KQJ5
    ♦ 5
    ♣ AQJ964

5. ♠ K
    ♥ AJ5
    ♦ Q976
    ♣ AJ1043

6. ♠ 5
    ♥ AKJ10743
    ♦ 104
    ♣ KQJ

7. ♠ Q92
    ♥ K4
    ♦ K763
    ♣ KQ108

8. ♠ AJ3
    ♥ 5
    ♦ Q842
    ♣ AK1098

9. ♠ 96
♥ 4
♦ AKQJ853
♣ 1083

10. ♠ 4
♥ Q1072
♦ Q10854
♣ AK3

You are responding to the opening bid of one club. What call do you make and why?

11. ♠ 1082
♥ Q54
♦ Q6
♣ Q10953

12. ♠ QJ62
♥ 85
♦ KJ10542
♣ 3

13. ♠ A3
♥ 952
♦ J87
♣ AQ1043

14. ♠ K52
♥ AJ3
♦ J7
♣ Q9876

15. ♠ 8
♥ K62
♦ 1043
♣ Q98754

16. ♠ 4
♥ Q109743
♦ J63
♣ 1062

17. ♠ QJ62
♥ A5
♦ KQJ54
♣ 93

18. ♠ 5
♥ A3
♦ KQJ4
♣ AQ10953

Partner opens one club and RHO doubles for takeout. What action do you take and why?

19. ♠ 5
♥ 83
♦ J765
♣ K107654

20. ♠ 62
♥ A102
♦ Q73
♣ KQ1074

You are responding to an opening bid of one heart. What call do you make if you are playing **Bergen Raises**? What call do you make if you are playing **Hardy Raises**?

21. ♠ K72
    ♥ AJ4
    ♦ K875
    ♣ 1062

22. ♠ 7
    ♥ Q9753
    ♦ 8642
    ♣ J106

23. ♠ K103
    ♥ AQ84
    ♦ 6
    ♣ A10972

24. ♠ KJ10854
    ♥ 6
    ♦ 973
    ♣ 432

25. ♠ KJ3
    ♥ AQ84
    ♦ 92
    ♣ A1093

26. ♠ 7
    ♥ AJ4
    ♦ K1098
    ♣ K7653

27. ♠ 7
    ♥ Q9753
    ♦ K642
    ♣ J106

28. ♠ 8
    ♥ QJ103
    ♦ 10942
    ♣ AK74

29. ♠ 1062
    ♥ J987
    ♦ 84
    ♣ AQ54

30. ♠ 84
    ♥ KQ83
    ♦ AQ4
    ♣ 9752

31. ♠ A6
    ♥ KQ83
    ♦ AQ4
    ♣ J975

32. ♠ 84
    ♥ J1085
    ♦ K963
    ♣ 1076

You are responding to an opening bid of one notrump. Plan your auction.

33. ♠ AJ62
    ♥ QJ8532
    ♦ 94
    ♣ 3

34. ♠ J6
    ♥ A52
    ♦ 4
    ♣ AKJ9753

35. ♠ 654
    ♥ J4
    ♦ 3
    ♣ QJ97543

36. ♠ K5
    ♥ 96
    ♦ AQ842
    ♣ KQ109

37. ♠ KQ6
    ♥ KQ8
    ♦ KQJ854
    ♣ 5

38. ♠ 6
    ♥ A5
    ♦ KJ963
    ♣ KQJ74

39. ♠ A3
    ♥ AQ104
    ♦ J105
    ♣ KQ62

40. ♠ KQ954
    ♥ AQ62
    ♦ 98
    ♣ 62

41. ♠ KQJ3
    ♥ 5
    ♦ AJ82
    ♣ A1093

42. ♠ KQ105
    ♥ AJ3
    ♦ KQ962
    ♣ 4

43. ♠ 6
    ♥ 753
    ♦ KJ87543
    ♣ 104

44. ♠ AQ102
    ♥ AKJ854
    ♦ —
    ♣ 863

45.   ♠ 4
     ♥ A6
     ♦ AJ98753
     ♣ K95

46.   ♠ AQ76
     ♥ QJ93
     ♦ AJ1054
     ♣ —

47.   ♠ —
     ♥ 82
     ♦ Q8754
     ♣ J97653

48.   ♠ 1074
     ♥ 6
     ♦ AKQJ853
     ♣ 82

49.   ♠ QJ84
     ♥ AK4
     ♦ 8
     ♣ KQJ73

50.   ♠ K5
     ♥ J6
     ♦ KQJ7
     ♣ AQ842

You are responding to the opening bid of two notrump. Plan your auction.

51.   ♠ J53
     ♥ K642
     ♦ 5
     ♣ Q10764

52.   ♠ Q852
     ♥ J654
     ♦ Q72
     ♣ 65

53.   ♠ Q85
     ♥ K63
     ♦ 108754
     ♣ J6

54.   ♠ KJ76
     ♥ A1054
     ♦ QJ73
     ♣ 4

You are responding to the opening bid of two clubs. What call do you make and why?

55.   ♠ AK1085
     ♥ 84
     ♦ Q102
     ♣ 987

56.   ♠ J1084
     ♥ Q52
     ♦ 8
     ♣ 107643

57. ♠ Q62
    ♥ 5
    ♦ AQ10983
    ♣ 842

58. ♠ J1084
    ♥ K52
    ♦ 8
    ♣ 107643

You have opened one diamond and partner has made an **Inverted Raise** to two diamonds. How do you continue?

59. ♠ K105
    ♥ Q1072
    ♦ AJ103
    ♣ Q9

60. ♠ KQ105
    ♥ A1076
    ♦ AJ103
    ♣ 5

61. ♠ KQ10
    ♥ AQ7
    ♦ AJ103
    ♣ K95

62. ♠ KQ105
    ♥ A82
    ♦ AJ103
    ♣ 95

You have opened two spades and partner has bid two notrump (**Ogust**) to ask for further description. What call do you make?

63. ♠ KQJ854
    ♥ J7
    ♦ J43
    ♣ Q8

64. ♠ AKQJ93
    ♥ 8
    ♦ 543
    ♣ 1072

65. ♠ KJ9765
    ♥ 8
    ♦ KJ102
    ♣ 92

66. ♠ Q109754
    ♥ 862
    ♦ K103
    ♣ Q

You have responded one diamond to the opening bid of one club and partner has rebid one heart. What call do you make and why?

67. ♠ 62
    ♥ QJ4
    ♦ AQJ954
    ♣ 83

68. ♠ 94
    ♥ 6
    ♦ AJ9754
    ♣ AKJ8

You have responded one heart to a one club opening bid and partner has rebid one spade. What call do you make and why?

69. ♠ 85
    ♥ K973
    ♦ QJ10765
    ♣ 3

70. ♠ 85
    ♥ QJ853
    ♦ AK954
    ♣ 3

You have responded to the opening bid of one spade by using the **forcing notrump**. Partner rebids two clubs in 71 and two hearts in 72. How do you continue in each case?

71. ♠ Q5
    ♥ K765
    ♦ 1076
    ♣ QJ102

72. ♠ Q5
    ♥ K75
    ♦ 10876
    ♣ QJ102

You have responded by using the **forcing notrump** to partner's opening bid of one heart in 73 and partner has rebid two clubs. You have responded one spade to partner's opening bid of one diamond in 74 and partner has rebid two clubs. What call do you make and why?

73. ♠ J104
    ♥ K3
    ♦ 10743
    ♣ QJ85

74. ♠ 109743
    ♥ K92
    ♦ J8
    ♣ Q64

You have responded two hearts, a **preemptive jump shift** to partner's opening bid of one club. Partner has continued by bidding two notrump to ask for an **Ogust** rebid. What call do you make and why?

75. ♠ 6
    ♥ KJ10973
    ♦ 10973
    ♣ 82

76. ♠ Q2
    ♥ 10987543
    ♦ Q3
    ♣ 104

77. ♠ —
    ♥ J1097542
    ♦ 83
    ♣ Q654

78. ♠ 84
    ♥ KJ10973
    ♦ 654
    ♣ 73

You have responded one spade to an opening bid of one diamond and partner has jump rebid two notrump. What call do you make and why?

79. ♠ K8754
    ♥ J10962
    ♦ 8
    ♣ 54

80. ♠ AJ1053
    ♥ K1093
    ♦ 7
    ♣ 643

81. ♠ K984
    ♥ 54
    ♦ J10962
    ♣ 82

82. ♠ AJ62
    ♥ 7
    ♦ KQ853
    ♣ J102

You have responded one heart to an opening bid of one diamond and partner has jump rebid two notrump. What call do you make and why?

83. ♠ K1084
    ♥ AJ63
    ♦ 92
    ♣ 1054

84. ♠ K1084
    ♥ AJ763
    ♦ 92
    ♣ 104

85. ♠ Q93
    ♥ KQ854
    ♦ J6
    ♣ 1043

86. ♠ 3
    ♥ QJ9643
    ♦ 1082
    ♣ J64

You have responded with a **forcing notrump** to partner's opening bid of one spade. Partner has rebid two clubs. Your partnership has agreed to play the **Bart** convention. How do you continue with each of these hands?

87. ♠ 8
    ♥ J94
    ♦ 10873
    ♣ KJ1052

88. ♠ A3
    ♥ A105
    ♦ Q973
    ♣ J542

89. ♠ 6
    ♥ J109854
    ♦ KQ4
    ♣ 1083

90. ♠ 86
    ♥ K102
    ♦ AQ10932
    ♣ 92

91. ♠ 5
    ♥ 987
    ♦ KQ10975
    ♣ 1063

92. ♠ 86
    ♥ K102
    ♦ Q2
    ♣ AQ10932

93. ♠ Q5
    ♥ K10963
    ♦ 854
    ♣ J62

94. ♠ J6
    ♥ Q1082
    ♦ Q43
    ♣ QJ63

You have responded with a **forcing notrump** to partner's opening bid of one spade. Partner has raised to two notrump showing 18 or 19 HCP. You have agreed to play transfers after the raise of the **forcing notrump**. What call do you make and why?

95. ♠ 85
    ♥ KJ93
    ♦ J86
    ♣ Q1062

96. ♠ 6
    ♥ J95
    ♦ KJ96543
    ♣ 82

97. ♠ QJ4
    ♥ 85
    ♦ KQJ3
    ♣ 9642

98. ♠ 873
    ♥ A65
    ♦ K943
    ♣ QJ2

99. ♠ 7
    ♥ 854
    ♦ 63
    ♣ KJ109754

100. ♠ KJ5
     ♥ 106
     ♦ 843
     ♣ AQJ84

101. ♠ 6
     ♥ QJ8763
     ♦ J93
     ♣ 842

102. ♠ 84
     ♥ QJ1085
     ♦ A96
     ♣ 842

You have agreed to play the **Hardy** defensive bidding complex with longer/stronger minor suits and shorter/weaker major suits. How do you compete against the opening bid of one club?

103. ♠ KJ104
    ♥ 2
    ♦ AK10643
    ♣ 93

104. ♠ 84
    ♥ 62
    ♦ AQJ9432
    ♣ 93

105. ♠ KQ1032
    ♥ 2
    ♦ AK10643
    ♣ 93

106. ♠ 63
    ♥ AQJ6
    ♦ KJ10983
    ♣ 8

How do you compete against the opening bid of one diamond?

107. ♠ 62
    ♥ AQJ6
    ♦ 8
    ♣ KJ10983

108. ♠ AQJ6
    ♥ 62
    ♦ 8
    ♣ KJ10983

How do you compete against the opening bid of one spade?

109. ♠ 8
    ♥ AQJ6
    ♦ 62
    ♣ KJ10983

110. ♠ 8
    ♥ AQJ6
    ♦ KJ10983
    ♣ 62

LHO has opened one club and rebid one notrump after a response of one heart. After two passes it is your turn to call. What action do you take and why?

111. ♠ KJ63
    ♥ 9
    ♦ KQ54
    ♣ J732

112. ♠ A6
    ♥ AQ1084
    ♦ 54
    ♣ A732

LHO has opened one spade, partner has doubled, and RHO has raised to two spades. What action do you take and why?

113. ♠ 874
    ♥ AK103
    ♦ 32
    ♣ KJ84

114. ♠ 874
    ♥ KJ103
    ♦ 32
    ♣ K1098

LHO has opened one diamond, partner has overcalled one heart, and RHO has raised to two diamonds. What action do you take and why?

115. ♠ J10854
♥ K2
♦ 3
♣ AJ976

116. ♠ AQJ76
♥ K2
♦ 3
♣ J10854

You have opened one club, LHO has overcalled one spade, partner has made a **negative double**, and RHO has raised to two spades. What action do you take and why?

117. ♠ 95
♥ AJ76
♦ Q82
♣ KQ84

118. ♠ 95
♥ AK76
♦ K82
♣ KQ84

LHO has opened one club, partner has overcalled one diamond, and RHO has bid one spade. What action do you take and why?

119. ♠ J94
♥ QJ843
♦ A6
♣ 1073

120. ♠ J94
♥ AJ984
♦ 63
♣ A107

121. ♠ J94
♥ QJ84
♦ A107
♣ 632

122. ♠ 4
♥ QJ843
♦ 10972
♣ A107

LHO has opened one club, partner has overcalled one spade, and RHO has made a **negative double**. What action do you take and why?

123. ♠ Q974
♥ 83
♦ J963
♣ 542

124. ♠ K3
♥ 874
♦ A963
♣ J1042

125. ♠ K8754
♥ 82
♦ 10963
♣ J4

126. ♠ J107
♥ 87
♦ A963
♣ J1042

Plan your auction under each of these circumstances:

1. RHO has opened one notrump and you have agreed to play **Hamilton**.
2. RHO has opened one notrump and you have agreed to play **Hello**.
3. RHO has opened with a forcing club and you have agreed to play **Mathe**.
4. RHO has opened with a forcing club and you have agreed to play **CRASH**.

127. ♠ 85
     ♥ A6
     ♦ KQ10874
     ♣ Q105

128. ♠ AQJ3
     ♥ KJ1074
     ♦ 86
     ♣ 42

129. ♠ K82
     ♥ 4
     ♦ 63
     ♣ AK109753

130. ♠ AQJ864
     ♥ 83
     ♦ KJ3
     ♣ 104

131. ♠ AJ9543
     ♥ KQ1087
     ♦ —
     ♣ A2

132. ♠ AQ1073
     ♥ 7
     ♦ K10984
     ♣ 62

133. ♠ 1054
     ♥ KQJ1073
     ♦ 6
     ♣ AJ2

134. ♠ 8
     ♥ 96
     ♦ KQJ63
     ♣ AQ1054

Partner has opened one notrump and RHO has made a natural overcall of two hearts. What call do you make and why?

135. ♠ KQ83
     ♥ 54
     ♦ A105
     ♣ J1093

136. ♠ 1032
     ♥ AJ4
     ♦ Q10973
     ♣ K6

137. ♠ KJ1074
     ♥ 862
     ♦ Q109
     ♣ 76

138. ♠ 1032
     ♥ 62
     ♦ AQJ954
     ♣ 85

139. ♠ KQ83
     ♥ A4
     ♦ 872
     ♣ J1062

140. ♠ KJ4
     ♥ 986
     ♦ AQ82
     ♣ 1043

141. ♠ AQJ106
     ♥ 54
     ♦ 102
     ♣ A1073

142. ♠ AQ1086
     ♥ 54
     ♦ 102
     ♣ Q1073

Partner has opened one notrump and RHO has bid two diamonds which is a takeout for major suits. What action do you take and why?

143. ♠ 52
     ♥ 87
     ♦ AKQ73
     ♣ J1062

144. ♠ A102
     ♥ 53
     ♦ KQJ6
     ♣ 9864

145. ♠ 53
     ♥ A102
     ♦ KQJ6
     ♣ 9864

146. ♠ A102
     ♥ KQ6
     ♦ 95
     ♣ J10952

Partner has opened two hearts and RHO has made a takeout double. What action do you take and why?

147. ♠ 84
     ♥ K95
     ♦ Q10763
     ♣ J82

148. ♠ K5
     ♥ 9872
     ♦ KQ6
     ♣ 8543

149. ♠ 1083
     ♥ —
     ♦ KQ87543
     ♣ J102

150. ♠ A54
     ♥ 1096
     ♦ 4
     ♣ 987652

151. ♠ K9
     ♥ 8653
     ♦ QJ102
     ♣ Q42

152. ♠ J107
     ♥ 952
     ♦ Q76
     ♣ AJ103

LHO has opened a weak two spade bid, partner has doubled for takeout, and RHO has passed. What action do you take and why?

153. ♠ 52
     ♥ AJ3
     ♦ K10762
     ♣ 854

154. ♠ 52
     ♥ QJ3
     ♦ QJ1063
     ♣ 954

155. ♠ 52
     ♥ AQ3
     ♦ KJ1072
     ♣ K54

156. ♠ 52
     ♥ AQJ3
     ♦ KJ1072
     ♣ 54

You have opened one diamond, LHO has passed and partner has responded one spade. RHO intrudes either by bidding two clubs or making a takeout double. What action do you take in each case?

157. ♠ K1073
     ♥ 976
     ♦ AQJ5
     ♣ A10

158. ♠ K7
     ♥ 106
     ♦ AQJ53
     ♣ AJ109

159. ♠ K103
     ♥ 986
     ♦ AQJ5
     ♣ A102

160. ♠ 103
     ♥ K86
     ♦ AQJ753
     ♣ A10

In each of these auctions what action do you take with hand 161?

1. 1♥ – 1♠ – 2♥ – 2♠, ?
2. 1♥ – 2♣ – 2♥ – 3♣, ?
3. 1♥ – 2♦ – 2♥ – 3♦, ?

In each of these auctions what action do you take with hand 162?

1. 1♠ – pass – 2♠ – 3♥, ?
2. 1♠ – dbl – 2♠ – 3♥, ?
3. 1♠ – 2♥ – 2♠ – 3♥, ?

161. ♠ A5
     ♥ AK10873
     ♦ A102
     ♣ J2

162. ♠ AK10873
     ♥ A5
     ♦ J2
     ♣ A102

You have opened one spade, LHO has passed, partner has bid a **forcing notrump**, and RHO has bid two diamonds. What action do you take and why?

163. ♠ AJ987
     ♥ KQ4
     ♦ 6
     ♣ A1093

164. ♠ AK1043
     ♥ A1093
     ♦ 6
     ♣ KQ4

You have opened one spade and partner has responded two diamonds. You have rebid two spades and partner has raised to three spades. What action do you take and why?

165. ♠ AJ1043
     ♥ J76
     ♦ K6
     ♣ A94

166. ♠ AK1043
     ♥ J76
     ♦ K6
     ♣ AJ2

You have responded by bidding two clubs—**Stayman**—to partner's opening bid of one notrump and partner has rebid two spades. What action do you take and why?

167. ♠ KQ93
     ♥ 6
     ♦ KQJ84
     ♣ KQ4

168. ♠ KQ93
     ♥ 6
     ♦ AQ942
     ♣ K108

169. ♠ KQ93
   ♥ J4
   ♦ AQ42
   ♣ K108

170. ♠ KQ93
   ♥ 6
   ♦ AQ942
   ♣ K108

You have opened one spade and partner has bid a **Jacoby two notrump**. You have rebid three spades to deny shortness and show a sixth spade. Partner bids four notrump. Plan your following auctions.

171. ♠ AQJ742
   ♥ A4
   ♦ K3
   ♣ A62

172. ♠ QJ10743
   ♥ KQ5
   ♦ KQ
   ♣ 105

You have opened one heart and partner has used a **Jacoby two notrump**. You have rebid three diamonds to show shortness there and partner has bid four spades which is **Kickback**. Plan your following auctions.

173. ♠ A932
   ♥ AQ1042
   ♦ —
   ♣ KQJ6

174. ♠ A93
   ♥ AQJ42
   ♦ 6
   ♣ KJ72

Partner has opened one club and you have made an **Inverted raise** to two clubs. Partner continues with a jump to four clubs which is **Roman Key Card**. Plan your following auctions.

175. ♠ A63
   ♥ 87
   ♦ KQ2
   ♣ AJ954

176. ♠ AK3
   ♥ 7
   ♦ A862
   ♣ AQ954

You have opened two spades and partner has jumped to four clubs which is an **Asking bid**. What response do you make?

177. ♠ KJ10743
   ♥ 85
   ♦ KQ63
   ♣ 4

178. ♠ KJ10743
   ♥ 85
   ♦ KQ6
   ♣ 43

179. ♠ KJ10743
    ♥ 85
    ♦ 63
    ♣ K82

180. ♠ KJ10743
    ♥ 852
    ♦ J63
    ♣ A

Answers _____

1. One diamond. You have a prepared rebid of two clubs. **Page 10, also Example 14a).**

2. One spade. If partner responds with a **forcing notrump**, your rebid will be two hearts. **Page 12, also Example 15b).**

3. One club in any of the first three seats. In fourth seat this is an **Acol three notrump** opening bid. If partner responds one spade, jump rebid three notrump. If partner responds one heart, **reverse** to two diamonds—your hand is too good to jump rebid three clubs which might be passed. If partner responds one diamond, you have no good rebid—perhaps the best would be a **splinter** jump to three spades. **Page 157, also Example 88a); page 17, also Example 19.**

4. One club. If partner responds one diamond, rebid one heart. If partner responds one spade or one notrump, rebid two clubs. If partner responds one heart, jump rebid four clubs. **Page 15, also Example 17a).**

5. One notrump. If you open one club you have no reasonable rebid. If you open one diamond planning a two club rebid, partner may take a **false preference** back to diamonds which would leave you in a poor trump fit. Opening one notrump—the least of evils—solves your rebid problem. **Page 14, also Example 16b).**

6. Four clubs. A perfect hand for the **Namyats** convention. Your hand is worth eight and one half tricks with hearts as trumps. **Page 160, also Example 90a).**

7. One club. You plan a rebid of one notrump. With four cards in each minor you have a choice, so bid the one you want partner to lead if your side defends. **Page 10, also Example 13a).**

8. One club. Again, your diamonds are too poor to chance a **false preference** if you open one diamond and rebid two clubs. If partner responds one diamond, you can raise. If partner responds one heart or one notrump, rebid two clubs. If partner responds one spade, you should raise with good three card support. **Page 10, also Example 14b).**

9. Three notrump if your agreement is that opening bid is **Gambling**. Without that agreement, open one diamond. **Page 154, also Example 87a).**

10. One diamond. Raise if partner responds one heart, but if the response is one spade or one notrump, rebid two clubs. Partner will not pass unless short in diamonds and holding a lot of clubs. **Page 14, also Example 16d).**

11. One diamond. Do not jump to three clubs with this balanced hand. Your values are not enough to bid one notrump, so temporize. **Page 112.**

12. One spade, a **Walsh Response**. We bid four card majors with less than game going values. If partner rebids one notrump, jump to three diamonds. This shows a weak hand with only four spades and six diamonds. **Page 64, also Example 45c).**

13. Two clubs. This **Inverted** raise shows at least game invitational values and is forcing for one round. **Page 114.**

14. Two notrump. Even though you have good club support, you need to protect your tenaces and become declarer at the probable notrump contract. **Page 118, also Example 66a).**

15. Three clubs. This is an **Inverted** preemptive raise. **Page 112.**

16. Two hearts. A **preemptive jump shift. Page 74.**

17. One diamond. Prepare a **reverse** rather than bid your four card major since you have game forcing values. **Page 64, also Example 45d).**

18. Four clubs. This is **Roman Key Card.** If partner shows two **key cards**, you can bid a small slam; if three, you can bid a grand slam in clubs. **Page 272.**

19. Three clubs unless you have agreed to play **Flip-Flop.** With that agreement, make a preemptive jump to two notrump. **Page 252.**

20. Two notrump to show your limit raise unless you have agreed to play **Flip-Flop.** With that agreement, bid three clubs. **Page 252.**

21. Use the **forcing notrump**, then jump in hearts to show a three card **limit raise** without a ruffing value. **Bergen, Page 126; Hardy, Page 133.**

22. Jump to four hearts. **Bergen, Page 125, also Example 74b); Hardy, Page 132, also Example 78a).**

23. Jump to three spades to announce a **concealed splinter. Bergen, Page 123; Hardy, Page 141.**

24. Jump to two spades, a **preemptive jump shift. Page 74.**

25. Jump to two notrump **(Jacoby)**, **Bergen**, or jump to four clubs, **Inverted Trump Swiss**, if playing **Hardy, Bergen, Page 125; Hardy, Page 141.**

26. Bid one **forcing notrump** playing **Bergen.** A **Bergen** raise requires four trumps at the three level. Playing **Hardy**, jump to three clubs to show a **good limit raise** which includes a ruffing value despite only three trumps. **Page 142.** If you are a passed hand, bid two clubs which is three card **Drury. Page 127.**

27. Bid four diamonds if playing **Bergen.** The diamond king makes the hand too good for a jump to four hearts. Playing **Hardy**, start with a **forcing notrump**, then jump to four hearts for the same reason. **Bergen, Page 125, also Example 74a); Hardy, Page 132, also Example 78b).**

28. Playing **Bergen**, jump to three spades to show a **concealed splinter.** Playing **Hardy**, make an **under jump shift** of three diamonds to show a **concealed splinter** with a high card range of 9+ to 12-. **Bergen, Page 123; Hardy, Page 137.**

29. Playing **Bergen**, jump to three clubs to show the values of a good single raise with four card support. Playing **Hardy**, raise to two hearts but be prepared to bid again if the opponents balance. **Bergen, Page 121; Hardy, Page 131.**

30. Playing **Bergen,** jump to three diamonds to show a **limit raise** with four card support. Playing **Hardy** jump to three clubs to show a **good limit raise** with either four card support or three card support with a ruffing value. **Bergen, Page 121; Hardy, Page 134.**

31. Playing **Bergen,** jump to four clubs to show a big balanced raise. Playing **Hardy,** use the **Jacoby Two Notrump. Bergen, Page 125; Hardy, Page 139.**

32. Using either method, make a preemptive raise by jumping to three hearts. **Bergen, Page 121, also Example 70d); Hardy, Page 142, also Example 80).**

33. Two clubs—**Stayman.** If partner bids a major raise to game. If partner bids two diamonds jump to four diamonds. This **Texas transfer** is part of the **Smolen** convention. **Page 94.**

34. Bid two diamonds as the start of a **Walsh Relay.** If partner bids two hearts bid two spades to cancel the transfer and require two notrump. If partner bids two spades to show a super acceptance for hearts or if the relay has been completed, bid three hearts to show a club slam try with a one loser suit. **Page 280, also Example 130b).**

35. Bid two notrump to relay to three clubs, then pass. **Page 99.**

36. Bid two spades, **Minor Suit Stayman.** Regardless of partner's next call you will bid three notrump to show doubletons in both majors and only mild slam interest. **Page 96, also Example 58c).**

37. Jump to four clubs, the **Gerber** convention. This hand just needs to know about aces to know the level at which to play. **Page 266.**

38. Bid two spades, **Minor Suit Stayman.** Your next call will be three spades to show a spade **splinter. Page 96, also Example 58d).**

39. Bid two clubs, **Stayman.** If partner bids two diamonds or two spades, make a quantitative jump to four notrump. If partner bids two hearts jump to four diamonds to show a four card fit and interest in slam with a balanced hand. **Page 275.**

40. Bid two clubs, **Stayman** and raise to game if partner bids a major. If partner bids two diamonds jump to three hearts—the **Smolen** convention—to show four hearts and longer spades. **Page 94.**

41. Bid two notrump to relay to three clubs, then bid three hearts. This shows a three suited hand with heart shortness and slam interest. **Page 99, also Example 60b).**

42. Bid two clubs, **Stayman.** If partner bids either two diamonds or two hearts bid three diamonds to show interest in a diamond slam. If partner bids two spades bid three hearts to show a four card spade fit and slam interest with a **concealed splinter. Page 275.**

43. Bid two spades, **Minor Suit Stayman.** If partner bids three diamonds, pass. If partner bids either two notrump or three clubs, bid three diamonds which requires a pass to end the auction. **Page 96, also Example 58a).**

44. Bid two clubs, **Stayman**. If partner bids either major, bid the other major at the three level to announce a fit, slam interest, and shortness somewhere. If partner bids two diamonds jump to three spades to show four cards there and longer hearts. If partner bids four hearts make some slam try. If partner bids three notrump, bid four diamonds which is a **Texas Transfer** showing interest in reaching a slam. **Page 94.**

45. Bid two diamonds as the start of a **Walsh Relay**. After the relay bid three diamonds to show a broken diamond suit slam try. **Page 280, also Example 130a).**

46. Bid two notrump to relay to three clubs, then bid four clubs to show club shortness and strong interest in slam. **Page 99, also Example 60d)**

47. Bid two spades, **Minor Suit Stayman**. If partner bids either minor suit, pass. If partner bids two notrump, bid three clubs which asks partner to pass or correct to diamonds. **Page 96, also Example 58b)**

48. Bid two diamonds as the start of a **Walsh Relay**. When the relay has been completed bid three notrump to show a completely solid suit and exactly seven winners. **Page 280, also Example 130d) and 130f).**

49. Bid two clubs, **Stayman**. If partner bids two hearts, bid three clubs which is a natural slam try. If partner bids two spades, bid three hearts to announce a four card fit and a **concealed splinter** with slam interest. **Page 275.**

50. Bid two spades, **Minor Suit Stayman**. Regardless of partner's next call, continue by bidding four notrump to show two-two in the majors and strong interest in slam. **Page 96.**

51. Bid three clubs, **Puppet Stayman**. If partner bids three notrump to deny either a five or four card major, pass. If partner bids three of either major to show five, raise to game. If partner bids three diamonds to show a four card major, bid three spades which will allow partner to declare if there is a four-four fit in hearts. **Page 102.**

52. Bid three clubs, **Puppet Stayman**. If partner bids three notrump, pass. If partner bids three of a major suit, raise to game. If partner bids three diamonds to promise a four card major, bid four diamonds to show that you have both. **Page 102, also Example 62d).**

53. Bid three clubs, **Puppet Stayman**. If partner bids three notrump, pass. If partner bids three of either major, raise to game. If partner bids three diamonds to announce a four card major, bid three notrump. **Page 102, also Example 62a).**

54. Bid three clubs, **Puppet Stayman**. If partner bids three notrump, raise to four to invite slam. If partner bids three hearts, bid four spades which is **Kickback** to ask for controls. If partner bids three spades, cue bid four hearts to suggest a spade slam. If partner bids three diamonds to announce a four card major, bid four clubs which shows both majors and interest in slam. **Page 102, also Example 62f).**

55. Two spades. This promises a suit at least five cards long headed by two of the top three honors and some other value. **Page 172, also Example 97b).**

56. Two hearts. This is an artificial negative denying as much as an ace, a king, or two queens. **Page 172, also Example 97b).**

57. Three diamonds. This is a natural positive response which should show a six card suit headed by two of the top three honors and some other value. **Page 172, also Example 97d).**

58. Two diamonds. This is an artificial positive response promising at least an ace or a king or two queens. **Page 172, also Example 97h).**

59. Two notrump. This shows minimum values (12 or a bad 13 HCP) and promises that both majors are stopped. **Page 115, also Example 64a).**

60. Three clubs. This shows a sound hand with a club **splinter**. After the strong raise if opener bids any new suit at the three level, that call is a **splinter**. **Page 115, also Example 64f).**

61. Three notrump. This promises a balanced hand with 18 or 19 HCP. **Page 115, also Example 97b).**

62. Two hearts. You have too much for two notrump and not enough for three notrump. Bid your stoppers "up the line." **Page 115, also Example 64c).**

63. Three diamonds. This shows a bad hand with a good suit. Don't be fooled by counting points. You hold ten HCP but your outside queen and jacks are naked and your shape is the worst it could be. **Page 163, also Example 92a).**

64. Three notrump. This promises a completely solid suit. **Page 163, also Example** 92e).

65. Three hearts. This shows a good hand with a bad suit. **Page 163, also Example** 92b).

66. Three clubs. This shows a bad hand (even though you hold 9 HCP) with a bad suit. **Page 163, also Example 92g).**

67. Three diamonds. Jumps in previously bid suits are invitational. **Page 24.**

68. Three clubs. This is the single exception to having jumps in previously bid suits as invitational. When responder first bids one diamond, then jumps to three clubs, this jump in a previously bid suit is forcing. **Page 24, also Example 21a).**

69. Three diamonds. This unusual jump shows four cards in the major and six diamonds and is weak. **Page 26, also Example 23).**

70. Two diamonds, then three diamonds at your next turn. This repeat of the **fourth suit** is natural and highly invitational. **Page 26, also Example 22b).**

71. Two spades. This preference with a doubleton is standard in **forcing notrump** auctions. Partner may hold only three clubs. **Page 68, also Example 47b).**

72. Two spades. This **false preference** may lead to a superior trump fit, but most importantly it allows partner to move toward game when holding extra values. **Page 68, also Example 48b).**

73. Two hearts. Again in **forcing notrump** auctions the preference to the major with a doubleton is standard. In this auction partner might hold only two clubs. **Page 68, also Example 47b).**

74. Two diamonds. The **false preference** may allow partner to make a try for game when pass would probably end the auction. **Page 68, also Example 49b).**

75. Three spades. In this auction you have a good hand and a good suit. Do not fear bypassing hearts at the three level. If partner has enough in values to inquire you were going to reach game in any case. **Page 74, also Example 51d).**

76. Three clubs. Your hand pattern is terrible and so is your suit. **Page 74, also Example 51a).**

77. Three hearts. Your pattern is great but your suit quality is bad. **Page 74, also Example 51c).**

78. Three diamonds. You have a bad hand but your suit is great. **Page 74, also Example 51b).**

79. Three clubs. After the **Wolff Signoff** requires partner to bid three diamonds you will bid three hearts. Partner must then either pass or correct to three spades and you will not get too high. **Page 89, also Example 54b)**

80. Three diamonds. This will find a four-four fit in hearts if it exists, or a three card fit for spades when that exists. With neither partner will bid three notrump. **Page 91, also Example 51c).**

81. Three clubs. When partner bids three diamonds as required you will pass and play a comfortable part score. **Page 89, also Example 54c).**

82. Three clubs. After partner bids three diamonds as required you will bid three notrump which becomes a mild invitation to a diamond slam. **Page 89, also Example 55).**

83. Three diamonds. Your checkback is to uncover a four-four spade fit if it exists. If partner bids three hearts to show three card support you will bid three notrump and partner should understand that your checkback was not for a heart fit, but to find a spade fit. **Page 91, also Example 56b).**

84. Three diamonds. If opener bids either major suit (spades is the first option), raise to game. Pass if partner bids 3NT. **Page 91, also Example 56d).**

85. Three diamonds. A simple attempt to find a five-three fit in hearts. **Page 91, also Example 56c).**

86. Three clubs. After partner bids three diamonds as required you will sign off at three hearts. It appears that you and partner do not play **preemptive jump shifts** since your first call was only one heart. **Page 89, also Example 54a).**

87. Three clubs. A preemptive raise. **Page 47, also Example 34a).**

88. Two diamonds. This artificial call will usually bring two hearts from partner and you

will bid two spades to invite game with a doubleton spade honor. **Page 46, also Example 33b).**

89. Two hearts. Non-forcing and promising a six card suit. **Page 47, also Example 34c).**

90. Two diamonds, artificial, then three diamonds to invite game with a good diamond suit. **Page 46, also Example 33c).**

91. Three diamonds. Preemptive. **Page 47, also Example 34d).**

92. Two diamonds, then three clubs at your next turn to invite game with a good club suit. **Page 46, also Example 33d).**

93. Two diamonds. Partner will either bid two hearts with three or return to spades. You will pass in either case. **Page 46, also Example 33a).**

94. Two spades. A simple preference. **Page 47, also Example 34b).**

95. Three notrump. Play the obvious game. **Page 50.**

96. Three clubs. Transfer to diamonds and then pass. **Page 50, also Example 39a).**

97. Three clubs, then three spades. Show that you have a balanced **limit raise** with a concentration of values in diamonds. **Page 51, also Example 41a).**

98. Three hearts, then three notrump. Show a balanced **limit raise** with bad spades and flat distribution, and let partner choose which game to play. **Page 51, also Example 40a).**

99. Three spades, then pass four clubs. If partner has good clubs we may miss a notrump game, but this partscore should be the safest available. **Page 50, also Example 39a).**

100. Three hearts, then four clubs. Show a balanced **limit raise** for spades with a source of tricks in clubs. **Page 51, also Example 42a).**

101. Three diamonds, then pass and let partner play three hearts. **Page 50, also Example 39a).**

102. Three diamonds, then three notrump. Offer partner the choice of games. **Page 50, also Example 39b).**

103. Two clubs. A **Top and Bottom Cue Bid** to show longer/stronger diamonds and shorter/weaker spades. **Page 200, also Example 107c).**

104. Three diamonds. Maximum preemption is good. Two diamonds was not available since it would have been conventional. **Page 188.**

105. Double. Since **Michaels** is not available you double with the top two suits and use equal level correction if partner bids the other minor. **Page 191, also Example 101e).**

106. Two diamonds. Showing longer/stronger diamonds and shorter/weaker hearts. **Page 185, also Example 98.**

107. Two hearts. Showing longer/stronger clubs and shorter/weaker hearts. **Page 185, also Example 99.**

108. Two diamonds. A **Top and Bottom Cue Bid** to show longer/stronger clubs and shorter/weaker spades. **Page 200, also Example 107a).**

109. Two spades. A **Top and Bottom Cue Bid** to show longer/stronger clubs and shorter/ weaker hearts. **Page 200, also Example 107b).**

110. Double. If partner bids clubs you will use equal level correction by bidding diamonds. **Page 191, also Example 101d).**

111. Two clubs. An artificial takeout for the unbid suits. **Page 189, also Example 100d).**

112. Double. Tell partner that you want to defend with a heart lead. **Page 189, also Example 100c).**

113. Three hearts. Your values are sufficient to bid at the three level. **Page 194, also Example 102e).**

114. Double. With values that are not sufficient to bid freely, make a **responsive double**. You expect partner to bid a minor suit and you will correct to hearts. **Page 194, also Example 102d).**

115. Double. You show the two unbid suits. Partner is asked to bid one of them when holding three cards. **Page 196, also Example 103a).**

116. Two spades. You have the pattern to make a **responsive double**, but your spades are so good that you should bid them instead. Minor suits take a back seat. **Page 196.**

117. Double. You know that your side has a four-four fit in hearts but you do not have the values to bid freely at the three level. If partner bids a minor suit you will correct to hearts. **Page 248, also Example 118a).**

118. Three hearts. You have the extra values needed to bid freely at the three level. **Page 248, also Example 118b).**

119. Double. This is **Snapdragon** which shows at least five cards in the unbid suit and tolerance for the suit of partner's overcall. **Page 197, also Example 105d).**

120. Two hearts. By bidding instead of doubling you let partner know that you have no fit for the suit of the overcall. **Page 197, also Example 105a).**

121. Two diamonds. You have the fit and values to raise, but your raise denies as many as five hearts. **Page 197, also Example 105b).**

122. Double. You not only have five hearts, you have a very good fit for diamonds as well. If partner does not bid hearts, show your diamond support later. **Page 197, also Example 105c).**

123. Three spades. A preemptive raise of partner's overcall. **Volume I.**

124. Redouble. Promising ace or king of partner's suit at least doubleton. **Page 198, also Example 106d).**

125. Four spades. It is more important to preempt with this huge fit than to redouble to show a top honor. **Page 198, also Example 106b).**

126. Two spades. A simple raise that denies a top honor. **Volume I.**

127. When the opening bid has been one notrump—Two clubs. Playing **Hamilton**, this shows a single suiter. Playing **Hello**, this shows either diamonds or a major-minor two

suiter. **Page 203, also Example 109a).** When the opening bid has been a forcing club—Playing **Mathe** make a natural overcall of one diamond. Playing **CRASH** you will have to jump to three clubs to transfer to diamonds. **Page 208.**

128. When the opening bid has been one notrump—You want to show major suits. Bid two diamonds if playing **Hamilton**. Bid two hearts if playing **Hello**. **Page 203, also Example 109c).** When the opening bid has been a forcing club—Playing **Mathe** double to show the major suits. Playing **CRASH** bid two spades to show two suits of the same rank. **Page 208.**

129. When the opening bid has been one notrump—With a club suit this good, playing **Hamilton** do not bid two clubs first and three clubs later. Just jump to three clubs at once. Playing **Hello** bid two notrump to show a club suit. **Page 203, also Example 109e).** When the opening bid has been a forcing club—Playing **Mathe** make a natural overcall of two clubs. Playing **CRASH** jump to two spades to transfer to clubs. **Page 208.**

130. When the opening bid has been one notrump—Playing **Hamilton** you must bid two clubs to show a single suiter. One of the reasons for the creation of **Hello** was to allow major suits to be shown at intruder's first call. Bid two spades. **Page 203, also Example 109b).** When the opening bid has been a forcing club—Playing **Mathe** make a natural overcall of one spade. Playing **CRASH** make a transfer call of one heart to show spades. **Page 208.**

131. When the opening bid has been one notrump—Playing **Hamilton** bid two diamonds to show both majors. Playing **Hello** jump to three diamonds to announce both majors and a very good hand. **Page 203, also Example 109h).** When the opening bid has been a forcing club—Playing **Mathe** double to show the majors. Playing **CRASH** bid one spade to show two suits of the same rank. **Page 208.**

132. When the opening bid has been one notrump—Playing **Hamilton** bid two spades to show spades and a minor. Playing **Hello** you must bid two clubs to relay to diamonds, then bid two spades to show spades and a minor. **Page 203.** When the opening bid has been a forcing club—Playing **Mathe** make a natural overcall of one spade. You do not have a way to show both suits. Playing **CRASH** bid one notrump to show two suits of the same shape. **Page 208.**

133. When the opening bid has been one notrump—Playing **Hamilton** bid two clubs to show a single suiter. Playing **Hello** bid two diamonds to show a heart suit. **Page 203, also Example 109b).** When the opening bid has been a forcing club—Playing **Mathe** make a natural overcall of one heart. Playing **CRASH** make a transfer overcall of one diamond. **Page 208.**

134. When the opening bid has been one notrump—Playing **Hamilton** bid two notrump. Playing **Hello** bid three clubs. **Page 203, also Example 109f).** When the opening bid

has been a forcing club—Playing **Mathe** bid one notrump to show the minor suits. Playing **CRASH** bid one spade to show two suits of the same rank. **Page 208.**

135. Three hearts. This is **Stayman** denying a heart stopper. **Page 239, also Example 113b).**

136. Two notrump. Relay to three clubs, then bid three notrump to show a heart stopper. **Page 238, also Example 112b).**

137. Two spades. Natural and non-forcing. **Page 235, also Example 111c).**

138. Three diamonds. Natural and invitational. **Page 235, also Example 111f).**

139. Two notrump to relay to three clubs, then cue bid three hearts. This is **Stayman** promising a heart stopper. **Page 239, also Example 113a).**

140. Three notrump. You have the values to bid this game and you deny a heart stopper. **Page 238, also Example 112b).**

141. Three spades. Natural and forcing showing exactly five cards in your suit. If the suit were longer you would have used a **Texas Transfer. Page 235, also Example 111a).**

142. Two notrump. Relay to three clubs then bid three spades. This shows a five card suit and invitational values. **Page 235, also Example 111b).**

143. Three notrump. You deny a stopper in either major. **Page 238.**

144. Two spades. You show values that are at least game invitational and a stopper in spades while denying a stopper in hearts. **Page 238, also Example 112b).**

145. Two hearts. You show values that are at least game invitational and a stopper in hearts while denying a stopper in spades. **Page 238, also Example 112b).**

146. Two notrump to relay to three clubs, then three notrump. This auction promises stoppers in both suits shown by the intrusion. **Page 238, also Example 112a).**

147. Three hearts. This ups the ante and also tells partner that a heart lead will work well if our side defends. **Page 240, also Example 114a).**

148. Three diamonds. This shows a heart fit and suggests a diamond lead if partner needs help as opening leader. **Page 240, also Example 114c).**

149. Two notrump. A relay to three clubs as an escape from hearts to diamonds. You cannot bid three diamonds directly as that would show a heart fit. **Page 240, also Example 114d).**

150. Three diamonds. Against a probable spade contract you would like a diamond lead. You will be able to win the first spade and lead a heart to partner to get one or more ruffs in diamonds. **Page 240, also Example 114e).**

151. Two notrump to relay to three clubs, then bid three hearts. This auction suggests that partner find an opening lead on his own. At favorable vulnerability it is probably best to just preempt to four hearts which carries no lead implications. **Page 240, also Example 114b).**

152. Three clubs. Tell partner that a club lead will work well, but you are really raising hearts. **Page 240, also Example 114c).**

153. Three diamonds. Natural, promising values in the range of 7 to 11 HCP. **Page 242, also Example 115d).**

154. Two notrump to relay to three clubs. You will correct to three diamonds. You deny as much as seven HCP. **Page 242, also Example 115c).**

155. Three spades. Show the values of an opening hand. **Page 242, also Example 115e).**

156. Four hearts. You know what game to bid, so just bid it. **Page 242.**

157. Two spades. Show four card support for partner's suit. **Page 245, also Example 116b).**

158. Pass if there has been a two club overcall. Bid two clubs if there has been a takeout double. Both actions deny as many as three spades. **Page 245, also Example 116c).**

159. Double if there has been an overcall. Redouble if there has been a double. Either call shows three card spade support. **Page 245, also Example 116a).**

160. Two diamonds. This natural rebid denies as many as three spades. **Page 245.**

161. Competition in spades takes away no bidding space. You have an easy game try of three diamonds. If the competition is in clubs you can still make a game try in diamonds, but partner will not know whether it is natural or forced since it is the only game try available. If the competition is in diamonds you have no space in which to make a game try. Since the opponents have found a fit you can make a **maximal overcall double** to try for game. **Page 246, also Example 117.**

162. The three heart overcall leaves you no available game try. You must guess whether to bid three or four spades. Double would be for penalty since the opponents have not found a fit. When LHO has doubled for takeout and RHO has bid hearts at the three level, a fit has been found. Double by you would be a **maximal overcall double** which is an artificial game try. When both opponents have bid hearts and left you with no space, the **maximal overcall double** clearly applies as a game try. **Page 246, also Example 117.**

163. Double. This is an **Exclusion double** which is for takeout. **Page 249, also Example 119c).**

164. Two hearts. An **Exclusion double** will not express the fact that you hold bidable hearts. Majors are too important not to bid. **Page 249, also Example 119d).**

165. Four clubs. This cue bid is free since it is below the game level and does not announce serious slam interest. **Page 262, also Example 122.**

166. Three notrump. Announce that you have serious interest in trying for a spade slam. **Page 262.**

167. Four clubs. This is **Roman Key Card Gerber** with spades agreed as the trump suit. All you need to know is how many **key cards** partner has in order to know the level at which to play. **Page 275, also Example 129a).**

168. Three hearts. Announce a spade fit, interest in a slam, and possession of a **concealed**

splinter. If partner asks you will be able to show a singleton heart. **Page 275, also Example 129d).**

169. Four diamonds. Announce a spade fit, interest in reaching a slam, and that you hold a balanced hand. **Page 275, also Example 129b).**

170. Three hearts. Announce that you hold a spade fit, interest in reaching a slam, and shortness somewhere. If partner asks you will be able to show a diamond void. **Page 275, also Example 129c).**

171. Five clubs. If partner shows doubts by bidding five spades, continue to six spades since you do hold three **key cards**. If partner bids five notrump to try for a grand slam, you do not have the extras to bid it at this turn. Bid six diamonds to show the diamond king and deny the club king. If partner bids five diamonds to ask for the spade queen, bid six diamonds to show that card and the diamond king while you deny the heart and club kings. **Page 268, also Example 127.**

172. Five clubs. If partner shows doubt by bidding five spades, pass since you hold no **key cards**. If partner bids five notrump show the diamond king and deny the club king. If partner bids five diamonds to ask for the spade queen bid five hearts to show that card and the heart king. **Page 268, also Example 127.**

173. Five spades. Show that you hold two **key cards** and a working void. There is no reason for you to believe that this void is not working since you have already shown diamond shortness. **Page 272, Page 274, also Example 128.**

174. Five hearts. The fourth step shows two **key cards** and the trump queen. If partner bids five spades to try for a grand slam bid six clubs to show the club king and deny the spade king (five notrump would show the spade king). **Page 272.**

175. Four spades. The third step shows two **key cards** without the trump queen. **Page 273.**

176. Four diamonds. The first step shows zero or three **key cards**. If partner bids four hearts to ask for the club queen bid four spades to show that card and the spade king. If partner shows doubt by bidding four notrump (a provisional signoff) jump to six clubs. If partner uses **Kickback** at the five level, bidding five diamonds to ask for a grand slam, bid five spades to show the spade king and deny the heart king. **Page 273.**

177. Four hearts. The second step show second round control in clubs. **Page 281, also Example 132a).**

178. Four diamonds. The first step shows no control in clubs. **Page 281.**

179. Four notrump. This shows the protected club king. **Page 281, also Example 132e).**

180. Five clubs. This shows absolute control of clubs with spades as trumps. **Page 281.**

INDEX